LAKES AND WETLANDS

LAKES AND WETLANDS

SIVAPRAKASAM VASUDEVAN

PARTRIDGE
A Penguin Random House Company

To order additional copies of this book, contact
Partridge India
000 800 10062 62
orders.india@partridgepublishing.com

www.partridgepublishing.com/india

CONTENTS

PREFACE

Lakes and wetlands play a vital role as freshwater resources for drinking water, agricultural water, and industrial water. They include saline waters and serve for fishery resources and for recreational activities. They act as a shield against natural disasters, like floods (protecting downstream areas), droughts, and tsunami, and serve as sinks for sediments and contaminants. In developing countries, lakes and wetlands are often centres of livelihoods for small-scale local fishers as well as a base for much larger fishing operations. Despite knowing their environmental, social, and economic significance, these water bodies are being continuously ignored. In recent years, however, there is growing concern especially in developing countries about the degradation of lake and their basin environments caused by inappropriate management. Facts and figures of the recent knowledge and issues pertaining to the sustainable development of lakes and wetlands in India are of paramount importance for appropriate management and prospect planning. Considering this alarming situation of negligence of these water bodies, this book intends to evaluate the fundamental concepts to processes involved with respect to the water bodies in India.

The determination of this book is to explore the treasures of lakes and wetlands. The topics are intended to discuss and augment the understanding of this fragile ecosystem. Essentially, all the familiar facts from basic to high-level research appear here. The important topics like morphometric characteristics, water quality, hydrogeochemical characteristics, impact of urbanization, hydrodynamics, tank rehabilitation, ecology, textural and trace element geochemistry, environmental-impact assessment, heavy metals in Indian mangroves, pollution threads to coastal wetlands, ostracod distribution, environmental implications of foraminifer distribution, and physico-chemical changes in the coastal environments form key subjects.

S. Vasudevan

T. Ramkumar

R. K. Singhal

A. Rajanikanth

G. Ramesh

1 MORPHOMETRIC CHARACTERIZATION OF SUKHNA LAKE CATCHMENT USING GIS

Prabhat Semwal, Suhas Khobragade, C. P. Kumar, Sudhir Kumar, and R. D. Singh

National Institute of Hydrology, Roorkee 247 667 (Uttarakhand)

Email: suhas@nih.ernet.in

ABSTRACT

Morphometric analysis of catchments helps in comparing the forms and processes of the catchments and sub-catchments and thereby helps in prioritization of the catchment for various purposes, such as soil and water conservation and soil erosion assessment. The present investigations have been carried out for the catchment of Sukhna Lake, Chandigarh, with the objective of determining the various morphometric characteristics, such as linear, areal, and shape factors. The morphometric analysis has been carried out using remote sensing and geographical information system (GIS) techniques. The special catchment map of Sukhna Lake prepared by the Survey of India, which has a scale of 1:25,000, has been used.

The catchment area has been further divided into six sub-catchments, and different morphometric parameters have been computed for the catchment as a whole, as well as for the various sub-catchments. Land-use andand-cover map, drainage map, etc. have also been prepared. The major land use in the catchment area is forest, which is about 76.44% of the total catchment area.

A total of 731 streams have been identified in the catchment; 565 of which are first order streams. The drainage pattern in the catchment is mainly dendritic to sub-dendritic pattern. The average drainage density is estimated to be 5.5 per square kilometres. The stream length ratios of different sub-catchments show an increasing trend from lower order to higher order, which indicates their mature geomorphic stage, except for the lower foothill and foothill villages. The mean bifurcation ratio value of the catchment has been estimated to be 4.89, which indicates that, in general, the geological structures are not distorting the drainage pattern. The relief ratios indicate that the various sub-watersheds lie between low to gentle slope and exhibit small ridges. Form factor and circulatory ratios indicate that the sub-catchments are mostly elongated in shape. The various morphometric parameters obtained for the catchment of Sukhna Lake shall be helpful for detailed analysis of rainfall run-off process as well as for erosion assessment and watershed prioritization for erosion control.

INTRODUCTION

Hydrological investigations on a lake involve analysis of the complex interaction between various physical processes and morphometric parameters of the lake and its catchment, including their interactions with atmospheric processes of inputs of energy and matter like radiation and precipitation. Many of the processes—for example, erosion and run-off from the catchment—are determined by the physical character of the catchment, such as its geomorphology and land use, besides depending upon the atmospheric processes like rainfall and evaporation. As such, for any scientific investigations, data on physical characteristics of the study area under investigation (such as morphometric data and hydro-meteorological data) are required. Morphometric data, in particular, are crucial for such investigations and form as the starting points for many investigations. Morphometric analysis deals with the measurement, quantification, and analysis of the configuration, shape, and dimensions of a landform (Clarke 1966).

Morphometric analysis of drainage basins not only provides an elegant description of the landscape but also serves as a powerful means of comparing the form and processes of drainage basins that may be widely separated in space and time (Easterbrook 1993). Quantitative morphometric parameters throw light on lithology and structural control of basin, relative run-off and recharge, erosion, and stage of development of the basin. Quantitative and qualitative analyses of the interrelationships of the morphometric parameters with other hydro-meteorological data have proven their importance in watershed prioritization for various purposes, such soil and water conservation and soil erosion assessment.

Use of morphometric studies for hydrological analysis was initiated by Horton (1940) and Strahler (1950). Due to their flexibility and accuracy in processing and analysing spatial information and ability to integrate information from the various sources, geographical information system (GIS) techniques are fast becoming very popular and a powerful tool for morphometric characterization and analysis of the catchments and drainage basins in recent times.

SIGNIFICANCE AND OBJECTIVES OF THE STUDY

The Sukhna Lake is a very significant lake of Chandigarh because of being an important tourist attraction and centre of recreation. As such, the lake also has some contribution to the economy of the region. However, the lake is in limelight in recent years for various problems being faced by it. High rate of erosion in the catchment and subsequent siltation of the lake, land-use changes in the catchment which caused decline in water availability, etc. are some of the major problems in the lake. Being located in the foothills of Shivaliks, the catchment of the lake is subjected to severe erosion, leading to heavy sedimentation of the lake.

For proper understanding of the problem of water availability, it is pertinent to carry out analysis of the rainfall run-off process in the catchment. Similarly, for controlling erosion in the catchment, it is necessary to identify the high-potential erosion zones in the catchment so that measures for conservation of soils in the catchment can be suggested and taken up. Such analysis needs data on morphometric characteristics of the study area. Although few scattered studies on siltation and ecology of Sukhna Lake have been reported in the past, detailed hydrological investigations have not been reported for the lake and its catchment.

Some historical morphometric data generated by past investigations are available for the study area; however, the reported data show discrepancy and significant variation. Some of the data are very old, inconsistent, or not adequate. Moreover, the lake and its catchment are undergoing variations from time to time on account processes, such as sedimentation in the lake, erosion, and land-use changes in the catchment. As such, many of the data available may not be accurate or relevant in today's context. Therefore, the present investigations have been undertaken by the National Institute of Hydrology,

Roorkee, to determine the various morphometric parameters for the lake catchment so that the same can be used for further detailed hydrological investigations of the system.

STUDY AREA

Sukhna Lake is located at Chandigarh at 30° 44' 8.5" to 30° 49' 3.6" N and 76° 48' 16.8" to 76° 53' 42.8" E at an elevation of 349.15 m AMSL. The lake is kidney-shaped. It is a man-made lake constructed in 1958 across the Sukhna Choe. The lake has a surface area of about 157.6 ha and a maximum storage capacity of 525.23 ha m. It is a shallow lake with a mean depth of 3.3 m. The lake is 2.32 km long and 1.06 km wide. The lake is significant from the point of view of recreation, tourism, and fisheries. India's longest rowing channel (2,170 m long, 62.5 m wide, and 3 m deep) was constructed in the lake in 1988–1989 for holding the Third Asian Rowing Championship. The lake also serves as a sanctuary for a large number of birds. The lake was notified as wetland of national importance by Chandigarh administration in 1988. The lake has also been notified for conservation by the National Wetland Committee, Ministry of Environment and Forest, government of India.

The catchment area of the lake falls in the union territory of Chandigarh, Haryana, and Punjab (Grewal 2009). It is located in the foothills of the Shivalik hill ranges, which form part of the fragile Himalayan ecosystem called Kandi (Bhabhar) region. Geologically, the subsurface formation comprises of beds of boulders, pebbles, gravel, sand, silt, clay, and some *kankar* (www.chandigarh.nic.in). The catchment area is rugged terrain, and the soils are predominantly alluvial and sandy, embedded with layers of clay, and are highly susceptible to soil erosion (Singh 2002). As such, the water flowing into the lake is highly turbid. However, a number of soil conservation measures have been taken up in the catchment (Grewal 2009). The climate of the study area is humid subtropical in nature.

DATA AND METHODOLOGY

In the present study, morphometric analysis of the Sukhna Lake and its catchment has been carried out using remote sensing and geographical information system (GIS) techniques. The data have been processed using Erdas Imagine and ArcGIS (version 9.3). The special catchment map (toposheet) of Sukhna Lake prepared by the Survey of India, which has a scale of 1:25,000, has been used. This special toposheet map prepared by Survey of India was geo-referenced using ground control points (GCPs) with the root mean square error (RMSE) of 0.2, and the image was resampled by cubic convolution method. The digital elevation map (DEM) of the catchment area was prepared using topographic contours (10 m interval) and elevation points of the study area, digitized using Survey of India toposheet of 1:25,000 scale. The drainage map was prepared using digital elevation model, IRS P6 LISS-III data, and Survey of India toposheet.

The study area has been divided into six sub-catchments. The morphometric parameters have been determined for the catchment as a whole as well as for each individual sub-catchment. Land-use/land-cover map, drainage map, drainage order map, drainage density map, slope map, aspect map, etc. have also been prepared. The land-use/land-cover map of the catchment has been prepared using IRS P6 LISS-III satellite data. The land use has been classified using semi-unsupervised classification technique. The various results/maps obtained are presented and discussed in the section on results of morphometric analysis.

MORPHOMETRIC PARAMETERS

A number of parameters and indices exist for morphometric characterization of a landform. The parameters can be broadly divided into linear parameters, areal parameters, and shape parameters. The parameters may vary depending upon the landform as well as objective of the analysis. In case of the lake catchments, the important parameters may be basin and sub-basin shape and size, stream order, stream length, stream frequency, drainage density, drainage intensity, drainage pattern, etc. The catchment and sub-catchment shapes are determined by various shape factor indices, such as circularity ratio, elongation ratio, form factor, and basin perimeter. Other important parameters related to the catchments and sub-catchments are soil types, land use, slope, etc.

RESULTS OF MORPHOMETRIC ANALYSIS

Delineation of the Catchment and Sub-Catchments

In the present study, the lake catchment has been divided into six sub-catchments (sub-basins). The various sub-catchments are Kansal, Nepli, Naththawala, Ghareri, lower foothills, and foothill villages. These are shown in Figure 1.1. The details of the sub-catchments are given in Table 1.1.

Figure 1.1. Sub-catchments of Sukhna Lake catchment area.

Table 1.1 Sub-catchments in the Sukhna Lake catchment

Sub-catchment	Ghareri	Kansal	Nath-thawala	Nepli	Lower foothills	Foothill villages	Total
Perimeter (km)	13.32	18.43	16.20	18.91	14.11	12.83	30.72
Area (km²)	5.85	10.84	7.56	7.43	4.82	5.87	42.37
Percentage (%) of the catchment area	13.81	25.58	17.84	17.54	11.38	13.85	100

It can be seen from Table 1.1 that Kansal sub-catchment, with an area of about one-fourth of the total catchment area, is the largest of all the sub-catchments while the Nepli sub-catchment has the highest parameter of 18.91 km.

Major Land Uses

The land-use/land-cover map of the catchment is shown in Figure 1.2. The catchment area has been broadly classified into five major classes, viz. forest, agricultural land, barren/open land, check dams, and ponds, and settlement. The total area covered by each land use and its percentage with respect to the total catchment area is shown in Table 1.2. As can be seen from Table 1.2, the major land use in the catchment area is forest (32.32 km² area), which is about 76.44% of the total catchment area, followed by barren/open land and agricultural land with 4.46 km² (10.58%) and 3.6 km² (8.54%) area respectively.

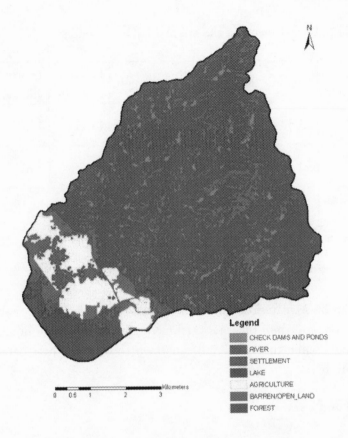

Figure 1.2. Land-use/land-cover map of the study area.

Table 1.2 Major land uses in the catchment

Land use	Area (km²)	Total area (%)
Check dams and ponds	0.74	1.76
Settlement	1.13	2.68
Forest	32.21	76.44
Barren/open land	4.46	10.58
Agricultural land	3.60	8.54
	42.14	100

Note: The total area shown here varies marginally when compared to the one shown in Table 1.2 above on account of error of digitization of the IRS LISS III data.

Drainage Characteristics

Figure 1.3 shows the drainage map of the study area. The various drainage characteristics of the lake are discussed below.

Drainage Order and Drainage Pattern

Drainage order has been given to each drain following Strahler (1964) stream ordering technique, wherein the smallest fingertip tributaries are designated as first-order drain. When two first-order drains join each other, a second-order stream is formed and so on. In the study area, up to fifth-order drainage basin has been observed. The total number of 731 streams has been identified, of which 565 are first-order streams, 133 are second-order streams, 27 are third-order streams, 5 are fourth-order streams, and 1 is a fifth-order stream. All of them ultimately drains into the lake. Table 1.3 presents the ordering of the drainage in the catchment. As the stream order increases, the number of stream segments decreases. If the number of streams is high, it generally indicates that the area is less permeable and has low infiltration rate. The drainage pattern in the study area is dendritic to sub-dendritic, and parallel to subparallel pattern has also developed in some places. The dendritic pattern indicates the homogeneity in texture and lack of natural (geological) structural control while parallel pattern indicates that the study area has a gentle and uniform slope with less resistant bedrock.

Figure 1.3. Drainage map of Sukhna Lake catchment.

Table 1.3 Ordering of drainages in catchment and sub-catchment area

Sub-catchment	Order				
	I	II	III	IV	V
Ghareri	114	32	7	1	-
Kansal	190	48	15	5	-
Naththawala	88	29	4	1	-
Nepli	93	31	5	3	-
Lower foothills	55	16	3	3	1
Foothill villages	26	9	1	-	-
Catchment	565	133	27	5	1

Drainage Density

The drainage density is the ratio of the total length of streams within a watershed to the total area of the watershed and indicates the closeness of spacing of channels (Horton 1932). Higher value of drainage density indicates a relatively high density of streams, weak or impermeable subsurface material, sparse vegetation, and mountainous relief. Lower value of drainage density indicates relatively low density of streams, highly resistant or permeable subsoil material, dense vegetation, and low relief. The types of rock also affect the drainage density. Massive, hard, and compact rocks with high specific gravity have high drainage density while the loose rock types have low drainage density. Also, rocks with clay minerals/particles may have high drainage density due to very low permeability. In the present study, the drainage density map of the catchment has been prepared using the ArcGIS line density function (Figure 1.4). The average drainage density of Sukhna Lake catchment is estimated to be 5.5m. The maximum drainage density is exhibited by Ghareri sub-catchment with 7.57 km/km^2 while foothill villages have a low value of 1.78 km/km^2 (Table 1.4).

Drainage Frequency and Drainage Texture

Drainage frequency, also called stream frequency, is the number of streams per unit area (Horton 1932). It is calculated by dividing the total number of streams in the catchment by the catchment area. The lesser the number of streams, the lower is the frequency. Conversely, the higher the number of streams, the higher is the drainage frequency. The drainage frequency is classified as the following: very poor (5–10), poor (11–15), moderate (16–20), high (21–30), and very high (31–45). The average drainage frequency of Sukhna Lake catchment is 16.64. The drainage frequencies of the sub-catchments vary from 6.13 for the foothill villages to 26.32 for the Ghareri sub-catchment (Table 1.4).

Figure 1.4. Drainage density map of Sukhna Lake catchment area.

Table 1.4 Drainage characteristics of Sukhna Lake catchment

Sub-catchment	Drainage density (km/km²)	Drainage frequency (No./km²)	Drainage texture	Drainage textural classification
Ghareri	7.57	26.32	11.56	Very fine
Kansal	6.49	23.81	14.00	Very fine
Naththawala	5.75	16.14	7.53	Fine
Nepli	6.09	17.76	6.98	Fine
Lower foothills	5.70	16.17	5.53	Moderate
Foothill villages	1.78	6.13	2.81	Coarse
Catchment	5.50	16.64	23.71	Very fine

Drainage texture of a catchment is defined as the total number of stream segments of all orders per perimeter of that area (Horton 1945). The drainage texture depends upon a number of natural factors, such as climate, rainfall, vegetation, rock and soil type, infiltration capacity, relief, and stage of development (Smith 1950). Smith further classified drainage density into five different textural classes, i.e. very coarse (<2), coarse (2–4), moderate (4–6), fine (6–8), and very fine (>8). As per the classification of Smith, drainage texture in the study area varies from coarse to very fine texture at individual sub-catchment levels (Table 1.4).

Stream Lengths and Mean Stream Lengths

Stream length is an important parameter to understand the surface run-off characteristics of any catchment area. In the present study, the stream lengths have been computed on the basis of the law proposed by Horton (1945). The length of a stream generally decreases with the increase in the order of the stream. If the length of the stream is long, it indicates flatter gradient. In the study area, the total length of the stream segments is at a maximum for the first order and decreases with the increase in stream order. However, the lengths of the streams segments of various order streams vary considerably in the different sub-catchments (Table 1.5). Kansal sub-catchment shows maximum length of the streams while foothill villages show minimum length. This indicates that the Kansal sub-catchment has high altitude, lithological variations, and maximum steep slope compared to other sub-basins.

Table 1.5 Stream lengths of the catchment and sub-catchments

Sub-catchment	Stream Length (km)					
	I	II	III	IV	V	Total
Ghareri	24.89	9.72	4.98	4.47	-	44.07
Kansal	39.21	16.07	9.0	6.07	-	70.35
Naththawala	24.35	10.24	2.37	6.49	-	43.47
Nepli	24.24	9.73	6.51	4.83	-	45.31
Lower foothills	14.92	5.79	1.70	2.54	2.53	27.49
Foothill villages	5.35	4.68	0.45	-	-	10.49
Catchment	132.99	56.23	25.02	24.4	2.53	241.17

The mean stream length is calculated by dividing the total stream length of any order by the number of stream segments of that order. Generally, the mean stream length of any given order is greater than that of the lower order and less than that of its next higher order. However, in some cases, variation to this generalization is possible, which may be due to variation in the slope and topography. The mean stream length of the Sukhna catchment varies from 0.24 to 4.88 km, with individual sub-catchments showing different variations as shown in Table 1.6. In the study area, mean stream length was found to increase with increasing order for the catchment as well as for all the individual sub-catchments (Table 1.6).

Table 1.6 Mean stream lengths of the catchment and sub-catchments

Sub-catchment	Mean stream length (km)					
	I	II	III	IV	V	Catchment
Ghareri	0.22	0.30	0.71	4.47	-	0.29
Kansal	0.21	0.33	0.60	1.21	-	0.27
Naththawala	0.28	0.35	0.59	6.49	-	0.36
Nepli	0.26	0.31	1.30	1.61	-	0.34
Lower foothills	0.27	0.36	0.57	0.85	2.53	0.35
Foothill villages	0.21	0.52	0.45	-	-	0.29
Total catchment	0.24	0.42	0.93	4.88	2.53	0.33

Stream Length Ratio

The stream length ratio is the ratio between mean stream lengths of any given order to the mean stream length of the lower-order streams of the same catchment. The stream length ratio shows important relationship between surface flow and discharge (Horton 1945). In the Sukhna Lake catchment, the stream length ratio of different sub-catchments (Table 1.7) except the lower foothill and foothill villages shows an increasing trend from lower order to higher order, which indicates their mature geomorphic stage. In the case of lower foothill and foothill villages, decreasing trend from higher order to lower order is observed in the stream length ratio, which indicates the late youth to mature stage of geomorphic development.

Table 1.7 Stream length ratios for different sub-catchments

Sub-catchment	Stream length ratio			
	2/1	3/2	4/3	5/4
Ghareri	0.39	0.51	0.90	-
Kansal	0.41	0.56	0.67	-
Naththawala	0.42	0.23	2.74	-
Nepli	0.40	0.67	0.74	-
Lower foothills	0.39	0.29	1.49	1
Foothill villages	0.87	0.10	-	-
Catchment	0.42	0.44	0.98	0.1

Bifurcation Ratio

The bifurcation ratio is the ratio of the number of stream segments of the given order to the number of segments of next higher order (Schumn 1956). The lower values of bifurcation ratio are indicators of less structural disturbance in the small sub-basins (Strahler 1964). Bifurcation ratios characteristically range between 3.0 and 5.0 for basins in which the geological structures do not distort the drainage pattern (Strahler 1964). The value of bifurcation ratio also indicates the shape of basin. High value of bifurcation ratio is basically an indicator of elongated basin while low values indicate the circular basins. Also, the low bifurcation ratio values signify a high drainage density and low permeability of the terrain and indicate areas with uniform surficial materials where geology is reasonably homogeneous (Yusuf et al. 2011). The mean bifurcation ratio value of the Sukhna Lake catchment (Table 1.8) has been determined to be 4.89, which indicates that, in general, the geological structures are not distorting the drainage pattern. However, the mean bifurcation ratio values of the Ghareri sub-basin (5.04) and foothill village basin (5.94) are showing little bit of distortion in the drainage pattern due to geological structure.

Table 1.8 Bifurcation ratio of the catchment and sub-catchments

Sub-catchment	Bifurcation ratio				Mean
Ghareri	3.56	4.57	7.00	-	5.04
Kansal	3.96	3.20	3.00	-	3.39
Naththawala	3.03	7.25	4.00	-	4.76
Nepli	3.00	6.20	1.67	-	3.62
Lower foothills	3.44	5.33	1.00	3.00	3.19
Foothill villages	2.89	9.00	-	-	5.94
Catchment	4.25	4.93	5.40	5.00	4.89

Aerial Aspects

Absolute Relief, Relative Relief, and Relief Ratio

The vertical difference in elevation between the highest and lowest points of a land surface within a specified horizontal distance or in a limited area is called relief. When the elevation difference is with respect to the mean sea levels, it is called absolute relief, whereas when the difference in elevation is with respect to the lowermost point of the land surface under consideration (e.g. outlet of the river), it is called relative relief or local relief. A relief map thus shows the topography of the area. The digital elevation model presents the absolute relief and is used to calculate relative relief. Figure 1.5 presents the relief maps of the Sukhna Lake catchment. The maximum relative relief of the Sukhna Lake catchment is estimated to be 266.73 m.

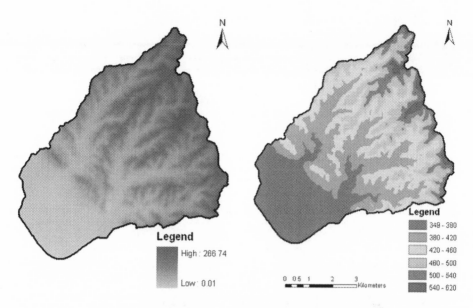

Figure 1.5. Relief maps of the Sukhna Lake catchment:
absolute relief (left) and relative relief (right).

The ratio of maximum relief to horizontal distance along the longest dimension of the basin parallel to the principle drainage line is termed as relief ratio (Schumn 1956). It is an indicator of the overall steepness of drainage basin and the intensity of degradation processes operating on slopes of the basin. Normally, with the decrease in drainage area and size of the catchment, the relief ratio increases (Gottschalk 1964). High value of the relative relief indicates steep slope and high relief while low value indicates low relief and gentle slope (GSI 1981). For the Sukhna Lake catchment, the relief ratio values have been estimated to be 0.03 (Table 1.9). However, the values for different sub-catchments vary within a range of 0.02 to 0.05, indicating that the various sub-catchments lie between low to gentle slope, exhibited by small ridges.

Table 1.9 Relief ratios of different sub-catchments

Sub-basins	Relief (m)	Relief ratio
Ghareri	242.91	0.05
Kansal	214.941	0.03
Naththawala	221.641	0.04
Nepli	254.325	0.05
Lower foothills	110.46	0.02
Foothill villages	112.287	0.03
Catchment	266.74	0.03

Slope and Aspect

Slope can be defined as the steepness or gradient of a unit of terrain, usually measured as an angle in degrees or as a percentage. *Aspect* can be defined as the direction in which a unit of terrain faces. Aspect is usually expressed in degrees from north. The slope and aspect maps of the catchment have been developed and are present in Figure 1.6 and Figure 1.7 respectively.

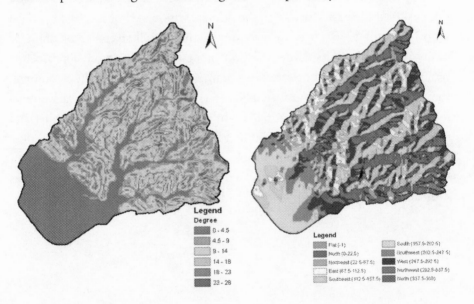

Figure 1.6. Slope map of the study area.

Figure 1.7. Aspect map of the study area.

Basin Shape Factors

The different shape factors, such as form factor, circulatory ratio, and elongation ratio, have been estimated for the lake catchment as a whole as well as for different sub-catchments. They are presented in Table 1.10 and are discussed below.

Table 1.10 Basin shape factors

Sub-catchment	Basin length (km)	Circulatory ratio	Elongation ratio	Form factor
Ghareri	4.95	0.41	0.55	0.24
Kansal	7.15	0.40	0.52	0.21
Naththawala	5.46	0.36	0.57	0.25
Nepli	5.44	0.26	0.57	0.25
Lower foothills	4.77	0.30	0.52	0.21
Foothill villages	4.06	0.45	0.67	0.36
Catchment	10.28	0.58	0.73	0.41

Form Factor

To express the shape of the basin quantitatively, Horton (1932) proposed the form factor. The form factor (F) is defined as the ratio between the area of the basin and square of the basin length (L^2). The value of form factor lies between 0 and 1. A value of 0 indicates highly elongated shape while a value of 1 indicates perfect circular shape. The value of form factor for the Sukhna Lake catchment area is 0.41 while the values for the various sub-catchments lie in the range of 0.24 to 0.36, which are on a lower scale. This indicates that the sub-catchments are mostly elongated in shape and have flatter peak flows for longer duration.

Circularity Ratio

The circularity ratio is the ratio of the area of the basin to the area of a circle having the same circumference as the perimeter of the basin (Miller 1953). The value of circularity ratio is dimensionless and expresses the degree of circularity of the basin. It is influenced by the length and frequency of streams and depends on the geological structures, land use/land cover, climate, relief, and slope of the basin. A circular basin is considered to be more efficient in the discharge of run-off than an elongated basin (Singh and Singh 1997). High circularity values indicate the circular shape while low circularity values indicate the low circularity in shape. The low, medium, and high values are also indicative of the youth, mature, and old stages of the life cycle of the basins (Sethupathi 2011). The value of circulatory ratio is 0.58 for the Sukhna Lake catchment as a whole while the values range from 0.26 to 0.45 for the various sub-catchments. This indicates low to moderate circularity in the shape of Sukhna catchment as a whole while the sub-catchments have elongated to moderately circular shapes.

Elongation Ratio

Elongation ratio is the ratio of diameter of a circle of the same area as the drainage basin and the maximum length of the basin (Schumm 1956). Areas with higher elongation ratio values generally have high infiltration capacity and low run-off (Sethupathi et al. 2011). The elongation ratio values generally range between 0.6 and 1.0. Values less than 0.7 indicate more or less elongated shape while the value more than 0.9 indicates circular shape. The value of elongation ratio is 0.73 for the lake catchment as a whole, which indicates moderately elongated shape. The values for the various sub-catchments range between 0.52 and 0.67, which indicate more or less elongated shape for most sub-catchments.

CONCLUSIONS

Catchments are integrated part of the lake systems. Morphometric analysis of catchments serves as a powerful means for understanding the hydrological regimes of the lake system. GIS, which has become a very popular and powerful tool in recent times for the morphometric characterization of landforms due to accuracy in mapping, measurements, and analysis, have been used in the present investigations. A number of morphometric parameters—such as drainage characteristics, stream length, stream order, stream length ratio, circularity ratio, elongation ratio, form factor, land use, relief, slope, and aspect—have been determined for the catchment. Thematic maps, such as land-use map, have been developed. The study area has been divided in six sub-catchments, and morphometric parameters have been estimated for the catchment as a whole as well as for various sub-catchments.

In the Sukhna Lake catchment, dendritic to sub-dendritic drainage pattern is observed to be most dominant, although parallel to sub-parallel drainage pattern is also found. It is observed that the lower-order drainage mostly dominate the basin compared to the higher-order drainage. It is also observed that the stream length decreases with the increase in stream order. The ratio of mean stream length to stream length shows stable slope and topography and maturity in geomorphic stage. The bifurcation ratio indicates that, in general, the geological structures in the study area are distorting the drainage pattern. The areal factors, like drainage density, drainage frequency, and drainage textures, show low to very high drainage density, poor to high drainage frequency, and coarse to very fine drainage texture, which may be due to the dominance of clay in the study area. Form factor, circularity ratio, and elongation ratio, etc. are showing flatter peaks, elongated to moderately circular shape, and low to gentle slope.

The various morphometric parameters obtained and the maps prepared for the catchment of Sukhna Lake shall be helpful in understanding the hydrologic behaviour of the catchment and for further detailed analysis of rainfall run-off process, erosion assessment, and watershed prioritization for erosion control as well as for hydrologic simulation of the catchment.

REFERENCES

Clarke, J. I. (1966), 'Morphometry from Maps' Essays in Geomorphology, Elsevier Publ. Co., New York, pp. 235–274.

Easthernbrook, D. J. (1993), 'Surface processes and landforms', Macmillan Publishing Co., New York, pp. 325.

GSI (1981), 'Geological and mineralogical map of Karnataka and Goa', Geological Survey of India.

Horton, R. E. (1932), 'Drainage basin characteristics', Trans. Am. Geophysics. Unions. 13, pp. 350–361.

Horton, R. E. (1940), 'An approach toward a physical interpretation of infiltration capacity', Proc. Soil Sci. Soc. Amer. 5, 399–417.

Horton, R. E. (1945), 'Erosional development of stream and their drainage basin', Hydrogeological approach to quantitative morphology, Bull. Geol. Societ. Amer., 5, pp. 275–370.

Gottschalk, L. C. (1964), 'reservoir Sedimentation. In: V. T. Chow (ed.), Handbook of Applied Hydrology', McGraw Hill Book Company, New York, Section 7I.

Miller, V. C. (1953), 'A Quantitative Geomorphic Study of Drainage basin Characteristics in the Clinch Mountains area, Virginia and Tennessee', Proj. NR pp. 389–402, Tech Rep 3, Columbia University, Department of geology, ONR, New York.

Singh, Yadvinder (2002), 'Siltation Problems in Sukhna Lake in Chandigarh, NW India and Comments on Geo-hydrological Changes in the Yamuna-Satluj Region'. Envis Bulletin, Vol. 10 (2): Himalayan Ecology, 2002, Pp 18–131, G. B. Pant Institute of Himalayan Environment and Development.

Smith, K. G. (1950), 'Standards for grading texture of erosional topography', Amer. Jour. Sci., 248, pp. 655–668.

Schumn, S. A. (1956), 'Evolution of Drainage Systems and Slopes in Badlands at Perth Amboy, New Jersey', Geol. Soc. Am. Bull., 67, pp. 597–646.

Strahler, A. N. (1964), 'Quantitative geomorphology of drainage basins and channel networks', In. Handbook of Applied Hydrology, McGraw Hill Book Company, New York, Section 4II.

Singh, S., and M. C. Singh (1997), 'Morphometric analysis of Kanhar River Basin', National Geographical Jour. of India 43 (1): 31–43.

Sethupathi, A. S., Lakshmi Narasimhan, C., Vasanthamohan, V., and S. P. Mohan (2011), 'Prioritization of miniwatersheds based on morphometric analysis using Remote Sensing and GIS techniques in a draught prone Bargur—Mathur subwatersheds, Ponnaiyar River basin, India', International Journal of Geomatics and Geosciences, Vol. 2, No. 2.

Yusuf, A., Rao Liaqat, A. K., and A. Z. Rehman (2011), 'Morphometric analysis of drainage basin using remote sensing and GIS techniques: A case study of Etmadpur Tehsil', Agra District, U. P. International Journal of Research in Chemistry and Environment, Vol. 1, Issue 2, pp. 36–45.

2 MORPHOMETRIC CHARACTERISTICS AND SHORELINE DEVELOPMENT IN TSOMORIRI, HIMALAYAS, INDIA, USING SRTM AND OPEN-SOURCE GEOSPATIAL TECHNIQUES

S. Vasudevan, C. V. Nishikanth, T. Ramkumar, R. K. Singhal, P. Balamurugan, R. Selvaganapathi, T. Pruthiviraj, G. Sathiyamoorthy, and G. Ramesh
Department of Earth Sciences, Annamalai University, Annamalainagar 608 002
Email: devansiva@gmail.com

ABSTRACT

Lake morphometry plays a vital role in understanding the lake morphology, which includes the study of lake forms and form elements, their origin, and role in a broad physical limnological perspective. The objective of this study is to demarcate the various morphometric characteristics of Tsomoriri using the open-source geospatial data and software. This study is the first of its kind to derive various morphometric features for Indian Himalayan Tsomoriri, using the geospatial techniques. The morphometric parameters for the Tsomoriri has been computed using SRTM and QGIS, which includes maximum length (26.0876 km), maximum effective length (25.6034 km), maximum width (7.9414 km), effective width or mean width (7.9130 km), relative depth (9.4m), length of shoreline (76.2604 km), shoreline development (1.799), and the total lake area (142.80 km). The results form as a basic database about the isolated lake in Himalayas and pave the way to explore more characteristics about the lakes located in the inaccessible regions.

Keywords: Tsomoriri, SRTM, open-source, morphometry, shoreline development, QGIS.

INTRODUCTION

Morphometry refers to the shape of the lake and involves the quantification and measurement of the lake. Measurement includes shape, length, width, depth, shoreline development, area, volume, etc. The size and shape of the lake can affect all the physical, chemical, and biological characteristics of the lake, like heat, thermal stability, light transmission, plants, fishes, insects, plankton, and chemical masses. Morphometric parameters are used for many applications, like evaluating nutrient loading, chemical balance, heat balance, biological productivity potential, and shoreline habitat. Lake morphometry can play a critical role on the dynamics of lacustrine systems and has long been recognized as one of the most significant characteristics in order to differentiate the properties of one lake from another. It is important to know the morphological features of a lake, since nearly all limnological characteristics (physical, chemical, and biological) are affected by the lake's shape (Duarte and Kalff 1989, Bezerra-Neto and Pinto-Coelho 2008, Johansson et al. 2007, Vijayakumar et al. 2014). Lake outlines may vary from nearly perfect circles to perimeters with very high length-to-width ratios. No matter how lakes are formed, the morphometric parameters related to them have a major impact on a series of physical processes (Kalff 2002). For instance, shoreline development may help in assessing the amount of potential wildlife habitat available for a lake. Surface area and maximum depth together have an effect on whether a lake may stratify, and the former can largely determine the thickness of the epilimnion in lakes that stratify as well as the distance over which the wind can blow and bring about turbulence (fetch).

The size and form of lakes regulate many general transport processes, such as sedimentation, internal loading, and outflow. These transport processes in turn regulate many abiotic state variables, such as concentrations of phosphorus, colour, water chemical variables, and water clarity, which regulate primary and secondary production. The aim of the present study is to demarcate the various morphometry parameters for Tsomoriri using Shuttle Radar Topographic Mission (SRTM) and geospatial techniques, morphometry parameters comparison with respect to SRTM and to determining the shoreline development.

STUDY AREA

Tsomoriri is located in northern plain area of Jammu and Kashmir (Figure 2.1) and falls entirely within India. The lake is at an altitude of 4,595 m (15,075 ft); it is the largest of the high-altitude lakes in the Trans-Himalayan biogeographic region. The lake is situated between Ladakh in the north, Tibet in the east, and Zanskar in the west. The spatial extent of the study area falls in between 7830' 54", 33 01' 26" and 78 26' 01", 32 98' 99" north and 78 29' 78", 32 80' 19" and 78 36' 19", 32 80' 35" south. The lake is fed by few springs and by a number of small glacial streams snowmelt from mountains on the Changthang plateau. The stream systems create alluvial cones with extensive marshes where they enter the lake. The lake is oligotrophic in nature, and its waters are alkaline. It formerly had an outlet in the southern part, but this has become blocked due to the sedimentation and the lake has become landlocked. As a result, the water is now becoming saline, and moreover, accessibility to the lake is limited to summer season only.

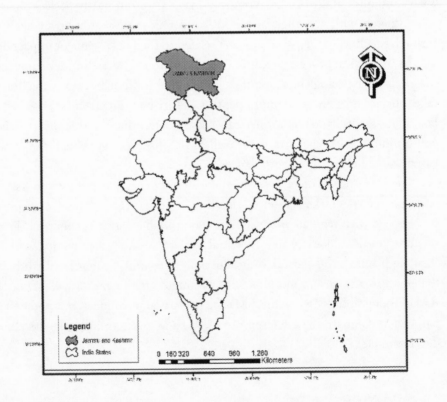

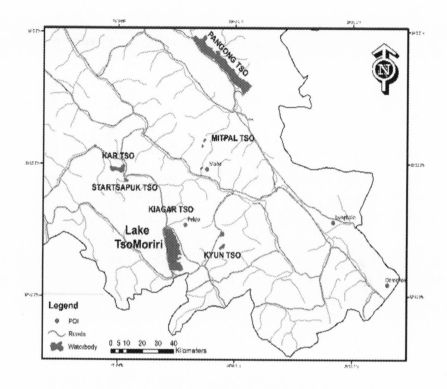

Figure 2.1. Study area map.

DATA AND METHODOLOGY

Shuttle Radar Topography Mission (SRTM) digital elevation data, originally produced by NASA, is a major breakthrough in digital mapping of the world and provides a major advance in the accessibility of high-quality elevation data for large portions of the tropics and other areas of the developing world. The SRTM, which is developed jointly by the National Aeronautics and Space Administration (NASA) and the National Geospatial-Intelligence Agency (NGA), provides elevation datasets for the globe at 3 arc second resolution (approximately 90 m at the equator) (USGS 2006). The original SRTM dataset was developed from raw radar echoes into DEMs, which are readily available at several resolutions—1 arc second resolution for the US and 3 arc seconds for the world (USGS 2006). The SRTM is projected into a geographic coordinate system (GCS) with the WGS84 horizontal datum

27

and the EGM96 vertical datum (USGS 2006). Quantum GIS, which is a very effective open-source desktop GIS software, has been used to process the SRTM, and various morphometric characters has been figured.

RESULTS AND DISCUSSIONS

Using the SRTM data, slope has been computed for northern plain area of Jammu and Kashmir, and the lake boundary of Tsomoriri has been delineated. Quantum GIS has been used to compute the slope and various other morphometric parameters, which include maximum length of the lake (*Lmax*), effective length (*Le*), maximum width (*Bmax*), effective width (*Be*), shore length, total area of the lake, according to Håkanson (1981). The geometry of Tsomoriri plays a key role in the processes occurring within the lake. The significant morphometrical characteristics of Tsomoriri are given in the Table 2.1.

Table 2.1 Morphometrical parameters of Tsomoriri

Morphometry parameter	SRTM-based output
Total lake area (*A*)	142.80 km
Maximum length (*Lmax*)	26.0876 km
Maximum effective length (*Le*)	25.6034 km
Maximum width (*Bmax*)	7.9414 km
Maximum effective width (*Be*)	7.9130 km
Direction	NE–SW
Lake depth (*Dm*)	40 m
Relative depth (*Dr*)	9.4
Length of shoreline (*l*)	76.2604 km
Shoreline development (*F*)	1.799

Computation of Slope Using SRTM

Slope can be described by a plane at a tangent to a point on the surface. Slope can be measured in degrees from horizontal (0 to 90°) or percent slope (which is the rise divided by the run, multiplied by 100). A slope of 45° equals 100% slope. As slope angle approaches vertical (90°), the percentage slope approaches infinity. Slope identifies the steepest downhill slope for a location on a surface. The SRTM is used to compute the slope, and Tsomoriri has been delineated as a vector data as shown in Figure 2.2. The slope generated through SRTM signifies the limited variation in the shorelines and also exhibits that the shorelines are the derivative of the slope angle.

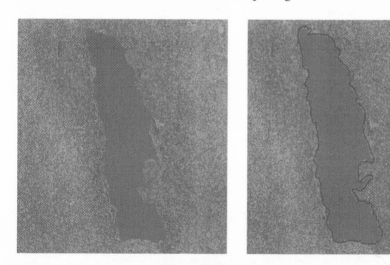

Figure 2.2. Slope computed using SRTM and slope delineated as vector using QGIS in Tsomoriri.

Length

Maximum length (*Lmax*), in kilometres, is the greatest distance between shoreline points, or it is the length of line connecting the two most remote extremities of a lake. Maximum effective length (*Le*), in kilometres, is the straight line connecting remote extremities along which wind and wave action can occur without land interruption (Figure 2.3). The maximum length (*Lmax*) and effective length (*Le*) for Tsomoriri is 26.0876 km and 25.6034 km respectively.

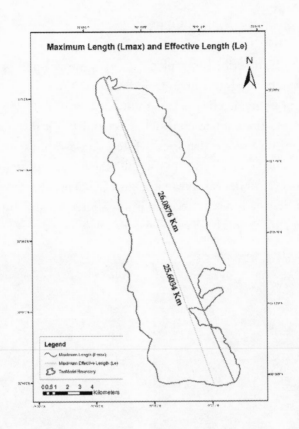

Figure 2.3. Maximum length and maximum effective length in Tsomoriri.

Width

Maximum width or breadth (*Bmax*), in kilometres, is the maximum distance on a lake surface at a right angle to the line of the maximum length between shores; in other words, *Bmax* is perpendicular to *Lmax*. The maximum effective width or mean width (*Be*), in kilometres, is defined by the straight line on the lake surface perpendicular to the maximum effective length (*Le*), which connects the two most distant points on the shoreline. Thus, the maximum effective width (*Be*) may not cross land or islands. The mean width (*B*), in kilometres, is defined by the ratio of lake area (*A*) in square kilometres to maximum length (*Lmax*) in kilometres. The maximum width (*Bmax*) and maximum effective width (*Be*) for Tsomoriri (in kilometres) is 7.941 km and 7.913 km respectively (Figure 2.4).

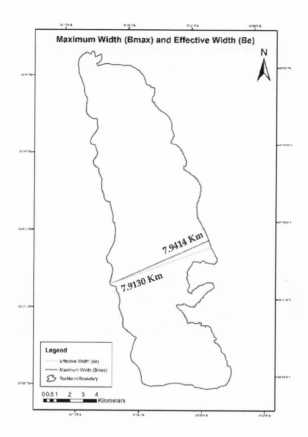

Figure 2.4. Maximum width and maximum effective width in Tsomoriri.

Direction of the Major Axis

Direction of the major axis is defined by the general compass direction of the maximum length (*Lmax*). It is the direction in which the lake is oriented. Tsomoriri is elongated, oval-shaped, and the long axis lies in the north-west–south-east orientation.

Lake Depth (*Dm* or *Zm*)

Among the morphometrical parameters, mean depth (*Dm*) is probably the most useful morphometric feature available because it could be related to the productivity and trophic status of lakes (Håkanson 1981). Mean depth is defined by the quotient of lake volume (*V*), in cubic kilometres, and lake area (*A*), in square kilometres. It serves as a surrogate for most morphometric attributes and a host of biological processes, but no correlate can provide unambiguous information on underlying causes (Kalff 2002). The mean depth derived from the SRTM slope angle for the Tsomoriri is 40 m (Table 2.1). The high value of mean depth in the Tsomoriri concludes that the lake has least potential for wave action and mixing events to disrupt the bottom sediments. Also, the high value of mean depth in Tsomoriri tends to show low levels of nutrients in water and consequently indicates less productivity.

The relative depth (*Dr*) is the maximum depth as a percentage of mean diameter. The relative depth may be used to describe stability of stratification of lakes. In general, most of the lakes are having *Dr* < 2%. The computed relative depth of the Tsomoriri is 9.4%, indicating that the Tsomoriri has the unique characteristics of the deep lake with small surface area. It also exhibits that it has greater resistance to mixing of water. The *Dr* has been computed based on the following formula:

$$Dr = \frac{\text{Dmax} \times \sqrt{\pi}}{\text{mean diameter} \times \sqrt{A}}$$

Where *A* is the lake area in square kilometres.

Shoreline Length (l_o) in Kilometres

Shoreline length is the linear extent of the lake margin or perimeter length of the shoreline, which has been derived with the help of QGIS (Figure 2.5). The derived shoreline length (l_o) of the Tsomoriri is 76.2604 km.

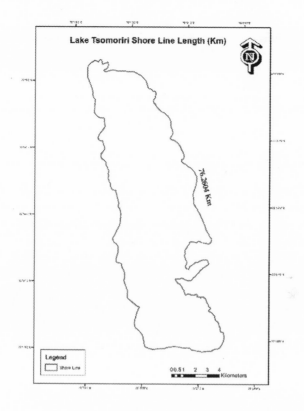

Figure 2.5. Shoreline length.

Total Lake Area (A) in Square Kilometres

The lake area (A) is within the limits of the shoreline. The derived Tsomoriri area value is 142.80 km. The lake area (A) value is used to determine the shoreline development (F), which is an important parameter in the optimization model for hydrographic surveys.

Shoreline Development (F)

It is the ratio of the shoreline to the circumference of a circle of area equal to that of the lake. It provides a measurement of the amount of interface between the lake and surrounding lands. Shoreline development is a measure of the degree of irregularity of the shoreline—i.e. how much the lakes surface shape deviates from being a perfect circle. The *F* value is defined by the following formula:

$$F = \frac{l_o}{2 \times \sqrt{\pi A}}$$

Where l_o is the normalized shoreline length in kilometers.
A is the total lake area in square kilometers.
V is volume in cubic kilometres.

The calculated shoreline development (*F*) for Tsomoriri is 1.799, and this value implies that the lake is having dendritic and devoid of semicircular nature.

CONCLUSION

The most important factor affecting the Tsomoriri ecosystem is mainly due to scarce and non-availability of vegetative matter on its shorelines. This implies possibility in frequent changes in morphometry parameters and destruction and substitution of littoral characteristics around the lake. The important factors responsible for its dynamic nature are the steep slope and soft sedimentary nature of the catchment and the great velocity and high erosional capability of the inlets. These factors lead to changes in depth, shoreline, and roughness of the lake, etc. Hence, this present study is an attempt; it is to document the present scenario of morphometric characteristics and also to emphasize the importance of morphological study in terms of possible future changes as a consequence of prospective impact in the Tsomoriri.

REFERENCES

Berlin Mishra, C., and B. Humbert-Droz (1998), Avifaunal Survey of Tsomoriri.

Bezerra-Neto, J. F., and Pinto-Coelho, R. M. (2008), Morphometric study of Lake Dom Helvécio, Parque Estadual do Rio Doce (PERD), Minas Gerais, Brazil: a re-evaluation. Acta Limnologica Brasiliensia, vol. 28, p. 161–167.

Duarte, C. M., and J. Kalff (1989), The influence of catchment geology and lake depth on phytoplankton biomass. Arch. Hydrobiol. 115: 27–40.

Håkanson, Lars. 1981. A Manual of Lake Morphometry. Springer-Verlag.

Johansson, H., Brolin, A. A., Håkanson, L., New approaches to the modelling of lake basin morphometry. Environmental Modelling and Assessment, v. 12, n. 3, p. 213–228, 2007.

Kalff, J., Limnology. Inland water ecosystems. Prentice-Hall, Inc New Jersey. 2002.

Lake and Adjoining NuroSumdo Wetland in Ladakh, Indian Trans-Himalaya. Forktail 14: 865–7.

Vijayakumar, V., S. Vasudevan, T. Pruthiviraj (2013), An Assessment of Morphometric Characteristics of Coastal Lakes of Cuddalore District, Tamilnadu, South East Coast of India, By Using GIS. International Journal of Advanced Research, Volume 1, Issue 4, 233–238.

USGS, 2006, Shuttle Radar Topography Mission (SRTM) 3 Arc Second (90 meter) Description http://seamless.usgs.gov/ website/seamless/products/ srtm3arc.asp (viewed 15/05/2006).

3 WATER QUALITY CHARACTERISTICS OF FRESHWATER LAKES AT GROVNES PROMONTORY, LARSEMANN HILLS, EAST ANTARCTICA

Pawan Kumar Bharti[1] and Khwairakpam Gajananda[2]

[1] Antarctica Laboratory, R and D Division, Shriram Institute for Industrial Research, 19, University Road, Delhi 110 007, India

[2] Center for Environmental Science, College of Natural of Sciences, Addis Ababa University, PO Box 1176, Addis Ababa, Ethiopia

Email: gurupawanbharti@gmail.com

ABSTRACT

Freshwater lakes of the Grovnes promontory (69° 24' to 69° 26' S, 76° 10' to 76° 15' E) at Larsemann Hills over East Antarctica were surveyed during the 26th Indian Scientific Expedition to Antarctica. Composite water samples from all the lakes were collected and analysed for various physico-chemical parameters to determine their quality and pollution load. The results were compared with WHO and BIS drinking-water standards. It is found that some of the lake waters are unfit for drinking purposes while majority of the freshwater lakes are unpolluted and the physico-chemical parameters are within the WHO and BIS limits. The data also suggested that the pH ranged between 6.6 and 7.8, colour and odour are <5 Hazen units and unobjectionable, suggesting palatable water. Most of the heavy metals are below the prescribed limits, and no growth is observed for coliform bacteria. However, the chloride contents are large, ranging from 84 mgl^{-1} in L3 to 1848 mgl^{-1} in L4. Lead (Pb) in L4, L6, L7, and L7A are 0.06, 0.04, 0.02, and 0.02 mgl^{-1}, which is higher than the prescribed permissible limits of WHO and BIS. Manganese (Mn) in L3 and L7 are also above the limit, with the values of 1.2 and 0.8 mgl^{-1}.

Contamination of the lakes water is unlikely; therefore, analysis for further confirmation of the results is recommended.

Keywords: Antarctica, freshwater lakes, water quality, environmental pollution.

INTRODUCTION

Grovnes promontory (GP) (69° 24' to 69° 26' S, 76° 10' to 76° 15' E) is situated over the Larsemann Hills of East Antarctica. The ice patches over the lake and the rocky regions are typical characteristics of the oasis regions. The polar ice is also seen in the background of the GP, which is one of the main feeders of fresh water to various lakes in this oasis region. This promontory is sandwiched by McLeod Island in the northern direction, the Quilty Bay in the eastern direction, Fisher Island in the north-eastern direction, the Stornes Peninsula in the western direction, and the Antarctic continent and polar ice caps in the southern direction. The ecosystem of this area is simple and in the primary stage of ecological succession. The area is devoid of any higher organisms and plants except for some seabirds, seals, penguins, skuas, algae, lichen, and mosses. Thick mosses, algae, and lichens crusts were observed mainly near the lakes' banks. Most of the areas are free from ice/snow. The lakes were frozen in the present study periods. The deepest lake observed is Lake No. 7 (Figure 3.1), which is about 16 m deep.

In the Antarctic periphery, there are about eight major oasis regions, which become ice-free during austral summer. The melted ice gets accumulated in depressions, forming freshwater lakes and streams of varying sizes. Coastal valleys drain parts of the mainland into the sea. Moreover, during local summer the polar ices melt to supply fresh water to the existing lakes. Sometimes, the melting become large, forming streams over the oasis regions, and adds significant quantity of water into the lakes. Due to overflow of lakes, the streams transport water to the shelf, thereby changing the physico-chemical characteristics of the water.

In this continent, average annual precipitation (expressed in terms of water) is between 50 and 150 mm, most of which falls as snow (Schwerdtfeger 1979). However, due to low temperature, the water is frozen and locked into the vast polar ice caps, making Antarctica the largest stock of fresh water on earth.

The aim of the present study is to understand the quality of the water in the lakes present in the Grovnes promontory (GP hereafter) for drinking purpose. There is a dearth of published data on the lake water quality of GP; therefore, in this study, we attempt to quantify the various biophysico-chemical parameters required for drinking water. We also compare the results with two important drinking-water quality guidelines provided by World Health Organization (WHO) and Bureau of Indian Standards (BIS). We hope this data will give some insight of the water quality of this promontory; however, we recommend further investigation for far-reaching conclusion.

STUDY AREA

The elevation of GP ranges between 0 and 101 m, with an average elevation of about 50 m (NCAOR 2007). It is oriented approximately in the east–west direction and forms a small obstruction to the flow of the glacier. Towards the north of it lays the shelf ice while towards its south lays the polar ice.

The remarkable characteristic of the Larsemann Hills is the absence of moraine deposits as in most coastal areas of East Antarctica (Gasparon et al. 2004). Due to low temperatures, weak chemical weathering processes take place, resulting in the enrichment and migration of chemical elements. The soils are mainly sandy, having unconsolidated matrix of talus, moraines, beach deposits, and vegetation fragments. Rock outcrops are rich in lichen colonies; this was mainly observed in the Stornes Peninsula.

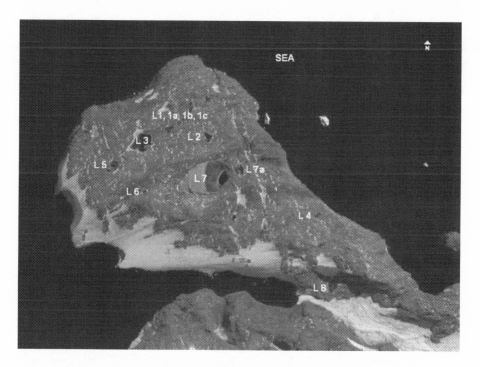

Figure 3.1. Photograph showing the lakes (L) water sampling sites at the Larsemann Hills, Ingrid Christensen Coast, East Antarctica.

The average ratio of SiO_2/Al_2O_3 is 5.79, which shows a weak chemical weathering property of the soil. Compared with the parent rock, SiO_2 and Al_2O_3 have been evaluated. There is a trend of increasingly strong weathering from south to north (Wang et al. 1997). Weak development of the weathering forms on the rock surfaces and fresh traces of glacial impact indicate recent ice disappearance. The weathering of rocks releases minerals, an essential component for the survival and development of the ecosystem (Hall and Walton 1992). It may be noted that the weathering of rocks leads to the formation of sandy soil, which cannot support normal forms of plant and animal lives. At the same time, brown rocks absorb solar energy, leading to a much higher temperature of the rock surfaces, thus providing a better habitat for the unique microflora and -fauna in Antarctica.

In summer, the surface of the oasis warms up due to the solar heating of the dark rocks having lower albedo. Daytime air temperatures from December to February frequently exceed 4 °C, with the mean monthly temperature a little above 0 °C. Pack ice is extensive inshore throughout summer, and the fjords and embayment are rarely ice-free. Snow cover is generally thicker and more persistent on Stornes Peninsula than Broknes Peninsula. Severe weather is experienced in the region with the occurrence of storms and the intensity of some lows exceeds that of a tropical cyclone/hurricane with central pressures as low as 930 hPa and maximum winds of 50 m/s. Extreme minimum temperature recorded so for is −40 °C (Turner and Pendlebury 2004).

Annual mean wind speed of 7 m/s and maximum wind speed of 50 m/s is recorded at the nearby Zhongshan Station. Annual mean gale days are about 171 (47%). Precipitation occurs as snow and is unlikely to exceed 250 mm water equivalent annually (Hogdson et al. 2001). Observations made at Zhongshang Station situated close to the site depicts that katabatic winds are dominant in January and October (Turner and Pendlebury 2004).

The relative humidity is 57% on a yearly basis. It is higher in the Larsemann Hills only when the temperature is above 0 °C, leading to a higher content of water in air during midsummer. Additionally, during a snowstorm or blowing snow episode, the relative humidity is higher and sometimes in excess of 90%, but absolute humidity remains low (Turner and Pendlebury 2004).

There are over 150 freshwater lakes in the Larsemann Hills, ranging from small ponds less than 1 m deep to glacial lakes up to 10 ha and 38 m deep. Some of these water bodies are ice-free for brief periods or partially ice-free in the summer months when their water temperature increase rapidly, reaching +8 °C in some of the shallower ones. For the remainder of the year (8−10 months), they are covered with 2 m of ice (Hodgson et al. 2006). The lakes around the Larsemann Hills site are in general young excepting the major lake (Gillieson et al. 1990). The waters have low conductivity and turbidity.

Human occupation commenced in this area in 1986, with the establishment of four scientific bases by Australia (Law Base), Russia (Progress I and II) and China (Zhongshan) situated around 10 km away in NE direction from the site. All these stations are situated within a radius of 2 km from each other. Ninety-three organic compounds including alkanes, lipidal isopentadienes, aromatic hydrocarbons, polycyclic aromatics, alcohols, aldehydes, ketones, esters, monocarboxylic acids, and phthalic esters in the range of 0.027–4.79 mg/l have been identified in the Mochou and Heart lakes of the of Broknes area. Organic compounds like BHC, DDT, and PCBs have also been detected in the water at concentrations of 0.012–0.356 mgl^{-1} (Li et al. 1997). Occasional ship-based tourist visits have also been made to the area since 1992.

MATERIALS AND METHOD

Sampling of lake's surface waters from 12 locations at GP, Larsemann Hills, East Antarctica, were carried out during 7–15 March 2007 (Table 3.1). A total of 12 (twelve) surface-water samples (composites, HNO_3 preserved) were collected and stored at 4 °C for further physico-chemical analysis. Preliminary field observations of certain vital data for surface waters were carried out onsite, and the data are presented in Table 3.2. Daytime ambient air temperatures during the study period (7–16 March 2007) ranged between –0.5 °C to –9 °C. The maximum wind speed recorded was about 8 ms^{-1}, blowing mainly from 90 to 135° directions. The average relative humidity was about 52.75%.

RESULTS AND DISCUSSION

Table 3.1 shows the onsite observation of the water quality of the 12 lakes at GP, Larsemann Hills of East Antarctica. Lakes present in the Larsemann Hills area are mostly saline in nature (Gillieson et al. 1990) and are characterized by low microbial diversity (Burgess and Kaup 1997).

Conductivity

Conductivity (also known as electrical conductivity or soluble salts) is a term used to measure the total concentration of salts in the water. The higher theconductivity, the more salts that are dissolved in the water. The conductivity of the water in the GP varied between 142.8 and 1,184 mscm^{-1}. However, another East Antarctic oasis (Schrimacher Oasis) has the conductivity of the water in the range between 8 and 15 mscm^{-1} (Gajananda et al. 2004).

Total Dissolve Solids (TDS)

A term closely related to conductivity is total dissolved solids or TDS. It is important to note that TDS measurements are used to determine the acceptability of drinking water. It is found that the TDS ranged between 158.4 and 6,257 ppm. The TDS of L4 is high (6,257 ppm), which may be due to the dissolution of salts from bedrock or sediment presence of algae and other invertebrate organisms. If the level of TDS exceeds the normal values, it may cause gastrointestinal irritation, and beyond the prescribed limit, it may reduce palatability on prolonged consumption of water.

Oxidation-Reduction Potential (ORP)

Redox or ORP is a measure of a systems capacity to oxidize material. In reduction-oxidation reactions, one chemical species loses electrons, and another gains. ORP is important as an indicator for understanding the mechanism of chemically supporting fish, plant, and invertebrate life. ORP is measured indirectly as the ability of an aquatic system to conduct electricity, in millivolts (mV). ORP changes rapidly; thus, it is necessary to monitor it on a continuous basis. ORP values above 400 mV are dangerous to life. In the present data (Table 3.1), the ORP values are in the range of 54 to 147 mV and suggestive of harmless nature.

Trophic Status

In terms of ecological status of the lakes, visual evaluation and sieving of the lake water are carried out to determine the trophic status. Bases on these observations, the following points are made: (a) the trophic status of the lakes ranged from oligotrophic to eutrophic in nature, (b) some coastal lakes are mesotrophic, and (c) inland lakes are mostly oligotrophic. L4 was slightly eutrophic with decomposed biological materials. This was also evident from the pungent smell (H_2S) coming out after agitating the lake bottom. The depth of L4 was approximately 3 m. With the above onsite observation, the detail analysis of the water samples collected from these 12 lakes was carried out. The results obtained from the analysis of the water samples of GP, Larsemann Hills of East Antarctica during March 2007 are presented in Table 3.2 along with WHO and BIS drinking-water standards (WHO 2006, BIS 1993).

Table 3.1 On-site observation of water quality of 12 lakes in Grovnes Promontory, Larsemann Hills, East Antarctica

S. ID	Date	Latitude	Longitude	Elev. (m)	Cond. (mS/cm)	Tem (°C)	pH	Total Dissolve Solids (ppm)	ORP (mV)	BP (mb)	Status of lakes
L1	7/3/07	69° 24.427' S	76° 11.293' E	35.1	255.1 at 0.9 °C	-0.3	7.14	175.9	95	-	Oligotrophic
L1A	9/3/07	69° 24.335' S	76° 11.5' E	27.7	505.5	2.6	7.52	356.4	115 at 2.6 °C	-	Mesotrophic
L1B	9/3/07	69° 24.310' S	76° 11.662' E	29	503.5	1.5	7.52 at 1.4 °C	356.8	97 at 1.4 °C	-	Oligotrophic
L1C	9/3/07	69° 24.365' S	76° 11.365' E	36	613.4 at 0.7 °C	0.4	7.82 at 0.7 °C	434.7 at 0.7 °C	121 at 0.7 °C	981.7	Oligotrophic
L2	9/3/07	69° 24.434' S	76° 11.709' E	28	1,066 at 1.9 °C	2.7	7.8 at 0.1 °C	769.3 at 1.9 °C	99 at 0.1 °C	980.2	Mesotrophic
L3	8/3/07	69° 24.458' S	76° 11.124' E	31	229.7 at 0.4 °C	0.4	7.4	158.4	75	987.5	Oligotrophic
L4	15/3/07	69° 25.084' S	76° 12.838' E	52	7,616		6.78	6,257	127 at 20 °C	-	Eutrophic
L5	10/3/07	69° 24.512' S	76° 10.823' E	38	366.6 at 0.5 °C	1.5	8.08 at 0.6 °C	258.6 at 0.6 °C	54 at 0.6 °C	976.5	Oligotrophic
L6	11/3/07	69° 24.613' S	76° 11.042' E	50	363.4 at 0.8 °C	-0.1	8.16 at 0.7 °C	282.7 at 0.9 °C	107 at 0.8 °C	983.3	Oligotrophic, crater-like feature
L7	8/3/07	69° 24.578' S	76° 11.593' E	35	142.8 at -0.6 °C	-0.4	7.08	997.2	147	986.1	Oligotrophic
L7A	9/3/07	69° 24.546' S	76° 11.917' E	54	1,184 at 0.6 °C	0.7	7.76	857.1	124	-	Oligotrophic, area not frozen
L8	10/3/07	69° 24.898' S	76° 12.733' E	06	531.5 at 0.3 °C	0	7.86 at 0 °C	377.2 at 0.3 °C	153 at 0 °C	992.7	Oligotrophic

ORP = Oxidation Reduction Potential.

BP = Barometric Pressure during the sampling period.

Table 3.2 Physicochemical parameters of 12 lakes in Grovnes promontory, Larsemann Hills, East Antarctica

S. No.	Date of sampling	9/3/07	9/3/07	9/3/07	9/3/07	9/3/07	8/3/07	15/3/07	10/3/07	11/3/07	8/3/07	9/3/07	10/3/07		
	Parameter	L1	L1A	L1B	L1C	L2	L3	L4	L5	L6	L7	L7A	L8	WHO*	BIS**
1	Colour (Hazen unit)	<5	<5	<5	<5	<5	<5	<5	<5	<5	<5	<5	<5	5	5
2	Odour	UO	UO	UO	UO	UO	UO	OB	UO	UO	UO	UO	OB	NG	UO
3	Turbidity as NTU	1	3	3	1	5	1	13.5	3	3	2	1	2	NG	5
4	rH	6.9	6.6	6.9	6.9	7.2	7.3	6.7	6.9	7.7	7.8	7.4	7.2	NG	6.5–8.5
5	Total Hardness as $CaCO_3$ (mg/l)	29	70	63.5	72	87	28	823.5	51	372	324	112	88	NG	300
6	Iron as Fe (mg/l)	0.03	0.04	0.04	0.05	0.03	0.03	0.50	0.04	0.1	0.07	0.06	0.06	NG	0.3
7	Chloride as Cl (mg/l)	112	156	93	166	198	84	1,848	107.5	1,060	704	340	144	NG	250
8	Fluoride as F (mg/l)	0.4	<0.1	0.6	0.4	0.5	<0.1	0.55	0.35	0.6	0.6	0.2	0.3	1.5	1
9	Dissolved solids (mg/l)	230	346	245	392	437	177	13,349.5	243.5	2,392	1,981	731	360	NG	500
10	Magnesium as Mg (mg/l)	3	6	7	6.5	8	4	113	4.5	34	33	9	8	NG	30
11	Calcium as Ca (mg/l)	7	18	14	17.5	21	5	141	13.5	91	74	30	22	NG	75
12	Copper as Cu (mg/l)	<0.01	<0.01	<0.01	0.01	<0.01	<0.01	0.02	<0.01	<0.01	<0.01	0.06	0.02	2	0.05
13	Manganese as Mn (mg/l)	<0.01	0.03	0.2	0.05	0.01	1.2	0.11	0.04	0.04	0.8	<0.01	0.1	0.4	0.1

#	Parameter														
14	Sulphates as SO$_4$ (mg/l)	9	19	21	30	44.5	13	408.25	14.5	147	409	45	28	NG	200
15	Nitrates as NO$_3$ (mg/l)	2	<1	1	3	9.5	<1	22.75	1	18	14	8	1	50	45
16	Mercury as Hg (mg/l)	<0.001	<0.001	<0.001	<0.001	<0.001	<0.001	<0.001	<0.001	<0.001	<0.001	<0.001	<0.001	0.006	0.001
17	Cadmium as Cd (mg/l)	<0.01	<0.01	<0.01	<0.01	<0.01	<0.01	<0.01	--	<0.01	<0.01	<0.01	<0.01	0.003	0.01
18	Selenium as Se (mg/l)	<0.005	<0.005	0.006	<0.005	<0.005	<0.005	0.007	0.006	<0.005	<0.005	<0.005	<0.005	0.01	0.01
19	Arsenic as As (mg/l)	<0.005	<0.005	<0.005	<0.005	<0.005	--	<0.005	<0.005	<0.005	<0.005	<0.005	<0.005	0.01	0.05
20	Cyanide as CN (mg/l)	<0.01	<0.01	<0.01	<0.01	<0.01	<0.01	--	<0.01	--	--	<0.01	<0.01	0.07	0.05
21	Lead as Pb (mg/l)	<0.01	<0.01	<0.01	<0.01	<0.01	<0.01	0.06	<0.01	0.04	0.02	0.02	<0.01	0.01	0.05
22	Zinc as Zn (mg/l)	0.2	0.1	0.2	0.25	0.1	0.1	0.23	0.1	0.1	0.1	0.2	<0.01	NG	5
23	Chromium as Cr^{+6} (mg/l)	<0.01	<0.01	<0.01	<0.01	<0.01	<0.01	<0.01	<0.01	<0.01	<0.01	<0.01	--	0.05	0.05
24	Alkalinity as CaCO$_3$ (mg/l)	8	10	11	7.5	29.5	9	176	9	72	74	48	34	NG	200
25	MPN coliforms/100 ml	NGO	NGO	NGO	NGO	NGO	NGO	NGO	NGO	NGO	NGO	NGO	NGO	ND	ND
26	Test for detection of *E. coli*	NA	NA	NA	NA	NA	NA	NA	NA	NA	NA	NA	NA	ND	ND

UO = unobjectionable, OB = objectionable, NG = no guidelines, NGO = no growth observed, NA = not applicable, ND = must not be detectable in any 100 ml (WHO) and 200 ml (BIS) sam.

General Physico-Chemical Characteristics

Analytical data of colour, odour, turbidity, TDS, pH, and total hardness parameters are summarized in Table 3.2. Following inferences can be drawn from the analytical values:

Colour and turbidity in water, if present above the permissible normal values, have unaesthetic impact value. Consumer acceptance decreases if water has high colour and turbidity levels. Samples collected from all the sources exhibit no colour, which is not detected as evident by the value below 5 Hazen units. Odours were detected in L4 and L8; however, other lakes water does not have any odour. The water of L4 was found to be turbid with the value of 13.5 NTU. Desirable limit of turbidity as per IS 10500-1991 is 5 NTU. The turbidity of other lake water is below the prescribed limit.

The pH value was found in range of 6.6–7.8 in all the samples, which is the acceptable range. As the Antarctic soils are sandy, the water drains easily, and leaching of nutrients occurs frequently. The waters of the GP show that the average value of pH is 7.1 for all the sites, whereas in L6 and L7 the pH is higher at 7.7 and 7.8. Total hardness is the measure of the water's ability to form scale in pipes, to produce suds from soap, or to leave spots on leaves. The units used to report hardness are calcium carbonate equivalents ($CaCO_3$). Hardness is the measure of the combined concentration of calcium and magnesium in the water, which are insoluble salts of ions, like calcium carbonate, that form scale. The total hardness ranges in the present samples are 28 to 823.5 mgl^{-1}. L4 has the highest value of 823.5 mgl^{-1} while L6 has the value of 372 mgl^{-1}, followed by L7 with the value of 324 mgl^{-1}, which are all above the prescribed BIS limit.

Inorganic Constituents

Inorganic constituents such as calcium, magnesium, chloride, sulphate, bicarbonate alkalinity, nitrate, and fluoride are summarized in Table 3.2. The inferences are drawn from the analytical values as follows:

Calcium was observed in range of 5–141 mgl^{-1} in all water samples. Desirable limit of calcium in drinking water is 75 mgl^{-1}. Analytical results indicate that calcium in all samples is within the desirable limit of drinking water except L4 and L6 with the values of 141 and 91 mgl^{-1}.

Magnesium (Mg) was found in range of 3–113 mgl^{-1} in all the samples. The desirable limit is 30. L4 and L6 exceed the limit with the values 113 and 34 mgl^{-1}. Higher concentration of calcium and magnesium in water may lead to encrustation in water supply structure and adverse effects on domestic use.

Chlorides (Cl) were in the range of 84–1848 mgl^{-1} in case of all the samples while the desirable limit is 250 mgl^{-1}. Beyond the permissible limits, taste, corrosion, and palatability of water may be affected. L4, L6, L7, and L8 exceed the permissible limit of chloride (Table 3.2). As there is intrusion of seawater, the average chloride concentration in the lakes is very high.

Sulphate occurs in all natural water sources. This is an important nutrient used by plants and animals. The source of this element may be due to parental bedrock. Sulphate (SO$_4$) was found in range of 9–409 mgl^{-1}. Desirable limit of sulphate is 200 mgl^{-1}. Beyond the permissible limits, sulphate may cause gastrointestinal irritation when magnesium and sodium are also present. Such lakes as L4 and L7 exceed the limit of BIS.

Desirable limit for alkalinity as CaCO$_3$ in drinking water is 200 mg/l. Analytical result indicates that alkalinity is within the permissible limit in all water samples.

Beyond desirable limits, nitrate (NO$_3$) may cause methaemoglobinaemia. In surface water, nitrate is a nutrient taken up by plants and assimilated into cell protein. Analytical results suggests that nitrate in all the samples are found well below the desirable limit of 45 mgl^{-1} and varied between <1 and 22.75 mgl^{-1}. Above the permissible limit of WHO 1.5 mg/l in drinking water, fluoride may cause fluorosis of varying nature. As indicated by analytical results, fluoride (as F) was found in the range <0.1 to 0.6 mgl^{-1}, which is within the limit.

Inorganic Metallic Constituents

If water sources are contaminated with toxic metals above the prescribed norms, water becomes toxic and in some cases carcinogenic. The analytical results are summarized in Table 3.2. The following inference can be drawn from the analytical values:

Copper in all samples is found in the range of <0.01 to 0.06 mgl^{-1}, which is below the limit. The permissible limit of copper is 2 mgl^{-1} according to WHO. Manganese in the lake water samples such as in L3 and L7 are higher than the permissible limit. Concentrations of the manganese above the guideline value may affect the appearance, taste, or odour of the water.

Iron is not hazardous to health, but aesthetic value of water may be reduced appreciably due to coloration of water, which may be yellowish-brown to black and turbidity formed by precipitation of oxides. Excess iron in water imparts bitter characteristics and metallic taste. In addition, carrying capacity of pipeline in the distribution system may reduce due to the deposition of iron oxide and bacterial slimes as a result of the growth of microorganism (iron bacteria) in iron-bearing water. BIS desirable limit of iron in water is 0.3 mgl^{-1}. Water samples drawn from L4 indicate higher concentration of iron (0.5 mgl^{-1}).

Mercury, cadmium, arsenic, selenium, and chromium were analysed and found to be below the detection limit. However, further study of various lake waters for heavy metals will help in determining the exact values and understand their circulation pattern, behaviour, fate, and sources.

Lead is found in the range of <0.01–0.06 mg/l, which is not desirable in comparison to WHO guidelines. Lake waters of L4, L6, L7, and L7a have the values of 0.06, 0.04, 0.02, and 0.02 mgl^{-1}. These values are above the international guideline of WHO; however, as per BIS the value of L4 exceeds the prescribed limits (Table 3.2). That is the matter of concern for consumption. Further investigation of the sources of the lead in the lakes water is also recommended. The source of lead may be parental metamorphic or igneous rocks.

Cyanide, if present beyond the acceptable level, imparts toxicity in water. As evident by analytical results, all the samples showed the value of <0.01 mgl^{-1} (Table 3.2), which is below the WHO and BIS permissible limit.

Microbiological Quality

Water samples shall be free from coliform group of bacteria. In the present study, all the surface lake water samples are free from coliform bacteria. The test for detection of *E. coli* showed no observed growth (Table 3.2). Therefore, the lake waters of GP were free from microbial contamination and safe to drink at the time of investigation.

CONCLUSION

The most undesirable constituents of drinking water are those capable of having a direct impact to the members of the Indian Antarctic Expeditions. In the present study, physico-chemical parameters are studied and evaluated for drinking-water quality. The following conclusions are made:

1. The present study shows that some of the lakes water sources of the Grovnes promontory (GP) have water of very high purity for drinking purposes as most of the parameters are within or below the permissible limit of drinking water set by World Health Organization (WHO) and Bureau of Indian Standards (BIS).
2. Some of the lakes have exceeded the prescribed limits of WHO and BIS. These are mainly due to eutrophic nature of the lakes.
3. The present work served as a primary data for the assessment of drinking-water quality from lakes of GP, and this data will help in further investigations.

ACKNOWLEDGEMENTS

We are thankful to the Management of Shriram Institute for Industrial Research for nominating K. G. and R. K. Singh to participate in the 26th ISEA. We also thank Dr Rasik Ravindra (director), Dr N. Khare, Dr Rahul Mohan, Dr Anoop Tiwari, and all the employees of the National Centre for Antarctic and Ocean Research, Goa, for giving assistance and supports to work at Larsemann Hills, East Antarctica. The support and cooperation rendered by the 26th Indian Scientific Expedition to Antarctica leaders, Mr Ajay Dhar (Larsemann), Shri Jaypaul D. (Maitri), and the entire members are thankfully acknowledged. The financial assistance given by the Ministry of Earth Sciences, government of India, is also thankfully acknowledged.

REFERENCES

Beg, J., Mihir, K., Shrivastava, M., Singh, J., and Wanganeo, A. (2005), Geological Studies in the Larsemann Hills Ingrid Chirstensen Coast, East Antarctica, *Report of Second Task Force to New Station Site*, NCAOR, India.

BIS (1991), Specification for Drinking Water, Bureau of Indian Standard (BIS: 10500–1991) http://www.wbphed.gov.in/Bureau%20of%20Indian.html.

Burgess, J. S., and Kaup, E. (1997), Some Aspects of Human Impact on Lakes in the Larsemann Hills, Princess Elizabeth Land, Eastern Antarctica, In Lyons, W. B., Howard-Williams, C., and Hawes, I., Eds. *Ecosystem Processes In Antarctic Ice-Free Landscapes*, Rotterdam: Balkema, 259–264.

Chapman, D. (1996), Water Quality Assessment: A guide to the use of Biotic, Sediments and Water in Environmental Monitoring. 2nd ed., Chapman and Hall, London.

Gajananda, K., Kaushik, A., Singh, B., Gupta, V., Gera, N., Dutta, H. N., Singh, J., Bishnoi, L., and Gopal, K. (2004), *Drinking water quality assessment over the Schirmacher Oasis, East Antarctica.* In: Singh VP and Yadava RN (Eds), Environmental Pollution (Water and Environment), *Allied Publishers Pvt. Ltd.*, New Delhi, pp. 19–28.

Gajananda, K. (2003), *Study of atmospheric parameters in relation to Antarctic ecosystem over the Schirmacher region of east Antarctica.* PhD Thesis, Department of Environmental Sciences, Guru Jambheshwar University, Hisar. India.

Gasparon, Massimo, Matschullat and Jörg (2004), Geogenic Sources and Sink of Trace Metals in the Larsemann Hills, East Antarctica: Natural Process and Human Impact, *Applied Geochemistry*, Vol. 21: 318–334.

Gillieson, D. S., Burgess, J., Spate, A., and Cochrane A. (1990), Atlas of the Lakes of the Larsemann Hills, Princess Elizabeth Land, Antarctica. *A N A R E Research Notes*, No. 74.

Hall, K. J., and Walton, D. W. H. (1992), Rock weathering, soil development and colonization under a changing climate. Philosophical Transactions of the Royal Society of London. Series B, Biological Sciences 338 (14): 269–277.

Hodgson, D. A., Verleyen, E., Squier, A., Sabbe, K., Brendan J. Keely, Krystyna M. Saunders., and Vyverman, W. (2006), Interglacial Environments of

Coastal East Antarctica: Comparison of MIS 1 (Holocene) and MIS 5e (Last Interglacial) Lake-Sediment Records, *Quaternary Science Reviews*, Vol. 25: 179–197.

Hodgson, D. A., Noon, P. E., Vyverman, W., Bryant, C. L., Gore, D. B., Appleby, P., Gilmour, M., Verleyen, E., Sabbe, K., Jones, V. J., Ellis-Evans, J. C., and Wood, P. B. (2001), Were The Larsemann Hills Ice-Free Through The Last Glacial Maximum? *Antarctic Science*, Vol. 13 (4): 440–454.

Li, Z. S., Wang, J., Lei, Z. H., Liang, X. M., Chen, X. D., and Liang, Y. L. (1997), Hydrochemical Properties of Lakes in Larsemann Hills, Antarctica. Jidi Yanjiu *Chinese Journal of Polar Research*, Vol. 9 (1): 71–77.

NCAOR (2007), Draft Comprehensive Environmental Evaluation of New Indian Research Base at Larsemann Hills, Antarctica. National Centre for Antarctic and Ocean Research, http://www.ncaor.gov.in.

Schwerdtfeger, P. (1979), Review on icebergs and their uses. Cold Regions Science and Technology 1:59–79.

Stüwe, K., Braun, H. M., and Peer, H. (1989), Geology and Structure of The Larsemann Hills Area, Prydz Bay, East Antarctica, *Australian Journal of Earth Sciences*, Vol. 36, 219–241.

Turner, J., and Pendlebury, S. (2004), The International Antarctic Weather Forecasting Handbook, BAS, UK.

Wang, Y. G., Zhao, J., Chen, C. S. (1997), Chemical Weathering at Stornes Peninsula, Larsemann Hills, East Antarctica. Jidi Yanjiu, Vol. 9 (4), 273–282.

WHO (2006), Guidelines for Drinking-water Quality, World Health Organization. First Addendum to Third Edition, Volume 1 Recommendations,_http://www.who.int/water_sanitation_health/dwq/gdwq0506.pdf.

**BIS = Bureau of Indian Standard/Specification for Drinking Water (BIS: 10500-1991) http://www.wbphed.gov.in/Bureau%20of%20Indian.htm.
*WHO = World Health Organization, Drinking Water Limits <http://www.who.int/water_sanitation_health/dwq/gdw>.

4 STUDY OF HYDROGEOCHEMICAL PARAMETER IN YERCAUD LAKE, SHEVAROY HILLS, TAMIL NADU, INDIA

G. Nanthakumar[1], P. Karthikeyan[2], and R. Venkatachalapathy[2]

[1]Department of Geology, Periyar University Colleges of Art and Science, Mettur-636 401

[2]Department of Geology, Periyar University, Salem 636 011

Email: geologynantha@gmail.com

ABSTRACT

Lakes are most important water resource in India for purpose like drinking-water supplies, irrigation, and fisheries. The present study aims to study the hydrogeochemical parameter of Yercaud Lake and asses its environmental status. Thirty-six water samples are collected during pre- and post-monsoon seasons for the present study during 2011–2013. Water samples are assessed by analysing the various physico-chemical parameters, such as temperature (°C), total dissolved solids (TDS), electrical conductivity (EC) (µs/cm), pH, total alkalinity (TA) (mg/l), salinity (ppm), calcium hardness (CH) (mg/l), magnesium hardness (MH) (mg/l), total hardness (TH) (mg/l), and total solids (TS) (mg/l). The results of the present study indicate that the Yercaud Lake water is moderately polluted and are not safe for drinking water purpose as the values for different parameters beyond permissible limit suggested by CPCB (2008). The nutrients available including calcium, sulphates, phosphates, nitrates and potassium are in sufficient quantities for the growth of aquatic plants and animals in the lake. The study reveals that the Yercaud Lake can be placed under the category of meso-eutrophic water body.

Keywords: hydrogeochemical parameters, meso-eutrophic, Yercaud Lake, Shevaroy Hills.

INTRODUCTION

Water is a prime natural resource, a basic human need and a precious national asset. Water pollution has been a major issue as water forms an important component of our day-to-day activity. Contamination of fresh water by sewage is a common occurrence. Water is known to contain a large numbers of chemical elements. Physical parameters such as temperature, turbidity, and current are also known to operate in the lake's ecosystem. The interaction of both the physical and chemical properties of water plays a significant role in the composition, distribution, and abundance of aquatic ecosystem. Apart from this, it also gives an insight into the relationships between the organism and their environment and can be used in determining water quality and productivity of the lake. Globally, fresh water has become the fastest-depleting natural resource nowadays. Only a small percentage of water exists as fresh water, and the portion accessible to humans—the surface water bodies such as lakes and rivers—is again a negligible part of its global stock. The present work deals with water quality parameters in relation to hydrobiology of the Yercaud Lake, Shevaroy Hills, Tamil Nadu, India.

MATERIALS AND METHODS

Study Area Description

Yercaud is a hill station near Salem town in Tamil Nadu and situated at an altitude of 1,500 m above MSL in the Servarayan range (anglicized as Shevaroys) of hills in the Eastern Ghats (Figure 4.1). The town gets its name from Tamil words *yeri*, which means lake, and *kaadu*, which means forest—i.e. *yeri* + *kaadu* later became Yercaud. Yercaud is known for its coffee plantations and oranges in addition to bauxite and granite reserves. The climate of Yercaud is a moderate one, with a maximum temperature of 34 °C and a minimum of 16 °C. During winter, the hills are covered by mist and improve their aesthetic value.

Figure 4.1. Panoramic view of Yercaud Lake, Salem
District, Tamil Nadu (study area).

Yercaud sits on top of Archaean plutonic rocks of charnockite series, and these have weathered into the rugged masses of hills. There are three routes up to the hills. The Shevaroy Hills are covered with green grasses and have not any considerable growth of forests.

Sample Collection and Analytical Procedures

Water samples from three sites (inlet, middle, and outlet) were collected at 0.5 m (a depth representative of the mixed water columns) on February 2012 and January 2013 in Yercaud Lake. The samples were kept in 2 l polyethylene plastic bottles which had been previously cleaned with metal-free soap, rinsed repeatedly with distilled water, soaked in 10% nitric acid for 24 h, and finally rinsed with ultrapure water. The water samples were subjected to analysis.

The measurements of water quality parameters were determined on the basis of standard methods established for surface water (APHA 1998). All water samples were analysed for different physico-chemical parameters within 48 h of collection. Chemical oxygen demand (COD) was determined on the same sampling day while biological oxygen demand (BOD) was determined promptly to avoid time-induced changes in bacterial concentration. The BOD was determined by the dilution and seeding method. Chloride was determined by silver nitrate ($AgNO_3$) titration using potassium chromate (K_2CrO_4) solution as an indicator. SO_4 was determined spectrophotometrically by the barium sulphate turbidity method. NO_3-N was analysed by phenoldisulphonic acid colorimetry. The acid-treated water samples were analysed for the determination of major cations Ca, Na, and K, measured by flame photometry while Mg was determined by the flame atomic absorption spectrometer (FAAS).

RESULT AND DISCUSSION

The water samples were analysed for 12 parameters—namely, pH, electrical conductivity (μS/cm), dissolved solid (mg/l), biochemical oxygen demand (BOD), calcium (Ca), magnesium (Mg), sodium (Na), potassium (K), chloride (Cl), bicarbonate (HCO_3) and sulphate (SO_4). The water quality parameters are summarized in Table 4.1 (inlet), Table 4.2 (middle), and Table 4.3 (outlet) and its variations are shown in Figure 4.2 (inlet), Figure 4.3 (middle) and Figure 4.4 (outlet).

Table 4.1 Water quality characteristics of the Yercaud Lake (inlet)

Parameters	2011		2012		2013	
	Pre-monsoon	Post-monsoon	Pre-monsoon	Post-monsoon	Pre-monsoon	Post-monsoon
Temp (°C)	23	24	22	25	24	27
pH	7.17	7.02	8.7	8.0	8.2	9
EC (μS/cm)	137.87	150.66	143.87	169.52	160.23	176
DO (mg/l)	13.78	12.48	11.12	12.31	10.2	9.7
NO_3-N (mg/l)	0.32	0.62	0.41	0.97	0.81	0.72
TDS (mg/l)	179	188	160	172	167	160
PO_4-P (mg/l)	0.56	0.72	0.72	0.43	0.63	0.77
Total alkalinity (mg/l)	7.56	6.73	8.7	7.1	8.81	9
Ca (mg/l)	5.42	2.86	4.79	5.95	3	4.16
Mg (mg/l)	2.79	1.68	1.36	4.63	1.28	3.67
Total hardness (mg/l)	8.21	4.54	6.15	10.58	4.28	7.83
Na (mg/l)	6.49	5.9	7.93	5.9	3.42	3.21
K (mg/l)	0.37	0.15	0.74	0.5	0.3	0.25
Cl (mg/l)	5.14	3.42	6.13	6.13	2.3	3.06
HCO_3 (mg/l)	6.43	4.27	7.66	7.66	2.87	3.83

Table 4.2 Water quality characteristics of the Yercaud Lake (middle)

Parameters	2011		2012		2013	
	Pre-monsoon	Post-monsoon	Pre-monsoon	Post-monsoon	Pre-monsoon	Post-monsoon
Temp (°C)	23	24	19	24	25	26
pH	7.9	7.75	9.43	8.73	8.93	9.73
EC (μS/cm)	138.62	151.41	144.62	170.27	160.98	176.75
DO (mg/l)	14.53	13.23	11.87	13.06	10.95	10.45
NO_3-N (mg/l)	1.07	1.37	1.16	1.72	1.56	1.47
TDS (mg/l)	179.75	188.75	160.75	172.75	167.75	160.75
PO_4-P (mg/l)	1.31	1.47	1.47	1.18	1.38	1.52
Total alkalinity (mg/l)	8.31	7.48	9.45	7.85	9.56	9.75
Ca (mg/l)	6.17	3.61	5.54	6.7	3.75	4.91
Mg (mg/l)	3.54	2.43	2.11	5.38	2.03	4.42
Total hardness (mg/l)	8.96	5.29	6.9	11.33	5.03	8.58
Na (mg/l)	7.24	6.65	8.68	6.65	4.17	3.96
K (mg/l)	1.12	0.9	1.49	1.25	1.05	1
Cl (mg/l)	5.89	4.17	6.88	6.88	3.05	3.81
HCO_3 (mg/l)	7.18	5.02	8.41	8.41	3.62	4.58

Table 4.3 Water quality characteristics of the Yercaud Lake (outlet)

Parameters	2011		2012		2013	
	Pre-monsoon	Post-monsoon	Pre-monsoon	Post-monsoon	Pre-monsoon	Post-monsoon
Temp (°C)	23	24	21	23	25	26
pH	9.04	8.89	9.57	8.87	9.07	9.87
EC (μS/cm)	138.86	151.65	144.86	170.51	161.22	176.99
DO (mg/l)	14.77	13.47	12.11	13.3	11.19	10.69
NO_3-N (mg/l)	1.31	1.61	1.4	1.96	1.8	1.71
TDS (mg/l)	177	172	161	170	163	158
PO_4-P (mg/l)	1.55	1.71	1.71	1.42	1.62	1.76
Total alkalinity (mg/l)	8.55	7.72	9.69	8.09	9.8	9.99
Ca (mg/l)	6.41	3.85	5.78	6.94	3.99	5.15
Mg (mg/l)	3.78	2.67	2.35	5.62	2.27	4.66
Total hardness (mg/l)	10.19	6.52	8.13	12.56	6.26	9.81
Na (mg/l)	7.48	6.89	8.92	6.89	4.41	4.2
K (mg/l)	1.36	1.14	1.73	1.49	1.29	1.24
Cl (mg/l)	6.13	4.41	7.12	7.12	3.29	4.05
HCO_3 (mg/l)	7.42	5.26	8.65	8.65	3.86	4.82

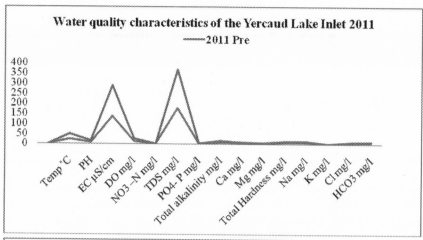

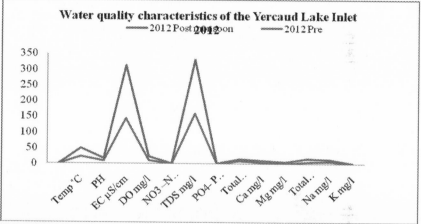

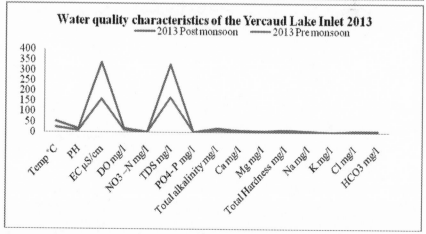

Figure 4.2 Water quality characteristics of the Yercaud Lake (inlet).

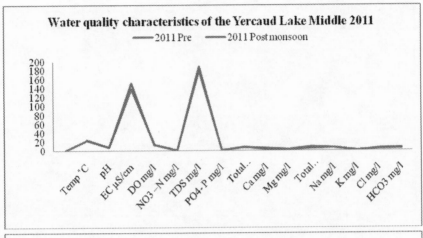

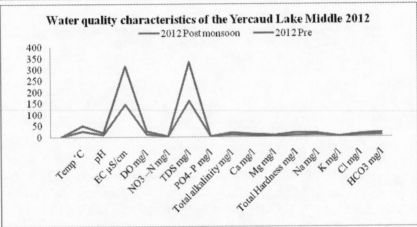

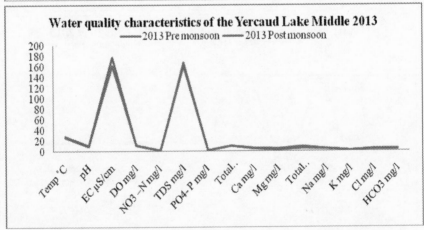

Figure 4.3 Water quality characteristics of the Yercaud Lake (middle).

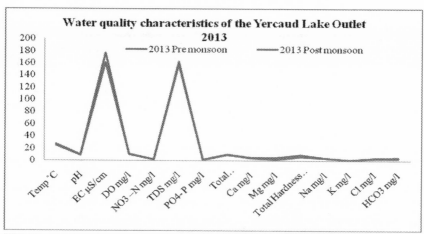

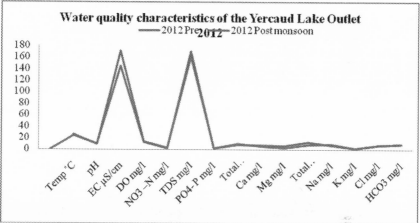

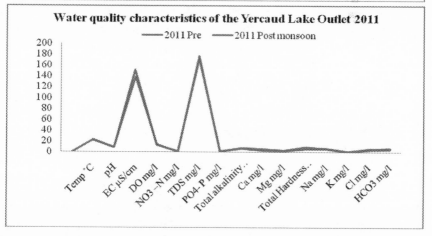

Figure 4.4 Water quality characteristics of the Yercaud Lake (outlet).

Temperature

Temperature of water may not be as important in pure water because of the wide range of temperature tolerance in aquatic life, but in polluted water, temperature can have profound effects on dissolved oxygen (DO) and biological oxygen demand (BOD). The fluctuation in lake water temperature usually depends on the season, geographic location, sampling time, and temperature of effluents entering the lake. Post-monsoon maxima (24 °C) and pre-monsoon minima (20 °C) are observed in inlet, middle, and outlet during 2011. Post-monsoon maxima (26 °C) and pre-monsoon minima (19 °C) are observed in inlet, middle during 2012. Pre-monsoon maxima (27 °C) and post-monsoon minima (24 °C) are observed in inlet and middle during 2013. This variation may be related to many environmental factors such as elevation, current velocity, and water depth.

pH

The pH is an important factor that determines the suitability of water for various purposes, including toxicity to animals and plants. In the present study, pH is found neutral to alkaline into inlet to outlet. It might be due to the increasing draining of domestic effluent water to the lake and microbial activities. The pH values in all the sites showed the same seasonal trend with summer minima and winter maxima (Table 4.1). The pre-monsoon maxima (9.04, 9.57, and 9.87 in post-monsoon) are due to the decreased decomposition rate, owing to the reduced microbial activity and increased algal productivity in outlet region (2011, 2012, and 2013). The post-monsoon minima (7.02 and 8) are due to increased decomposition rate, leading to acidification and lowered pH (Chetana and Somashekar 1997) in the inlet region (2011–2013).

Electrical Conductivity (EC)

Conductivity is the measure of the ability of an aqueous solution to carry an electric current. This ability depends on the presence of ions on their total concentration, mobility, and valence, and the temperature of measurement. In the present study, the outlet site during pre-monsoon (2013) showed higher values of EC and total dissolved solids in contrast to other sites. Increasing levels of conductivity and cations are the products of decomposition and mineralization of organic materials (Abida 2008). In the inlet region, EC with minima (137.87 μS/cm in 2011) was observed in pre-monsoon due to dilution with rainwater and maxima in summer, owing to evaporation and reduced discharge of sewage water to the lake.

Dissolved Oxygen

Dissolved oxygen content is one of the most important factors in stream health. Its deficiency directly affects the ecosystem of the lake due to bioaccumulation and biomagnifications. The oxygen content in water samples depends on a number of physical, chemical, biological, and microbiological processes. Dissolved oxygen values also change depending on the industrial activities of human. Oxygen is the single most important gas for most aquatic organisms; free oxygen (O_2) or dissolved oxygen is needed for respiration. Dissolved oxygen values are found maximum during winter and minimum during summer, which might be due to natural turbulence and higher algal productivity, which produces O_2 by photosynthesis in rainy period, and active utilization in bacterial decomposition of organic matter. The pre-monsoon maxima (14.77) and minima (9.7 in post-monsoon 2013) in the lake may caution increasing accumulation of organic load and human activities.

Phosphate and Nitrate

Phosphate and nitrate determinations are important in assessing the potential biological productivity of surface waters. Increasing concentration of phosphorus and nitrogen compounds in lakes and reservoirs leads to eutrophication. Phosphates and nitrates of all the sites showed pre-monsoon maxima and post-monsoon minima; this could be due to agricultural run-off during rainy season and utilization as nutrients by algae and other aquatic plants. A significant increasing trend was observed at the inlet, which could be due to the sewage water.

Chlorides

Chlorides occur naturally in all types of waters. High concentration of chlorides is considered to be the indicator of pollution due to organic wastes of animal. The levels of chlorides in the present investigation exhibit the values which are maximum in pre-monsoon (2013) and minimum in post-monsoon (2012) and ranged from 2.13 mg/l to 7.12 mg/l in the inlet and outlet region respectively.

Sodium and Potassium

Sodium and potassium of the present analysis showed pre-monsoon maxima and post-monsoon minima. All the three locations—viz. inlet, outlet, and middle—are showing higher concentration. Sodium and potassium showed increasing trend in all the sites and ranges from 3.21 mg/l to 8.92 mg/l and from 0.3 mg/l to 1.73 mg/l respectively.

Total Hardness

Total hardness of water is an important consideration in determining the suitability of water for domestic and industrial uses. Hardness is caused by multivalent metallic cations and with certain anions present in the water to form scale. Increasing trend of values is observed at all the sites, with the range of 4.28 to 12.56 mg/l during pre-monsoon (2013) in the inlet region and during post-monsoon (2012) in the outlet region respectively.

CONCLUSION

Thus, the present study concludes that the lake water of the study area that falls in the inlet and outlet regions are moderately polluted and the middle region is fairly polluted with respect to physico-chemical assessment. The pH, DO, bacteriological studies show that the lake water is not fit for drinking purposes due to great amount of sewage. The study concludes that the significance of continuous monitoring and treatment process is essential make the available water to be used for drinking purposes.

REFERENCES

Abida, B., and Harikrishna (2008), Study on the Quality of Water in Some Streams of Cauvery River, *E-Journal of Chemistry*, **5** (2): 377–384.

APHA American Public Health Association., Standard Methods For The Examination of Water and Wastewater. 20ᵗʰ Edition. APHA American Water Works Association. (AWWA), and Water Pollution Control Federation, Washington, DC (1998).

5 PHOSPHOROUS HYDROCHEMISTRY IN LAKES OF KUMAUN HIMALAYAS, INDIA

P. Purushothaman[1], S. P. Rai[2], and A. Manju[3]

[1] Department of Civil Engineering, Saveetha School of Engineering, Saveetha University, Chennai, Tamil Nadu, India 602105

[2] Hydrological Investigation Division, National Institute of Hydrology, Roorkee, Uttarakhand 247667

[3] Department of Embedded System Technology, SKP Engineering College, Tiruvannamali, Tamil Nadu 606611

Email: purus26@gmail.com

ABSTRACT

The Kumaun Himalayan lakes, situated in the administrative state of Uttarakhand, are one of the major tourist attractions in the northern part of India. The present study is aimed to understand phosphorus water chemistry in these lakes. The study was accomplished by the collection of water samples at different depths and interstitial water. The total concentration of nutrients (P, N, and S) in the water column, interstitial water, and the sediments varied differently. The oversaturation of minerals, hydroxyapite (in Nainital), and carbonate fluorapatite (in other lakes) in the water column indicates precipitation of phosphorous on to the sediments.

Keywords: hydrogeochemistry, phosphorous, Kumaun lakes.

INTRODUCTION

Most of the lakes are characterized by finite boundaries and comparatively limited mobility of materials and, hence, provide a more tractable venue as natural laboratories for mechanistic studies. Several concepts and processes of current interest in aquatic ecosystems were first defined and examined in lakes (Wetzel 2001). Lakes serve as a source of water for organisms living in it, and they also serve humans in several ways. They are used for drinking water, irrigation, fisheries, industrial and domestic needs, and socio-economy. The major sources of water for the lakes are precipitation and small streams/springs draining into the lake basin. The lake water composition depends mainly on the lithology of the catchment area. However, recent human activities around lakes have also imprinted their signatures on water flux and lake water quality. In addition to water, the sediments are also an important component of lakes and act as both source and sink for the contaminants (Forstner and Wittman 1983). The contaminants are transported both in solution and attached to the suspended matter from the catchment area (Salomons et al. 1987). The permanent accumulation of contaminants poses problems because sediments act as a source of pollution long after the pollution of overlying water has been abated (Harder et al. 2007). Natural processes and anthropogenic changes in external parameters may cause rapid mobilization of the accumulated pollutants.

The major nutrients, phosphorus, nitrogen, silica, and the metals cause eutrophication of lake ecosystems. The nutrients are introduced into a lake system through the streams and springs in both particulate and dissolved forms. In the solution phase, metals and nutrients are present as free ions or as inorganic and organic complexes. In the solid phase, the main absorbing phases are clay minerals, Fe, Mn and al-oxyhydroxides, organic matter, etc., and the elements are also present in mineral lattices.

The Kumaun Himalayan lakes in India, one of the frequently stopover places during vacation in the northern part of the country, has been experiencing vigorous urbanization. The diversified nature of these lakes, which are located very near to each other, has attracted many workers towards them. The posing problem of water deterioration and increasing population have made Lake Nainital one of the most extensively studied lakes. Pant et al. (1980) observed that the Lake Nainital is undergoing rapid eutrophication and reported that N, CO_2, and the hardness of the water have increased quite alarmingly during the last two decades. Handa et al. (1982) reported phosphate (PO_4-P) concentration to be above critical levels in the Nainital Lake. Pandey et al. (1983) observed that rainfall contributed significant amounts of phosphorous and nitrogen and also found that the forestland lost nutrients very quickly compared to the non-forested land. Khanna and Jalal (1985) studied the physico-limnological aspects in Naukuchiatal Lake. Pant and Joshi (1987) studied the phytoplankton population in the Sattal Lake. Gupta and Pant (1989) have documented the elemental chemistry of sediments in the Nainital Lake. Singh and Gopal (1999) observed the productivity of Nainital Lake to be very high (>8) in Bhimtal Lake. Ali et al. (1999) in their study on the Nainital Lake observed the lake water to be rich in nutrients and metals and found that the macrophytes in the lake act as a good remover of these metals in the lake. Nachaiappan et al. (2000) studied the hydrodynamics of the Nainital Lake using numerical modelling and stable isotopes. Bartarya (1993) studied the water chemistry of the Kumaun Himalayan lakes. Das et al. (1995), Chakrapani (2002), and Das (2005) studied the major ion chemistry of the Kumaun Lakes. Das et al. (1995) estimated the rate of sedimentation on core sediments using ^{210}Pb isotope method and observed that, among all the lakes in the region, the Nainital Lake has higher sedimentation rate as compared to the other lakes. However, detailed investigations of nutrients in water and interstitial water in these lakes are still lacking, and hence, the present study is aimed at filling the gap.

METHODOLOGY

Sample Collection

Water samples were collected from the surface of the lake in 2006, and both surface- and deep-water samples at three depth intervals were collected during 2008 (Figure 5.1). The interstitial water samples were collected by centrifuging the sediments at 7,500 rpm for 1 h. The water samples were filtered through 0.45 μm cellulose nitrate membrane filter papers using a powered vacuum filtration unit. The water samples for the metal analysis were filtered immediately in the field by a hand-powered vacuum of 250 ml volume filter unit and were acidified to <2.0 pH by adding a few drops of pure nitric acid.

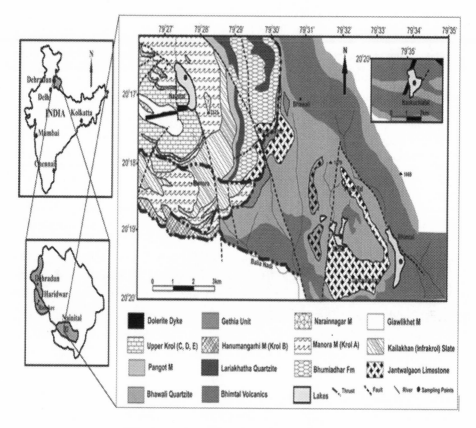

Figure 5.1. Location map of the study area.

Sample Analysis

The initial measurements of pH, Eh, and temperature were carried out in the water and sediment samples immediately after the sample collection in the field. Briefly, alkalinity in the water samples were analysed by acid titration (Gran plot). The major cations and anions in the water samples were measured using Metrohm basic ion chromatography after calibrating the instrument with the standards prepared in the laboratory. Dissolved phosphorous and silica were analysed using UVIS spectrophotometer. Dissolved trace elements (Fe, Al, Mn) in the water were analysed using DRC 3000 Elan, PerkinElmer ICP-MS. The laboratory standards procured from PerkinElmer were used to calibrate the instrument.

RESULTS AND DISCUSSION

The major cations chemistry vary widely between the lakes with magnesium (>55%) dominating the water column of the Nainital Lake and calcium (>50%) dominating in the other lakes (Figure 5.2). Calcium is the next abundant element to dominate the Nainital Lake. On the other hand, presence of magnesium was noted in other lakes (20–40%) (Figure 5.2), and sodium, and potassium were present in low concentrations in all the lakes. The interstitial water and the sediment-water interface show high concentrations compared to the water column. Calcium and magnesium dominate in Nainital, whereas calcium and sodium dominate interstitial water chemistry of the other three lakes. This might be due to the dominance of minerals such as dolomite and calcite in the catchment rocks (composed of limestone of Krol–Tal formation) of the Nainital Lake (Purushothaman et al. 2012, Purushothaman and Chakrapani, 2012, 2014) and the presence of Bhimtal volcanics and the metamorphic rocks in the catchment of the other lakes. The water chemistry of Nainital falls in magnesium bicarbonate facies and other lakes in the calcium bicarbonate facies (Bartarya 1993). The sodium and potassium concentration in the water column of the lakes is very low as compared to calcium and magnesium. Sodium is almost constant throughout the water column in the lakes except Naukuchiatal, which shows high concentration in the anoxic water column. This might be due to the dissociation of sodium from the organic matter by a sudden change in Eh (Boyle 2001). The concentration of potassium is low in all the lakes, which might be due to the low mobility of potassium. The interstitial water shows high concentration of calcium in all the lakes, but the dominance of calcium and magnesium in the Nainital may be due to the dissolution of minerals, calcite, and dolomite (limestone) from the sediments. The dominance of sodium in interstitial water of other lakes, especially in the Sattal and Naukuchiatal, may be due to the release of sodium from the dissolution of feldspar and other silicate minerals and dissociation from the organic matter in the sediments.

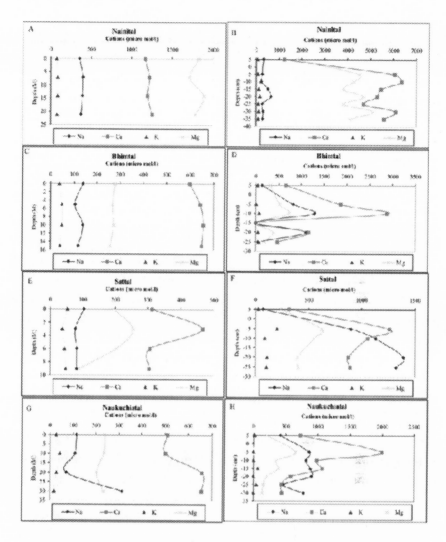

Figure 5.2. Cation variation in the water and interstitial waters in the lakes (A, C, E, G for water column; B, D, F, H for interstitial water).

Among the anions, bicarbonate dominates the water column in all the lakes, which constitute >75% of the total anions in Nainital lake and >95% in the other lakes (Figure 5.2). Sulphate (~20%) is the next dominant anion in Nainital and chloride (~10–15%) in the other lakes. Phosphorus concentrations in the lakes are very less (0.05–0.3 μmol/l), although the concentration in the Nainital Lake is much higher (3.78 μmol/l). The anions concentration in the sediment–water interface and the top 10 cm of the sediment column increase dramatically. Bicarbonate and sulphate show very high concentration in the interstitial water, and chloride shows high concentration in the sediment–water interface. This may be due to the dissolution of gypsum or oxidation of pyrite (in Nainital) derived from the catchment. Phosphorus concentration is less in the interstitial water column of the Nainital Lake, and the other lakes show increased concentration in the interstitial water column. The concentration of nitrate reduces in the interstitial water, and the concentration of ammonium increases with depth. This indicates denitrification in the anoxic zone, where nitrate reduces to form ammonia-free nitrogen (Schwientek et al. 2008). The high concentration of dissolved sulphate (Table 5.1) in the interstitial water can also be attributed to the reduction of iron and nitrate in the anoxic zone, resulting in the oxidation of sulphide minerals (Lucassen et al. 2005, Schwientek et al. 2008). The high concentration of phosphate in the water column of the Nainital can be attributed to the weathering of the country rocks (apatite in the Krol formation) or the domestic sewage draining into the lake. The phosphorus-bearing mineral apatite is not abundant in the catchment; hence, anthropogenic source, such as domestic waste disposal into the lake, may play a significant role in the increase of phosphorus concentration in the lake water. The low concentration of phosphorous (Nainital Lake) (Figure 5.3) in the interstitial water may also sequester phosphorus by carbonate fluorapatite. The other three lakes show high concentration of phosphorus in the water column above sediment layer and interstitial water. This may be due to the release of phosphorus by the reduction of the iron–manganese oxides, which is co-precipitated from the oxic layer in the anoxic lake layer.

Saturation of Minerals in the Water Column and Interstitial Water

The WATEQ4F speciation model was used to find the saturation indices of various minerals in the lakes. The minerals calcite, siderite, aragonite, and dolomite are oversaturated in the Nainital Lake (Table 5.1), whereas these minerals are absent in the other three lakes (Table 5.1). This indicates the precipitation of these minerals from the water column in Nainital Lake. The phosphorus in the water column mainly remains as orthophosphate and manganese phosphate. The mineral hydroxyapatite is undersaturated in the lakes other than Nainital (SI = 1). The oversaturation of the carbonate fluorapatite (FCO$_3$ apatite) (Table 5.1 and 5.2) shows that this mineral acts as main sink for phosphorus in these lakes. Silica generally occurs as silicate ion in the water and interstitial column. The minerals quartz, chalcedony, and amorphous quartz mostly show undersaturation in the water column, and shows oversaturation in the interstitial water column in Nainital Lake (tables 5.1 and 5.2), thus indicating precipitation in the sediment column. The other lakes show undersaturation of these phases in the entire lake.

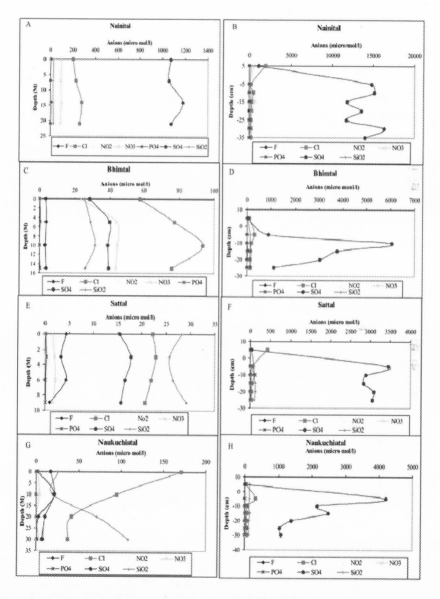

Figure 5.3. Anion variation in the water and interstitial water in the lakes (A, C, E, G for water column; B, D, F, H for interstitial water).

Table 5.1 Saturation indices of different minerals in the water column

Minerals	Nainital	Bhimtal, Sattal, and Naukuchiatal
$Al(OH)_3$ (a)	–1	–0.8 to –0.7
Aragonite	0.3 to 0.2	–0.8 to –0.7
Calcite	0.4 to 0.45	–0.6
Chalcedony	–0.8 to –0.7	–0.8 to –0.7
Cristobalite	–0.7 to –0.6	–0.7 to –0.6
Cupric ferrite	9	14 to 13
Cuprite	1.9	–7 to –5
Cuprous ferrite	14	12
Dolomite (d)	0.3 to 0.2	–2
Dolomite (c)	0.9	–1.8
FCO_3 apatite	16	4 to 3
$Fe_3(OH)_8$	2	5 to 4.5
$Fe(OH)_{2.7}Cl_{0.3}$	5	7.5
Ferrihydrite	0.8	3
Fluorapatite	2	–4.5
Goethite	5.9	8
Hematite	13.7	18.5
Hydroxyapatite	1	–6
Illite	1.2	1 to 0.5
Kaolinite	3.8	4
Kmica	7.9	8 to 7.5
Magnetite	15.8	19 to 18
$MnHPO_4$	0.25	–0.7
Montmoril BF	1.8	2.5 to 2.1
Montmoril AB	1.7	1.7 to 2
Montmoril Ca	1.3	1.9 to 1.4
Quartz	–0.3	–0.3
Siderite (d)	0.12	–1.4
Siderite (c)	0.43	–1
Vivianite	–0.95	–7 to –6

Amorphous (a), crystalline (c), disordered solids (d).

Table 5.2 Saturation indices of different minerals in interstitial water column

Minerals	Nainital	Bhimtal, Sattal, and Naukuchiatal
$Al(OH)_3$ (a)	–1.2 to –0.5	–0.27 to –0.08
Aragonite	0.4 to 0.2	–1.2 to –0.6
Calcite	0.6 to 0.3	–1.5 to –0.5
Chalcedony	–0.08 to –0.08	–0.8 to –0.2
Cristobalite	0.18 to 0.05	0.1 to 0.07
Cupric ferrite	-	–7
Cuprite	1.8 to 1.1	1.8 to 0.6
Cuprous ferrite	8 to 6	6 to 9
Dolomite (d)	0.143	–4.5 to –2.5
Dolomite (c)	0.8 to 0.4	–3.5 to –1.5
FCO_3 apatite	11 to 7	6 to 1.5
$Fe_3(OH)_8$	-	-
$Fe(OH)_{2.7}Cl_{0.3}$	-	0.7 to –0.3
Ferrihydrite	–6 to –5	–6.5 to –3.5
Fluorapatite	–4 to –1	–10 to –4
Goethite	–1.5 to –0.2	–1.5 to –0.5
Hematite	–1 to –0.5	5 to –1.5
Hydroxyapatite	–6 to –4	–12 to –7
Illite	4.5 to 2.5	5 to 3
Kaolinite	5 to 6	8 to 6.5
Kmica	9 to 11	11
Magnetite	1.8 to –1.09	6 to –2
$MnHPO_4$	–2	0.01 to -0.14
Montmoril BF	3 to 1.88	4 to 2.5
Montmoril AB	1.7 to 0.3	2.1 to 0.89
Montmoril Ca	5.5 to 4.5	6.8 to 4.2
Quartz	0.6 to 0.4	0.6 to 0.45
Siderite (d)	0.12	–1.8 to –0.8
Siderite (c)	0.4 to 0.2	–0.4 to –0.6
Vivianite	–4.5	–9 to –4.5

Amorphous (a), crystalline (c), disordered solids (d).

CONCLUSION

The water composition Ca+Mg:Na+K shows the major influence of carbonate rock weathering in water chemistry of the lakes. The increasing concentration of chloride in the anoxic layer shows formation of mono- and bisulphides in the anoxic condition. The increasing concentration of ammonia shows denitrification/ammonox process. The high concentration of dissolved sulphate in the Nainital Lake may be due to the oxidation of mono- and bisulphides. The Nainital Lake also shows high concentration dissolved phosphate compared to the other three lakes. Dissolved phosphate precipitates from the water column as carbonate fluorapatite, resulting in low concentration in the interstitial water. The high concentration of phosphorus in the sediments of Nainital and Sattal lakes may be due to the weathering of apatite-bearing calcareous rocks in the catchment. The oversaturation of carbonate minerals calcite, dolomite, and aragonite in the water column of Nainital Lake and their presence in the sediments indicate a possible precipitation. The oversaturation of minerals, hydroxyapatite (in Nainital), and carbonate fluorapatite (in other lakes) in the water column indicates precipitation of phosphorus on to the sediments.

ACKNOWLEDGEMENTS

The first author specially acknowledges MoEF, CSIR, India, for support through fellowship. The authors also thank Prof. Chakrapani, Ravi, Yadav, and Vijay for their help in the field and lab.

REFERENCES

Ali, M. B., Tripathi, R. D., Rai, U. N., Pal, A., and Singh, S. P. (1999), Physico-chemical characteristics and pollution level of Lake Nainital (UP, India): Role of macrophytes and phytoplankton in biomonitoring and phytoremediation of toxic metal ions. *Chemosphere*, 39, 2171–2182.

Bartarya, S. K. 1993. Hydrochemistry and rock weathering in a sub-tropical Lesser Himalayan river basin in Kumaun, India. *Journal of Hydrology*, 146, 149–174.

Boyle, J. 2001. Redox remobilization and the heavy metal record in Lake sediments: A Modelling approach. *Journal of Paleolimnology*, 26, 423–431.

Chakrapani, G. J. 2002. Water and sediment geochemistry of major Kumaun Himalayan lakes, India. *Environmental Geology*, 43, 99–107.

Das, B. K. 2005. Environmental pollution impact on water and sediments of Kumaun lakes, Lesser Himalaya, India: a comparative study. *Environmental Geology*, 49, 230–239.

Das, B. K., Singh, M., and van Grieken, R. (1995), The elemental chemistry of sediments in the Nainital Lake, Kumaun Himalaya, India. *Science of the Total Environment*, 168, 85–90.

Forstner, U., and Wittmann, G. T. W. (1983), *Metal Pollution in the Aquatic Environment*, 2nd Revised Edition, Springer Verlag, p 486.

Gupta, P. K., and Pant, M. C. (1989), Sediment chemistry of Lake Bhimtal, UP, India. *International Revue Hydrobiology*, 74, 679–687.

Handa, B. K., Kumar, A., and Goel, D. K. (1982), Eutrophication of Nainital lake. *IAWPC Tech manual IX*, 110–120.

Harder, S. V., Amatya, D. M., Callahan, T. J., Trettin, C. C., and Hakkila, J. (2007), Hydrology and water budget for a first order forested coastal plain watershed, South Carolina. *Journal of American Water Resources Association*, 43, 563–575.

Khanna, L. S., and Jalal, D. S. (1985), Physico-limnological analysis of Naukuchiatal Lake, Kumaun Himalaya. *Mountain Research Development*, 4, 51–54.

Lucassen, E. C. H. E. T., Smolders, A. J. P., Lamers, L. P. M., and Roelofs, J. G. M. (2005), Water table fluctuations and groundwater supply are important in preventing phosphate-eutrophication in sulphate-rich fens: Consequences for wetland restoration. *Plant and Soil*, 269, 109–115.

Nachiappan, P. R., Kumar, B., Saravanakumar, U., Jacob, N., Sharma, S., Joseph, T. B., Navada, S. V., and Manickavasagam, R. M. (2000), Estimation of sub-surface components in the water balance of lake Nainital (Kumaun Himalaya, India) using environmental isotopes. *Proceedings of International Conference on Integrated Water resources Management for Sustainable Development*, New Delhi, 239–254.

Pandey, A. N., Pathak, P. C., and Singh, J. S. (1983), Water, sediment and nutrient movement in forested and non-forested catchments in Kumaun Himalaya. *Forest Ecology and Management*, 7, 19–29.

Pant, M. C., and Joshi, A. (1987), Phytoplankton analysis in Lake Sattal, UP, India. *International Revue of Hydrobiology*, 72, 307–324.

Pant, M. C., Sharma, A. P., and Sharma, P. C. (1980), Evidence for the increased eutrophication of lake Nainital as a result of human interference, *Environmental Pollution (Series B)*, 1, 149–161.

P. Purushothaman, S. Mishra, A. Das, and G. J. Chakrapani (2012), Sediment and Hydro Biogeochemistry of Lake Nainital, Kumaun Himalaya, India. Environmental Earth Sciences, 65, 775–788.

P. Purushothaman and G. J. Chakrapani (2012), Trace Metal Biogeochemistry in Kumaun Himalayan lakes. Environmental Monitoring and Assessment, 184, 2947–2965.

P. Purushothaman, G. J. Chakrapani. Phosphorous Biogeochemistry in sediments of High Altitude Lakes, Kumaun Himalayas, India. Arabian Journal of Geosciences (In Press).

Salomons, W., de Rooij, N. M., Kerdijk, H., and Bril, J. (1987), Sediments as a source for Contaminants? *Hydrobiologia*, 149, 13–30.

Schwientek, M., Einsiedl, F., Stichler, W., Stogbauer, A., Strauss, H., and Maloszewski, P. (2008), Evidence for denitrification regulated by pyrite oxidation in heterogeneous porous groundwater system. *Chemical Geology*, doi: 10.1016/j.chemgeo.2008.06.005.

Singh, S. P., and Brij, Gopal, eds., (1999), *Nainital and Himalayan Lakes*. NIE and WWF Publications, New Delhi, India, p. 62.

6 IMPACT OF URBANIZATION ON HESARAGHATTA LAKE (RESERVOIR): A CASE STUDY OF ARKAVATHY RIVER

H. V. Rekha and Asima Nusrath
Department of GIS, Maharaja's College, University of Mysore, Mysore
Email: rekhashreenivasu@gmail.com

ABSTRACT

The drying of lakes and rivers at the vicinity of a big metropolitan area is one of the most common dangers of urbanization in recent times. This problem is more in case of surface water; however, in the case of groundwater, it is overexploited and insufficiently recharged. The river Arkavathy is a tributary of Cauvery, and it draws water from the south-western portion of the Nandi Hills. Though the river is not exactly a seasonal stream, in the summer months it presents as a sandy bed with a small current of water flowing on one side.

The study deals with the present form of the Hesaraghatta lake, the causes for its drying, and the impacts on land-use changes. The impacts are mainly felt on the forest cover and groundwater condition. Because of the drying of lakes and rivers, groundwater level dropped more than 1,000 ft. At this level, water contains dangerous chemicals which affects human life.

INTRODUCTION

The availability and quality of water determine not only the nature of human activity but also the quality of life. However, as a consequence of the diverse activities of humans, a serious problem of lakes and rivers drying as a result of uncontained urbanization seems to be a growing fear. The Arkavathy is a tributary of the Cauvery, and its source is a well in the south-western portion of the Nandi Hills. Taking a south-westerly route, the river enters Doddballapur taluk, passes through the Hesaraghatta and eastern portions of Nelamangala taluk, receives the rivulet Kumudvathi from the west at Thippagondanahalli, and flows through the Magadi taluk, passing east of Savandurga. Penetrating between the hills Ramagiri and Shivanagiri, it runs through Ramanagara District and then through Kanakapura taluk. Another tributary, the Vrishabhavathi, meets the river near Maduvadidurga, and finally the river flows into the Cauvery on the southern borders of the district in Kanakapura taluk at Sangam. The length of the main stream is about 190 km. Sir K. Seshadri Iyer, the then diwan of erstwhile Mysore province, thought of providing water supply to Bangalore through a source of perennial character by building a reservoir across river Arkavathy, which could store three years' supply to the city. In accordance with the above, the first scheme of protected water supply, Chamarajendra Water Works, was undertaken in 1894, the source of supply being Hesaraghatta lake on the Arkavathy river.

The present study aims to identify land use and land cover or Hesaraghatta lake/reservoir catchment and to assess the impact of urbanization on the lakes of Arkavathy catchment using remote sensing techniques.

METHODOLOGY

Resourcesat LISS III data downloaded from Bhuvan for 2008 (12 November 2008) and 2011 (09 November 2011) are used to know the land use, land cover, and its changes in the study area using supervised classification method in Erdas Imagine 9.1.. MS Excel was used to generate the graphs.

STUDY AREA

The study area is situated about 23 km north-west of the Bangalore City and is drained by the river Arkavathy. The catchment extends up to Doddaballapur, which is part of Devanahalli, north part of Bangalore North District. The catchment covers an area of 564.64 km^2 and is covered in the Survey of India toposheet Nos. 57 G/7, G/8, G/11, G/12. The area lies between 13° to 13° 30' N and 77° 15' to 77° 45' E. The catchment occupies an area of 569.49 km^2 (13.77% of the total catchment).

RESULTS AND DISCUSSION

Water bodies of the study area are extracted from the satellite images of 2008 and 2011, and using Erdas Imagine 9.1, supervised classification has been performed. In the 2008 images, there were a number of lakes, but in the 2011 images, after Doddaballapur the lakes disappear. Land use and land cover broadly connote everything land is used for as expressed in the vegetation and other human interventions covering the land surface. Land-use pattern generally reflects the extent of resources utilization and indicates productivity of the area. Therefore, inventory of various land-use and land-cover categories and their spatial distribution and understanding the changes in their pattern are very important for resources management and conservations efforts.

The study area has been delineated into different categories such as built-up lands, plantation, agricultural fields, open lands with grass, and water body. Figures 6.1 and 6.2 enable a quick relational perception of the different land-use/land-cover categories and the changes over a period of three years.

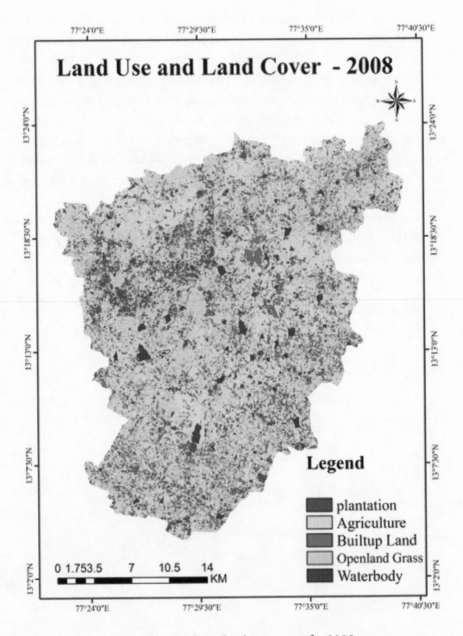

Figure 6.1. Land-use/land-cover map for 2008.

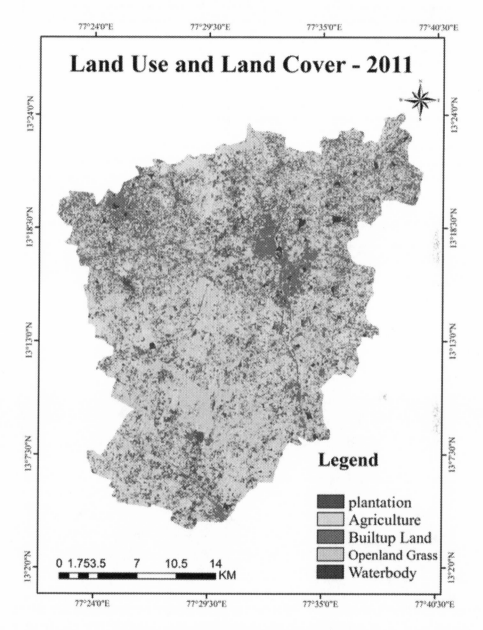

Figure 6.2. Land-use/land-cover map for 2011.

Built-Up Land

In the study area, built-up land includes urban/rural settlements and industrial lands. The total area occupied by built-up land in 2008 is 4,994.03 ha (7.05%). This was increased to 9,085.70 ha (12.082%) in 2011, showing an increase in area by 4,091.66 ha during the last three years. The different categories of build-up lands within the catchment are village settlements, towns, urban areas, and industrial land, which increased especially in Doddaballupur District.

Agricultural Land

Within the study area, crops in the agricultural lands were identified through field observation. Paddy, ragi, groundnut, pulses, oilseed, ornamental flowers, and vegetables are generally grown. Area under this category is 37,948.89 ha (53.57%) in 2008 is decreased to 37,670.11 ha (53.18%) in 2011, showing a decrease of 278.78 ha during the last three years.

Plantation

Plantations (such as coconut, areca nut, vegetable, and ornamental-flower plantations) and orchards (mainly mango, guava, pomegranate, grape, mulberry orchards) are included in this category. There is a gradual decrease in the area occupied by these crops during the last three years. It has declined from 9,413.91 ha (13.29%) in 2008 to 7,176.10 ha (10.13%) in 2011.

Open Land with Grass

Open lands with grass are degraded areas which are underutilized or have undergone degradation either due to natural or anthropogenic causes. These are covered by thorny scrubs, grass, bushes, and small trees. The degraded open land with grass during 2008–2011 was 17,249.38 ha (24.35%) to 16,354.06 ha (23.08%) respectively.

Water Body

Water body comprises of the areas under tanks (tanks with water) and reservoirs in the study area. Surface water spread in the tanks/reservoirs during 2008 and 2011 were 1,228.12 ha (1.733%) and 548.36 ha (0.77%) respectively.

Land-Use/Land-Cover Change Detection

Through the change detection analysis, decreased area and increased area were identified (Figure 6.3). Agriculture, water body, and open lands are under decreased category. Only the build-up lands are under the increasing land use (Figure 6.4). As per the output image of change detection for 2008–2011, area under decreasing land use and land cover is 29,275.81 ha. Unchanged land use and land cover are 53,760.03 ha, and increased land use and land cover are 36,619.2 ha (Table 6.1 and Figure 6.5).

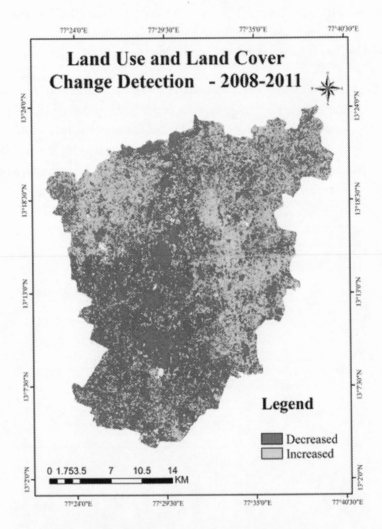

Figure 6.3. Land-use/land-cover changes with respect to
decreased area and increased area (2008 to 2013).

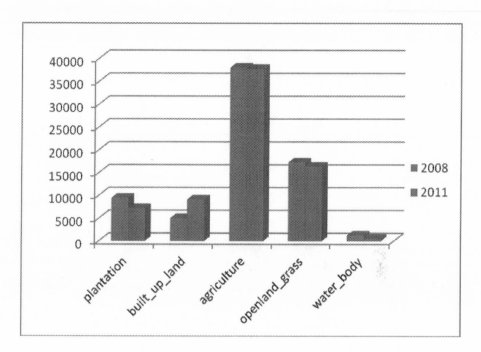

Figure 6.4. Land-use and land-cover change detection for 2008–2011.

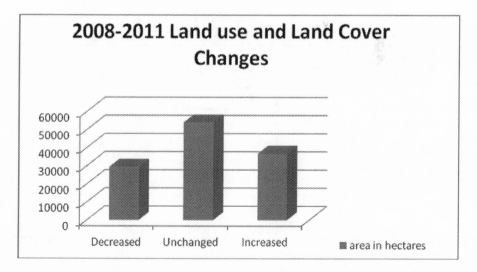

Figure6.5. Land-use and land-cover pattern.

Misuse of Lakebed due to Urbanization

Bangalore is one of the fastest-growing cities in India due to the demand of land for residential and industrial sector. Bangalore extends its area to the surrounding region north of Doddaballapur taluk as a result of urbanization and industrialization. Devanahalli International Airport is also a cause of changes in land use. Its impact on lakes is very dangerous. Lakes are occupied by the people for agriculture purpose in Doddaballapur. Some people building apartments at the lake were identified during the field visit. Some parts of the lake are filled with waste or garbage of the town, and some parts of the forest near the lake have been planted with trees under afforestation programmes, which are bound to disturb water flow of the Hesaraghatta Lake. Due to urbanization and the huge demand for water, there are 21 borewells drilled at the Hesaraghatta Lake. Groundwater level crossed more than 750 ft. There is no proper groundwater recharge because of all these reasons. Surface water is almost gone in Hesaraghatta Lake in 2011. The direct effect of urbanization is the conversion of agricultural/garden lands into residential or industrial layouts. Doddaballapur and Devanahalli also play a major role in the urbanization. They are also in the same condition, and due to these reasons, Hesaraghatta Lake is drying up.

Table 6.1 Land-use/land-cover characteristics

land use/ land cover	2008	2008 (%)	2011	2011 (%)
Plantation	9,413.914	13.29004	7,176.103	10.13082
Built-up land	4,994.034	7.050301	9,085.703	12.82669
Agriculture	37,948.89	53.57414	37,670.11	53.18058
Open land with grass	17,249.38	24.35172	16,354.06	23.08775
Water body	1,228.126	1.7338	548.3655	0.774152
Total	**70,834.34**	**100**	**70,834.34**	**100**

CONCLUSION

Water is very important to sustain life. Water not only sustains life but also determines the quality of life; however, as a consequence of diversified human activities, a serious problem of lakes and rivers drying arises in the study area. This problem is more serious in the case of surface water due to the urbanization. In the case of groundwater, it is overexploited, and recharging is not going properly. Certain preventive measures are necessarily called for to preserve the Hesarghatta Lake and its catchment. Keeping in view the importance of the Hesaraghatta reservoir as a vital source of water supply to Bangalore City in the years to come and Arkavathy as a natural source of water for agriculture to its surrounding regions, the following recommendations are made: (1) creating awareness among the public (especially those within the vicinity of the catchment) on the importance of water conservation and conjunctive utilization of surface water and groundwater, (2) considering the entire catchment as a conservation zone and adopting a suitable land utilization strategy therein, especially from the point of view of regulating the urbanization/industrialization, (3) declaring a zone of about 10 km. radius around the Hesaraghatta as a reservoir area, and (4) regulating a buffer of around 2 km on either side of the Arkavathy course for protecting the river from further deterioration.

REFERENCES

Bangalore District Gazetteer (1990), Govt of Karnatakapublication.

Bangalore Rural District Gazetteer (1990) (2000), Govt. of Karnataka.

Bangalore, Published in the Seminar volume 'Infrastructure Key to Growth, is Karnataka geared up?'

Gajanana Bhat Sangeetha (2003), Environmental Impact Assessment of Water Quality in the River Arkavathi, Karnataka India.

Indian Space Research Organization (ISRO) (2000), Reduced inflow into Tippagondanahalli Reservoir (TGR) A Remote Sensing based evaluation.

In-RIMT and BMRDA (1995), Technical Report—Integrated Resources Analysis to Water Resources and Sustainable Development: Challenges of 21 Century/edited by Kamta Prasad. Delhi, Shipra Pub., 2003, xxvi, 468 p. Vol.

7 HYDRODYNAMICS OF MANSAR LAKE, UDHAMPUR DISTRICT, JAMMU AND KASHMIR, USING STABLE ISOTOPE (δ^{18}O AND δ^2H)

S. P. Rai, C. P. Kumar, Omkar Singh, and S. K. Verma
National Institute of Hydrology, Roorkee 247 667 (Uttarakhand)
Email: spr@nih.ernet.in

ABSTRACT

An attempt has been made to study the isotopic composition (δ^{18}O and δ^2H) of Mansar Lake, a natural lake located in the Himalayan foothill of Jammu and Kashmir, India. The δ^{18}O and δ^2H compositions of the local precipitation, springs, groundwater, and the lake are used to understand the hydrodynamics of Mansar Lake. It has been observed that the lake exhibits a distinct hydrothermal behaviour. The lake water mixes completely during the months of January and February and remains stratified in the remaining months. The δ^{18}O values of the lake water varies from +1‰ to +4‰ in surface water and from +1.1‰ to +2.6‰ in bottom water while the average values for rainwater and groundwater are in the order of −6.8 ‰ and −5.3‰ respectively. The lake's δ^{18}O values show enrichment of lake water in comparison to groundwater. The δ^{18}O and δ^2H relationship shows that the slope of the lake's meteoric waterline is 4.7. The D-excess values for the lake are observed to vary between 0 ‰ and −15‰, which confirm the significant effect of non-equilibrium fractionation. The enrichment of the lake water's δ^{18}O clearly reveals that the lake water has undergone significant evaporative fractionation. The enrichment of δ^{18}O of the lake's bottom water reveals that the contribution of groundwater to the lake water is insignificant. It implies that the lake is sustained mainly through the rainfall-derived run-off. The present study reveals the hydrodynamic aspect of Mansar Lake, which is important for proper management of the lake.

INTRODUCTION

A large number of natural lakes in Himalayas are famous for their picturesque views, and most of them are utilized for drinking and irrigation purposes. For example, Nainital, Dal, and Mansar lakes are used to meet the drinking water supply to the respective cities. Lakes are important in maintaining the hydrological, ecological, and environmental balance of the region. However, the increasing anthropogenic activities in recent years have greatly affected the hydrological regime of the lakes in the country and inflow of eroded materials, and other contaminants from the lakes' catchment have accelerated eutrophication process and rate of sedimentation (Dansgaard 1964, Gopal and Zutshi 1998). This higher rate of sedimentation has diminished the useful life of several small lakes within the country, and others are shrinking at an alarming rate. Hence, knowledge on hydrological conditions of these lakes becomes utmost importance for appropriate management and future planning of them. Physico-chemical and biological characteristics of various lakes in the Himalayas have been studied by Goyal et al. (2002), Ishaq and Kaul (1988), Kaul (1977), Kumar et al. (1999a, b), Nachiappan et al. (2002), Pant et al. (1985), Rai et al. (1998), Rai et al. (2007), Rai et al. (2002), and Rai et al. (2006a) in detail. However, complete water balance study of any of the Himalayan lakes is not reported using conventional techniques. In Indian Himalayas, Nainital Lake is the first example where all the parameters of the lake's water balance have been estimated using isotopic techniques (Pant et al. 1985 and Rozanski et al. 1993). The complete water balance of any lake reveals its hydrological status. In the present study, isotopic composition of Mansar Lake has been used to understand the hydrological status of the lake.

STUDY AREA

Mansar Lake (75° 05' 11.5" to 75° 5' 12.5" E and 32° 40' 58.25" to 32° 40' 59.25" N) is located 60 km east of Jammu City at an elevation of 666 m AMSL in the Siwalik terrain (Figure 7.1). The suboval-shaped lake covers an area of 0.59 km^2. The maximum depth of the lake is 38.25 m, and it has a capacity of 11.57×10^6 m^3 (Rai et al. 2007). The lake's mean width and depth are 490 m and 20.23 m respectively.

Climatically, the area is subtropical, and the average annual rainfall is 1,500 mm; the air temperature varies between 3 °C (minimum) in winter and 43 °C (maximum) during peak summer while the lake water temperature at the surface varies between 14 °C (minimum) in January and 31 °C (maximum) in July. There is no surface inflow channel into the lake. The excess water from the lake drains to a small tributary of the Tawi River through piped outlet. The lake's water level varies within 1.5 m to 2 m in a year. An initial water balance of this lake indicated that the lake is also fed by groundwater (Singh and Sharma 1999).

Geologically, the Mansar Lake catchment is composed of fine-grained sandstone alternating with siltstone, mudstone, and clay of the lower Siwalik (Figure 7.1). Both the Mansar and Surinsar (a nearby lake) lakes are located at the crestal part of the WNW–NW to ESE–SE trending subhorizontal anticlinorium. Associated with upright fold plunging 5° towards S 52° E, the NNE–SSW trending faults have displaced the anticlinorial axes at several places (Trisal 1987) and are responsible for the fragile nature of the lower Siwalik. These crushed rocks form the porous and permeable zone for recharge of the lakes.

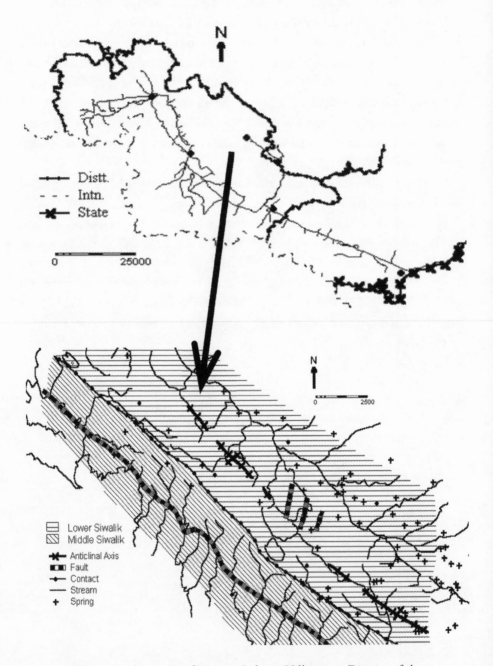

Figure 7.1. Location of Mansar Lake in Udhampur District of the Jammu and Kashmir, showing hydrogeological setup of the area.

The lake has a small catchment area of 1.67 km². Habitation and agricultural fields cover the northern and eastern parts of the lake catchment. The north-west flank is mainly covered by agricultural fields (25%). The reserve forest on the western and southern parts of the catchment covers 0.39 km² (Figure 7.2 and Table 7.1) is mainly represented by *Mangifera indica*, *Ficus religiosa*, *Pinus roxburghii*, and other subtropical type of plants, but the forest cover is scattered and degraded. Agriculture land area is extensively used mainly for paddy, wheat, and maize productions. There is a rapid increase in the urban area due to the construction of hotels and guest houses.

METHODOLOGY

In order to assess the lake water isotopic composition, samples were collected from different locations in the lakes at different depth intervals. To characterize groundwater, samples were collected on monthly and on different seasons from various handpumps and springs located nearby the lake, within the lake catchment, or outside the lake catchment. Water samples were collected in pre-cleaned 60 ml polypropylene bottles (Tarsons make). These were rinsed profusely at the site with sample water and filled with water samples, tightly capped (to prevent evaporation and exchange with the atmospheric moisture), and brought to the laboratory for isotopic analysis. The oxygen and hydrogen isotope measurements were carried out using a dual-inlet isotope ratio mass spectrometer (GV instruments, UK) with automatic sample preparation units. For oxygen and hydrogen isotopes, 400 mL water samples were taken, and Hokko beads were used as the catalyst. Along with each batch of samples, secondary standards developed with reference to primary standards (i.e. V-SMOW, SLAP, GISP) were also measured, and the final δ-values were calculated using a triple-point calibration equation. The overall precision based on 10 points repeated measurements of each sample was with the error limits of ±0.1‰ for $\delta^{18}O$ and ±1‰ for $\delta^{2}H$.

RESULTS AND DISCUSSION

Thermal Characteristics

The depth-versus-temperature plots (Figure 7.2) of the Mansar Lake depict that the temperature decreases with depth from April to November. In these months, the relatively warm and wind-mixed upper layer called the epilimnion ranges up to a depth of 6 m, and below the epilimnion, between a depth of 6 and 10 m, the temperature decreases rapidly. This plane of maximum temperature change is called thermocline. Lying below a depth of 10 m, a relatively cold layer that is not mixed by wind comes under the hypolimnion. The stable stratification that persists from April to November tends to become unstable during early winter (i.e. December) because of the falling air temperature, resulting in the decrease of water temperature of epilimnion and thermocline zone due to net heat loss from the lake. The development of uniform temperature conditions in January–February starts the process of convection, which, coupled with the increased action of wind, results in the deepening of surface layer (sinking of thermocline), and complete mixing of the lake takes place. This period of vertical mixing of Mansar Lake is called 'winter overturn', when the lake may be considered well mixed. As a consequence of the rise in air temperature in March, thermal stratification starts and establishes in April, and the lake remains stratified till November. Therefore, Mansar Lake undergoes two distinct stages, namely completely mixed stage and a stratified stage of minimal vertical mixing.

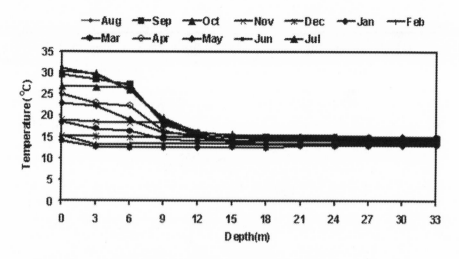

Figure 7.2. Temperature profile of the lake.

Variations of $\delta^{18}O$ with Time

The depth profile of $\delta^{18}O$ (Figure 7.3) with time reveals the isotopic composition of the lake water occurring at different depths, i.e. epilimnion, metalimnion, and hypolimnion. The $\delta^{18}O$ of the surface water in Mansar Lake varies between +1.0‰ (minimum) during the month of August and +4.2‰ (maximum) during the month of June. The higher temperature during May and June causes maximum evaporation, which results in maximum enriched value in the month of June. The observed minimum $\delta^{18}O$ value of the surface water during the month of August in Mansar Lake is due to the direct rainfall on the lake surface and run-off generated in the lake catchment with depleted $\delta^{18}O$ values (average of –6.8‰) join the lake water and dilute isotopic composition of surface water from +4.2 to +1.1‰. The temporal variation in the isotopic composition of the epilimnion is significant than in the hypolimnion as an effect of the evaporative enrichment and depletion due to the addition of run-off water during the monsoon period. However, $\delta^{18}O$ in lake metalimnion and hypolimnion varies from +1.6‰ during the month of June to +2.2‰ during the month of August (Figure 7.3). The enrichment in the bottom of the lake during the month of the August reveals that the subsurface inflow into the lake is negligible.

δ²H–δ¹⁸O Relationship

The δ^2H–$\delta^{18}O$ plots (Figure 7.4) show the isotopic composition of Mansar Lake. The local meteoric water line (LMWL) developed using the rainfall data of Jammu (Zutshi and Khan 1977) is as follows:

$$\delta^2H = 8.1 \times \delta^{18}O + 9.3 \ (n = 24, \ r^2 = 0.99)$$
Equation 1

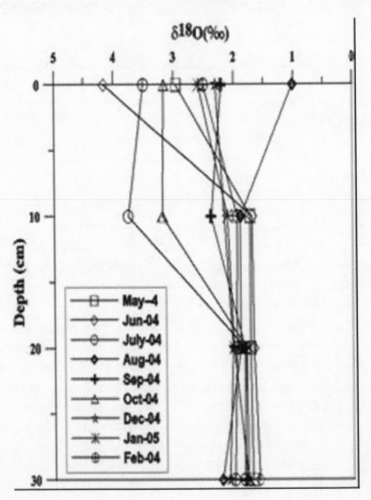

Figure 7.3. Depth profile of $\delta^{18}O$ in different months at Mansar Lake.

The slope of LMWL is very close to GMWL [δ^2H = (8.2 ± 0.1) × $\delta^{18}O$ + (10.6 ± 0.6) (Zutshi et al. 1972), which shows that the condensation process occurring at the two lakes' catchment is in equilibrium conditions. As seen in Figure 7.4, all samples from Mansar Lake fall below the LMWL, indicating its evaporative enrichment—a lower slope, i.e. 4.7 (vide Equation 2) and 4.6 (vide Equation 3), compared to that of its LMWL, i.e. 8.1 (vide Equation 2). The water balance study showed that the average annual evaporation loss is about 1.0 m in case of Mansar Lake (Rai et al. 2006b). Significant evaporative signatures indicate low groundwater contribution to the lake.

δ^2H = 4.7 × $\delta^{18}O$ – 3.7 (n = 20, r^2 = 0.66) (Equation 2, for epilimnion zone)

δ^2H = 4.6 × $\delta^{18}O$ – 3.6 (n = 30, r^2 = 0.66) (Equation 3, for hypolimnion zone)

The enriched isotopic composition reveals that the subsurface inflow is very low and, hence, not sufficient to dilute the isotopically enriched water due to evaporation. Also, the retention time of the Mansar Lake is comparatively very high as its hypolimnion waters do not show seasonal variations in their isotopic signatures (Figure 7.3).

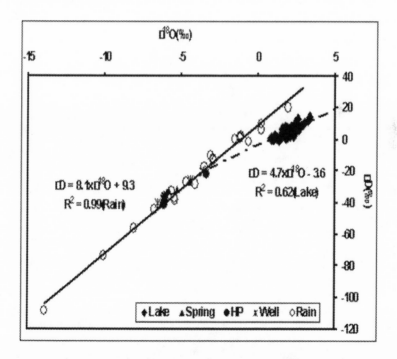

Figure 7.4. δ^2H–$\delta^{18}O$ plot of Mansar Lake along with groundwater samples.

D-Excess

The isotopic imprints of evaporation are also recorded in the form of a parameter called D-excess. The D-excess or D-index means the surplus deuterium relative to the Craig's line (Zutshi et al. 1980). The characteristics of the D-index are the following: (a) equilibrium processes do not change the D-index for any of the phases and (b) non-equilibrium evaporation from a limited amount of water reduces the D-index of the water as long as exchange is not a dominating factor. The extent to which ^{18}O is more fractionated compared to D can be defined by Dansgaard (1964) as below:

$d = \delta^2H - 8 \times \delta^{18}O$ (‰)   (Equation 4)

The D-excess (d) as defined above represents the excess δ^2H than eight times $\delta^{18}O$ for any water body or vapour. The magnitude of equilibrium fractionation (condensation) for ^2H is about eight times to that for $\delta^{18}O$. Thus, due to evaporation (non-equilibrium fractionation) from a water body, the D-excess of the evaporating water decreases while it increases in water vapour. The D-excess in the Mansar Lake is varying between 0 and –15‰ (Figure 7.5). The more negative D-excess of Mansar Lake shows significant effect of non-equilibrium fractionation of the lake water.

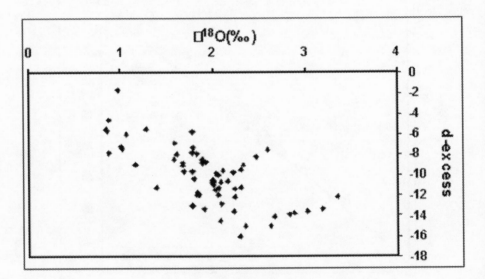

Figure 7.5. $\delta^{18}O$–D-excess of Mansar Lake.

The Mansar Lake, situated in the lower Siwalik rocks, is composed of sandstone alternating with clay bands of 1–2 m thickness. These clay bands act as impermeable layer and reduce the infiltration rate. This results in the reduction of subsurface inflow into the lake and subsurface outflow from the lake. On the other hand, Mansar Lake catchment area is very small of only 1.67 km^2. Out of which, 0.60 km^2 is the lake's surface area, and the lake volume of Mansar Lake is 12.3 × 10^6 m^3, which is greater than that of Nainital Lake. Therefore, it is obvious that the catchment input in form of subsurface inflow will be less in comparison to that of Nainital Lake. The isotopic composition of open wells and springs located in close vicinity of Mansar Lake is in the range of −4.5‰ to −6.1‰. It clearly reveals that seepage from the lakes in downstream side is negligible. Thus, Mansar Lake's groundwater interaction appears to be very poor.

Another factor responsible for this enrichment is the sedimentation rate. The sedimentation rate in Mansar Lake is in comparison to other Lesser Himalayan lakes of Kumaun region (i.e. Nainital, Bhimtal, Naukuchiatal, and Sattal). The sediment accumulation rate in Nainital, Bhimtal, Naukuchiatal, Sattal, and Mansar lakes are 860 m^{3}y^{-1}km^{-2}, 224 m^{3}y^{-1}km^{-2}, 424 m^{3}y^{-1}km^{-2}, 307 m^{3}y^{-1}km^{-2}, and 893 m^{3}y^{-1}km^{-2} respectively (Zutshi 1985). This reveals that sediment accumulation rate in Mansar Lake is higher than that of the Lesser Himalayan lakes of Kumaun. This is because rocks of Siwalik terrain (made up of fine-grained sandstone alternating with siltstone, mudstone, and clay) are more prone to erosion than the Lesser Himalayan rocks. Nainital Lake catchment is made up of limestone, dolomites, shales, with marlite. Bhimtal Lake catchment consists of metabasites associated with quartzites, grits, conglomerates, and phyllites. Naukuchiatal Lake catchment is made up of metavolcanics. And Sattal Lake catchment is made up of quartzites. Thus, it is revealed that the siltation rate in lakes of the Siwalik terrain is comparatively higher than that in the Lesser Himalayan lakes. The higher sedimentation rate in Mansar Lake has clogged the subsurface pathways by the deposition of finer sediments. This has resulted into the lake.

CONCLUSIONS

The variation of δ^2H and $\delta^{18}O$ and results clearly show that Mansar Lake is subjected to more evaporative enrichment. The D-excess in the Mansar Lake is varying between 0‰ and –15‰. Mansar Lake groundwater interaction appears to be very poor. The enriched isotopic composition of Mansar Lake is due to higher residence time of the Mansar Lake. The results point out that higher rate of sedimentation does not reduce only the volume of the lake but also the lake subsurface inflow and outflow due to clogging the subsurface pathways by the deposition of finer sediments. Thus, the present study demonstrates the usefulness of stable environmental isotopes as useful tools to understand the hydrological status of the lake systems.

ACKNOWLEDGEMENTS

The authors are thankful to Shri R. D. Singh, director of National Institute of Hydrology, Roorkee, for providing the necessary support and permission to submit this study. The support provided by Shri Y. S. Rawat for preparing the figures is also acknowledged.

REFERENCES

Dansgaard, W., Stable isotopes in precipitation, Tellus, 16, 1964, pp. 436–468.

Gopal, B., and Zutshi, D. P., Fifty years of hydrobiological research in India. Hydrobiolgia, 384, 1998, pp. 267–290.

Goyal, V. C., Rai, S. P., and Vijay Kumar, Hydrological evaluation of groundwater contribution in Mansar Lake, Jammu and Kashmir), Hydrology Journal, 25 (4), 2002, pp. 81–88.

Ishaq, M., and Kaul, V., Distribution of minerals in Himalayan lake, Trop. Ecol., 29, 1988, pp. 41–49.

Kaul, V., Limnological survey of Kashmir lakes with reference to tropic status and conservation, Int. J. Ecol. Envir. Sci., 3, 1977, pp. 24–44.

Kumar, B., Jain, S. K., Nachiappan, Rm. P., Rai, S. P., Kumar, V., Dungrakoto, V. C., and Rawat, Y. S., Hydrological studies of lake Nainital, Kumaun Himalayas, Uttar Pradesh, Project Report, National Institute of Hydrology, Roorkee, India, 1999a.

Kumar, B., Nachiappan, Rm, P., Rai, S. P., Kumar, U. S., and Navada, S. V., Improved prediction of life of a Himalayan lake, Mountain Research and Development, 19 (2), 1999b, pp. 113–121.

Nachiappan, Rm. P., Bhishm Kumar and Rm. Manickavasagam, Estimation of sub-surface components of water balance of lake Nainital (Kumaun Himalayas, India) using environmental isotopes. Hydrol. Sciences J. 2002, pp.

Pant, M. C., Sharma, P. C., and Sharma, A. P., Physico-chemical limnology of a Himalayan lake (lake Nainital, India). Acta Hydrochim. Hydrobiol. 13, 1985, pp. 331–349.

Rai, S. P., Omkar, Vijay Kumar and Jain, S. K., Water quality variations in Mansar lake, District Udhampur, Jammu and Kashmir, Proc. National Seminar GWR-98, Banaras Hindu University, Varanasi, 1998, pp. 47–54.

Rai, S. P., Kumar, V., Omkar, and Jain, S. K., Hydrochemical characteristics of Mansar Lake, Jammu and Kashmir in India, IE (I) Journal, 88, 2007, pp. 16–22.

Rai, S. P., Kumar, V., Omkar, Kumar, B., and Jain, S. K., Limnological study of the Mansar Lake, District Udhampur, J and K, Project Report, National Institute of Hydrology, Roorkee, India. 2002.

Rai, S. P., Kumar, V., Omkar, Kumar, B., and Jain, S. K., Bathymetry, Sedimentation and physico-chemical characteristic of Mansar Lake in the Himalayan foothills, Journal of Geological society of India, 56, 2006a, pp. 211–220.

Rai, S. P., Vijay Kumar and Bhishm Kumar () Sedimentation rate and pattern of a Himalayan foothill lake using ^{137}Cs and ^{210}Pb, Hydrological Sciences Journal, 52 (1), 2006b, pp. 181–192.

Rozanski, K., Araguas, L., Gonfiantini, R., Isotopic patterns in modern global precipitation, In Climate Change in the Isotopic records, Monograph 78, American Geophysical Union: Washington, DC, 1993, 1–36.

Singh, R., and Sharma, V. K., Geoenvironmental appraisal of Mansar and Surinsar lakes, Udhampur and Jammu Districts, Records of the Geological Survey of India, 131, Part-8, 1999, pp. 19–24.

Trisal, C. L., Ecology and conservation of Dal Lake, Kashmir. Water Resour. Dev., 3, 1987, pp. 44–54.

Zutshi, D. P., and Khan, M. A., Limnological investigation of two subtropical lakes. Geobios, 4, 1977, pp. 45–48.

Zutshi, D. P., Kaul, V., and Vass, K. K., Limnology of high altitude Kashmir Lakes, Verh. Int. Ver Limnol., 18, 1972, pp. 599–604.

Zutshi, D. P., Subla, B. A., Khan, M. A., and Wanganeo, A., Comparative limnology of nine lakes of Jammu and Kashmir Himalayas, Hydrobiologia, 72, 1980, pp. 101–112.

Zutshi, D. P., The Himalayan lake ecosystem, In: Singh, J. S. (eds.) Environmental Regeneration in Himalaya: Concept and Strategies, The Central Himalayan Environmental Association and Gyanodaya Prakashan, Nainital, 1985, pp. 325–342.

8 DRINKING-WATER SAFETY THROUGH TANK REHABILITATION IN KOVILAMBAKKAM: A PARTICIPATORY AND GIS APPROACH

S. P. Saravanan and Soorya Vennila

Centre for Water Resources, Anna University, Chennai 600 025, India
Email: sooryavennila@gmail.com, spsaransp@gmail.com

ABSTRACT

Drinking water is a basic requirement for life and a determinant of standard of living. The present study carried out in Kovilambakkam, a peri-urban village in Chennai, the capital of Tamil Nadu, transpires the fact that drinking water has become a perennial problem due to urban sprawl. The study aims to address the best bets found in Kovilambakkam in providing safe drinking water to the community through securing the local water bodies. Also, the study emerged to analyse suitable measures to improve the water quality and tank quality and to examine ways to suggest sustainable and cost-effective drinking water.

Integrated water resources and management (IWRM) approaches best fit the situation of integrating governance and community members in this village. In addition to it, participatory rural appraisal (PRA) tools were used to identify, analyse, and prioritize the local resources in an empirically sound way. The specific tools used were transect walk, focus group discussion, key informant interview, resource map, semi-structured interview, creating awareness, and capacity building. To ensure drinking water safety, reliability, and affordability, a natural system of drinking water treatment process called community-based bio-sand filter was developed. This not only ensures the community safe drinking water but also provides sustainable solution with cost-effective drinking water.

Keywords: bio-sand filter, PRA tools, capacity building, drinking water.

INTRODUCTION

Water has always been an important life-sustaining drink to humans and is essential for the survival of all organisms. It is rather difficult to imagine the well being of life without access to safe drinking water. Earth is estimated to have 1,400 million cubic kilometres of water, of which 97.3% is saltwater in the oceans and 2.7% is fresh water. A major portion (75%) of fresh water is frozen in the polar regions. Of the remaining 25%, groundwater constitutes 23%, and surface water forms a meagre 2%. Water is the elixir of life and agriculture. Tanks are the traditional water-harvesting structures which were formed many centuries ago by the kings or local chieftains for storing rainwater. Tanks occupied a prominent place in the rural economy, and in times of drought, they served as the main multiple sources. There are as many as 40,000 tanks present in Tamil Nadu (of varying sizes and types). Water resources are increasingly scarce today, and the water crisis is ever more severe. Water resource has become a scarce natural and economic resource and even a crucial strategic resource. Tu et al. (2007) suggested that urbanized watersheds with high population density, high percentage of developed land use, and low per capita developed land use tended to have high concentrations of water pollutants.

The basic types of drinking water sources were groundwater, water supplied through pipes, packaged water, and home-purified water. The quality of groundwater can be directly or indirectly affected by the deterioration of surface water quality. This groundwater was the resource for all the four types of drinking water sources. Preservation and protection of water resources is a central imperative to prevent future risk on health due to contamination and to prevent the existing water resource. Hence, there is an urgent need to transform over traditional water resources management methods. One of the important changes is to encourage the public and interest parties to participate in water resources management (Zhang Xueying et al. 2007).

MATERIALS AND METHODS

Study Area

Kancheepuram District is situated on the north-east coast of Tamil Nadu and is adjacent to the Bay of Bengal and Chennai City. It is bounded in the west by Vellore and Thiruvannamalai District, in the north by Thiruvallur District and Chennai District, in the south by Villuppuram District, in the east by the Bay of Bengal. Figure 8.1 shows the blocks map of Kancheepuram District. The district has a total geographical area of 4393.37 km^2 and a coastline of 57 km. Kancheepuram, the temple town, is the district headquarters. Figure 8.2 shows St Thomas block's panchayat villages. Kovilambakkam is a village panchayat coming under St Thomas block of Kancheepuram District. It is located at the longitude of 80.2 and the latitude of 12.9. Figure 8.3 shows the base map of Kovilambakkam and its surrounding watershed region. Kovilambakkam village has a population of about 45,000 according to the 2011 census, which was only about 9,270 in 2001, indicating that the rate of urbanization is high in this area. The number of houses in the area is 5,300. It has 1 higher secondary school, 1 private matriculation school, 1 nursery and primary government school, 1 primary health centre, 1 private hospital, 10 clinics and private buildings, 9 common wells, 2,300 pipe connections, 40 borewells, 12 overhead tanks, 1 lake, and 1 pond.

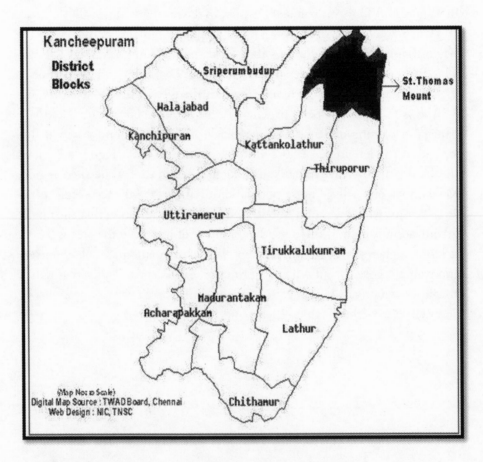

Figure 8.1. Blocks map of Kancheepuram District (source: www.tnmaps.nic.in).

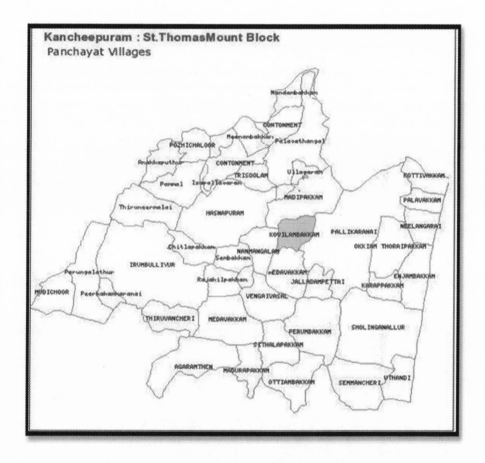

Figure 8.2. St Thomas Mount block's panchayat
villages map (source: www.tnmaps.nic.in).

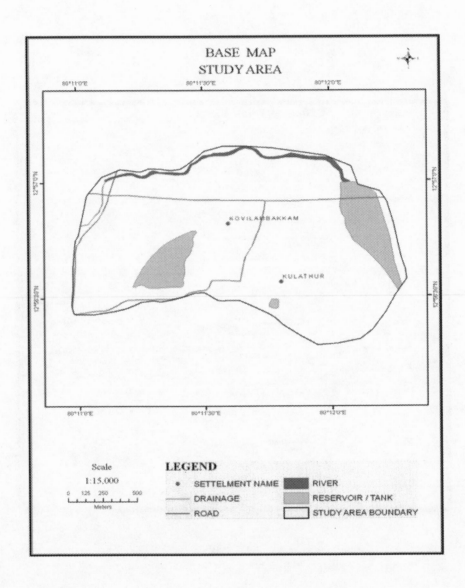

Figure 8.3. Base map of Kovilambakkam (source: Institute of
Remote Sensing (IRS), Anna University, Chennai 2012).

METHODOLOGY

The methodology adopted in the present study has been given in the form of a flowchart (Figure 8.4). The schematic diagram is as follows:

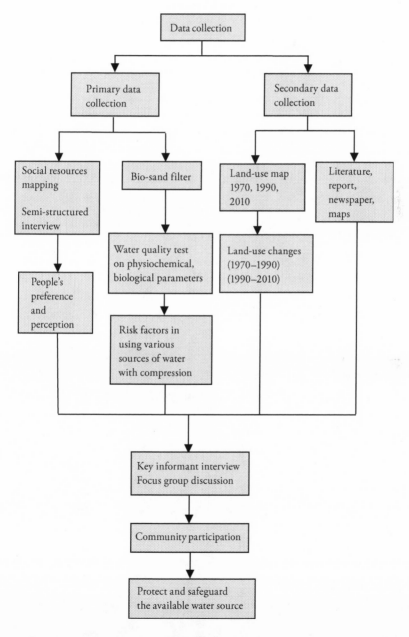

Figure 8.4. Methodology framework.

Primary Data

Primary data has been collected using PRA tools through water quality test by bio-sand filter and creating the public–private partnership. PRA tools, such as transect walk, social-resource mapping, semi-structured interview, and focus group discussion, are to be carried. Land-use changes in Kovilambakkam village were depicted using the satellite image of the area for three years 1970, 1990, and 2010.

PRA Tools

Participatory rural appraisal (PRA) tools facilitate collection and analysis of information by and for community members. PRA emphasizes local knowledge and involves communities in the inventorying, monitoring, and planning.

Transect Walk

This is a systematic walk along one line (transect) across the community area together with the people involved to explore the spatial differences by observing, asking, listening, looking, and producing a transect diagram. The transect walk is normally done during the initial phase of the fieldwork. It is best to choose a route which will cover the greatest diversity in resources, land use, geographical conditions, etc. It facilitates discussion on the status, problems, and potential of different land types and land use.

Resource Map

The village resource map is a tool that helps us to learn about a community and its resource base. The primary concern is not to develop an accurate map but to get useful information about local perceptions of the resources. Figure 8.5 shows the resource map.

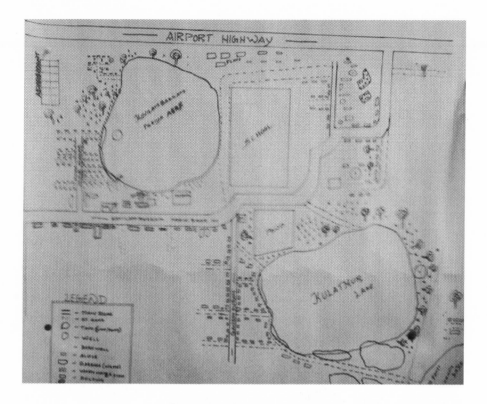

Figure 8.5. Resources map.

Community Participation

The Kovilambakkam tank was getting polluted a lot, and pollution abatement was necessary. The encroachments in the tank have been evicted except the government buildings, including the government higher secondary school which comprises a large ground. There is a graveyard-cum-dump that is very near to this tank which contributes pollution to this tank. The surplus course from Medavakkam tank, which has to serve as the storm water drainage, is now carrying the sewage water from the residents and is draining into the Kovilambakkam tank, which serves major pollution to the tank. A part of the tank (around 60% of the tank area) has been deepened; due to which the tanks storage capacity has been increased. There is no water quality monitoring system in this village. The risk factors involved in accessing the supplied water were also discussed and safety measures for accessing the supplied water and suggestions to safeguard and protect the tank were given.

RESULTS AND DISCUSSION

The sewage intrusion in the lake is the major issue in the contamination of water. This sewage is coming from the residents through the storm water drain and getting mixed with the lake. Strom water drain is being flooded with sewage as there is no underground drainage system in this village, so all the residents and the commercial buildings are letting the sewage into this.

Bio-Sand Filter

The household bio-sand filter (BSF) was first conceptualized by Dr David Manz in the late 1980s at the University of Calgary–Canada. The system was developed from the slow sand filter, a technology used for drinking water purification for almost 200 years. Initial lab and field tests were conducted in 1991, and the system was patented in 1993. That same year, the first BSF was implemented in Nicaragua. Subsequent developments on the filters have included circular designs using concrete and plastic housings. In 2001 Dr David Manz co-founded CAWST (Centre for Affordable Water and Sanitation Technology) as a worldwide distributor of BSFs. It is estimated that over 200,000 BSFs are currently in use worldwide.

Most bio-sand filters consist of similar components. At the top of the filter, there is a tightly fitted lid, which prevents contamination and unwanted pests from entering the filter. Below is the diffuser plate, which prevents disturbance of the filtration sand layer and protects the bio-layer when water is poured into the filter. Next is the filtration sand layer; it removes pathogens and suspended solids. Below the sand is a layer of smaller gravels called the separating gravel layer. This prevents filtration sand from entering the drainage gravel layer and clogging the outlet tube. Right below this separating layer is the drainage gravel layer, which supports the separating gravel layer and helps water flow by preventing clogging near the base of the outlet tube.

Filtration Process

Pathogens and suspended solids are removed through a combination of biological and physical processes that take place in the bio-layer and within the sand layer. These processes include the following:

- *Mechanical trapping.* Suspended solids and pathogens are physically trapped in the spaces between the sand grains.
- *Predation.* Pathogens are consumed by other microorganisms in the bio-layer.
- *Adsorption.* Pathogens become attached to each other, suspended solids in the water and the sand grains.
- *Natural death.* Pathogens finish their life cycle or die because there is not enough food or oxygen for them to survive.

As was referenced earlier, different processes occur during different points in the filter running process.

Maintenance

The cleaning method known as the 'swirl and dump' or wet harrowing is used to restore flow rate. To do this, about one gallon of water is added into the filter before cleaning (assuming the filter is empty). The upper layer of sand is then swirled in a circular motion. Dirty water from the swirling is dumped out, and the sand is smoothed out at the top. This process is repeated until flow rate is restored. It is also recommended to clean the diffuser plate, outlet tube, lid, and outside surfaces of the filters regularly.

Removal of Contaminants

The bio-sand filter has been studied in the field and in labs. It has been shown to remove the following from contaminated water: up to 100% of helminths (worms), up to 100% of protozoa, up to 98.5% of bacteria, 70–99% of viruses, up to 95% of turbidity (dirt and cloudiness), and up to 95% of iron.

Like other filters, the bio-sand filter cannot remove dissolved contaminants or chemicals, such as salt, arsenic, or fluoride.

Drinking-Water Sample

Water quality test were carried out with six samples (packaged water, home-purified water, before and after purification of lake water, and tap water) collected from the study area (Kovilambakkam village). Analyses were done with reference to BIS drinking-water specification (2009, second revision of IS 10500).

The parameters that were considered are pH, TDS, hardness, alkalinity, sodium, potassium, iron, manganese, sulphate, nitrate, chloride, fluoride, zinc, total coliform bacteria, and faecal coliform bacteria. The water quality test results of the six drinking water samples were given in the tables.

Table 8.1 Water quality test results

SAMPLE	pH	TDS (mg/l)	Alkalinity (mg/l)	Na (mg/l)	k (mg/l)	Cl (mg/l)	Ca (mg/l)	Mg (mg/l)	Sulphate (mg/l)
Desirable limit	6.5–8.5	500	200	20	20	250	--	--	200
Permissible limit	no re-laxation	2000	600	200	200	1000	200	100	400
Tap water (before)	8.04	576	488	16.3	3.9	74.9768	40	3.8	106.12
Tap water (after)	7.02	409.6	125	9.8	2.3	19.9845	10	5	10.56
Lake water (before)	8.26	614.4	244	15.2	4.6	62.4806	40	38	154.66
Lake water (after)	7.29	449.3	157	10.5	2.8	22.4806	10	12	56.7
Packaged water	7.48	431.4	91.5	9	1.8	12.4961	0	1.2	0.168
Home purified water	6.20	210.6	36.6	11	2.5	10.635	0	4.8	1.129

Land-Use Changes

Land-use maps for 1970, 990, 2010 and the statistics for 1970, 1990, and 2010 were depicted. Land-use change detection maps between 1970–1990 and 1990–2010 were prepared, and the statistics of land-use changes were also presented. Figure 8.6 shows the land-use pattern of the Kovilambakkam Village for 1970, 1990, and 2010. Figure 8.7 shows the land-use change deduction map (1970–1990 and 1990–2010). Total area of the study area, i.e. Kovilambakkam, and its surrounding watershed was 274.76 ha. The changes from cropland to residential area were found to be about 49.98 ha in 1970 to 1990 and about 52.17 ha in 1990 to 2010. Between 1990 and 2010, the identified changes from cropland to fallow were 55.27 ha; from cropland to industrial area, 2.20 ha; from cropland to vacant land, 10.55 ha; from cropland to scrubland, 21 ha.

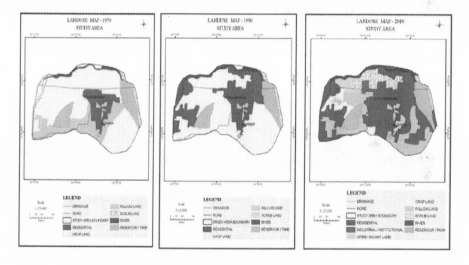

Figure 8.6. Land-use pattern of the Kovilambakkam
Village for 1970, 1990, and 2010.

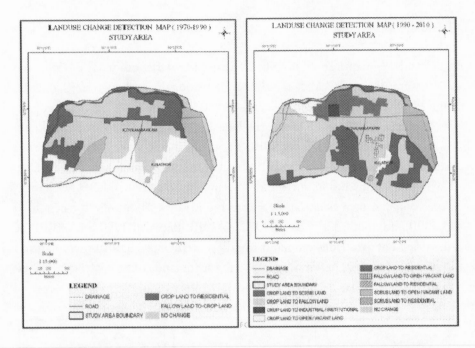

Figure 8.7. Land-use change deduction map (1970–1990 and 1990–2010).

CONCLUSION

The water resources such as lakes, wells, and ponds are maintained to utilize in a sustainable way. Water availability in Kovilambakkam Village is sustainably secured by tank rehabilitation through participatory approach. Safe and easy access of drinking water is achieved by natural system of drinking water process called bio-sand filter. It gives potable quality of water to community people which is cost-effective.

REFERENCES

Adriana Allen, Julio D. Davila, and Pascale Hofmann (2006), 'Goverence of water and sanitation services for the peri-urban. Poor, afrance work for understanding and action in metropolitan regions', *development planning unit London, ISBN 1 874502 60 9, <http://www.bartleft.ucl.ac.uk/dpu/ latest/publication/ dpu> accessed on 4 january 2011.*

Anuradha, B., and N. K. Ambujam (Oct 2009), 'Impact Of Tank Rehabilitation: An Analytical Study Of Peri-Urban Tanks In *Tamil nadu*', *Water and Energy International, Vol. 66, No. 4.*

David Manz co-founded CAWST (Center for Affordable Water and Sanitation Technology), *www.cawst.org.*

Kancheepuram district profile (2004), *<http://www.kanchi.nic.in/ district_profile_ pro.html>* Accessed on October 18th 2012.

Kiruthika (2009), 'Study on Degradation of Water Bodies and the Field Implementation of Policies for Protection', Unpublished ME Thesis, Centre for Water Resources, Department of Civil Engineering, Anna University, Chennai.

Murugan (2012), Kovilambakkam Panchayat Board.

Pankajavalli, T. (2007), 'Water Budgeting And Gender Issues In Drinking Water Supply In Chennai City,' Unpublished ME Thesis, Centre For Water Resources, Department of Civil Engineering, Anna University, Chennai.

Palanisami, K., and Ruth Meinzen (2001), 'Tank Performance And Multiple Uses In Tamil Nadu, South India' *Irrigation And Drainage Systems* 15: 173–195.

Priyanga (2012), 'Urban Sprawl And Drinking Water Safety: A Participatory Study In Chennai City'. Unpublished ME Thesis, Centre For Water Resources, Department of Civil Engineering, Anna University, Chennai.

Radha (2012), Assistant Engineer, PWD, Chengalpattu.

Ranganathan (2012), Village president, Kovilambakkam.

Themba O. Mahlangu, Lizzy Mpenyana-Monyatsi (2011), 'A simplified cost-effective bio-sand filter (BSFZ) for removal of chemical contaminants from water' Journal of Chemical Engineering and Materials Science Vol. 2 (10), pp. 156–167, November 2011.

9 ENUMERATION OF TANKS AND PRIORITIZATION OF TANKS IN UPPER THURINJALAR WATERSHED OF PONNAIYAR RIVER BASIN IN TAMIL NADU USING REMOTE SENSING AND GIS TECHNIQUES

K. Santhanam[1], P. Mohana, T. Sivasubramaniam[2], and K. Venugopal[1]
[1] Centre for Water Research, Sathyabama University, Chennai
[2] Centre for Remote Sensing, Sathyabama University, Chennai
Email: gissanthanam@gmail.com

ABSTRACT

Tanks have been a major source of irrigation in Tamil Nadu for several centuries. Further, tank irrigation constitutes the most important component of minor irrigation. Some tanks may be natural depressions, but most of them have been formed by man-made activities. These tanks are not only utilized for irrigation but also to increase groundwater recharge. Among the 17 river basins of Tamil Nadu, Ponnaiyar basin is one of the major ones. Upper Thurinjalar watershed is one of the 67 watersheds of Ponnaiyar basin which lies in eastern part of Ponnaiyar river basin. Using GPS, each and every tank is located in the watershed in order to know the exact number of tanks in the area which are alive. Using aerial photographs from and a toposheet which is 1 in to 1 mi. (1:67,360 scale), the number of tanks for 1978 was derived. By interpreting IRS 1D satellite imagery, the number of tanks for 1998 was derived. Using IRS P6 LISS-4 satellite data and GPS survey, the number of tanks as to date was derived. Based on remote sensing satellite data interpretation, thematic layers on geology, geomorphology land use, and fault/lineament maps were generated. From the geophysical resistivity survey results, depth to bedrock contour layer was prepared. Based on GIS overlay analysis, suitable tanks favourable for desilting and modernization were prioritized to increase the groundwater potential and storage capacity of the tanks.

INTRODUCTION

Water is a very important deciding factor for the production of crops in the irrigation sector. Cultivation of land in Tamil Nadu depends on the availability of water. The various sources of irrigation are canals, tanks, and irrigation wells. Tanks with more than 40 ha of ayacut are being maintained by PWD. Tanks which have ayacut less than 40 ha are being maintained by Revenue Department. There are 7,933 PWD tanks and 32,386 Revenue Department tanks. Totally, 40,319 irrigation tanks are reported to be functioning in Tamil Nadu as per PWD and Revenue Department records, but in reality, many tanks were converted to habitations and irrigated lands. To know the correct number of tanks alive as to date, field check of each and every tank was carried out with GPS. For comparison, 1978 and 1998 tank census was compared with this current number of tanks to know the deductions and additions. Huge amount of fund is sanctioned either as free assistance or loan assistance and allotted to the state government for modernization and desilting by the World Bank, Asian Development Bank and funds from Europe and Japan. Modernization and desiltation work are being carried out in the haphazard manner without scientific background. In this study, using the latest scientific techniques like remote sensing, GIS, and GPS techniques, suitable tanks that really fit for modernization and destination were selected. The exact number of tanks alive as to date in the Upper Thurinjalar watershed in the Ponnaiyar basin was also determined. The aim of the present study is to know the exact number of irrigation tanks which are alive as to date and to compare the location of tanks in 1978, 1998, and 2012 in order to know their status, whether they still exist or have disappeared due to man-made activities. It also aims to prioritize tanks which are favourable and suitable for desilting and modernization using remote sensing and GIS techniques.

STUDY AREA

The total geographical area of the Upper Thurinjalar watershed of Ponnaiyar basin is 323.31 km^2. It lies within the coordinates 78° 57' 23" to 79° 09' 23" E and 12° 9' 08" to 12° 21' 17" N. The watershed is surrounded by Upper Cheyyar to the north-west, Varahanadhi river basin to the east, lower Thurinjalar watershed to the south, and Alliyar watershed of Ponnaiyar basin to the west. The study area lies in Thiruvannamalai, Thurinjapuram, Kilpennathur, Chengam, and Thandarampattu blocks of Thiruvannamalai District (Figure 9.1).

Geology

The Archean crystalline rocks of the area have charnockites, pyroxenites, pyroxene granulites, magnetite quartzite, hornblende–biotite gneiss, granites. Major part of the watershed is covered by charnockites. Granite rocks occur as patches (Figure 9.2).

Figure 9.1. Administrative map.

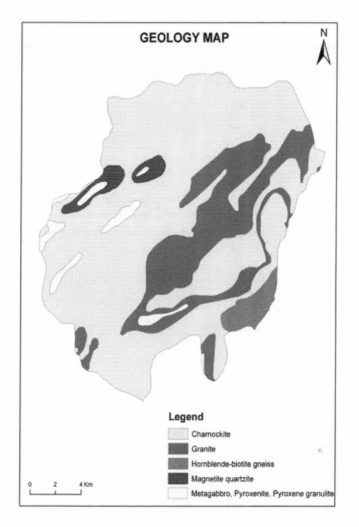

Figure 9.2. Geology map of the study area.

Subsurface Lithology

From the hydrogeological investigation and geophysical resistivity survey results, it is inferred that topsoil occurs from ground level to 2–3 m. Weathered formation occurs below topsoil to 25–30 m below ground level (bgl) partially weathered formation occurs up to 40 m bgl. Jointed and fractured rocks occur up to 75 m, and in certain locations up to 90 m (Figure 9.3). In central and southern parts of the watershed, thickness of jointed and fractured zone is more.

Figure 9.3. Map of the depth to the bedrock.

Geomorphology

The following geomorphic features are found out by interpreting the IRS P6 LISS-IV resource satellite data using image processing techniques. Geomorphology map of watershed was generated. Six types of geomorphological features have been identified (Figure 9.4) as (1) moderately buried pediplain, (2) pediment, (3) pediment–inselberg complex, (4) residual hill, (5) structural hills, and (6) weathered/buried pediplain.

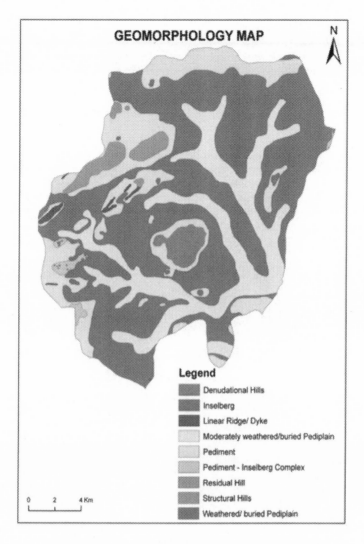

Figure 9.4. Geomorphology map of the study area.

Drainage

Thurinjallar is flowing north-west to south-east, and its tributary Oliyr is flowing west to east. Other streams are flowing west–east, north-west–south-east, and north–south, and the drainage density is more in the north-west (Figure 9.5). There are 115 tanks. Out of which, 22 tanks are maintained by PWD, and the 93 other tanks are maintained by Revenue Department. The PWD tanks have more than 40 ha of ayacut area. Revenue Department tanks are having less than 40 ha of ayacut area. The list of the tanks present is verified physically village-wise (Figure 9.6).

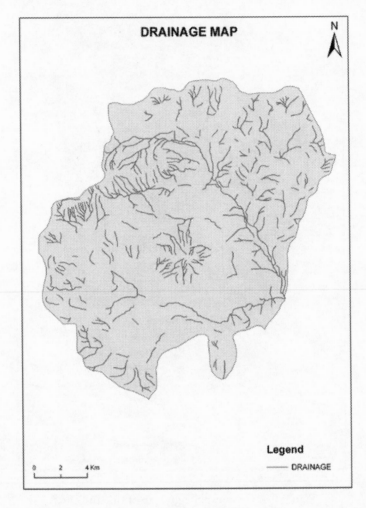

Figure 9.5. Drainage map.

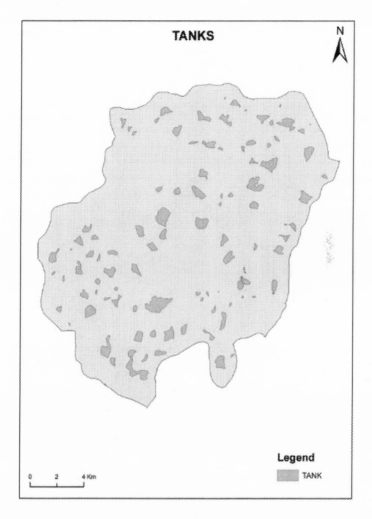

Figure 9.6. Tank layer map.

Land Use/Land Cover

By interpreting the remote sensing data, land-use/land-cover map was prepared. From this map, extent of wasteland can be derived as the government is interested in converting wastelands into productive lands. The land use is classified as cropland, forestland, surface water bodies, and settlements (Figure 9.7). The following is the land-use classification:

Land use	Area in square kilometres
Wet crop	47.931
Dry crop	59.031
Wasteland	150.108
Forestland	39.011
Tank	19.307
Settlement	8.202
Total area	323.32

(Around 50% of the total area is covered by wasteland.)

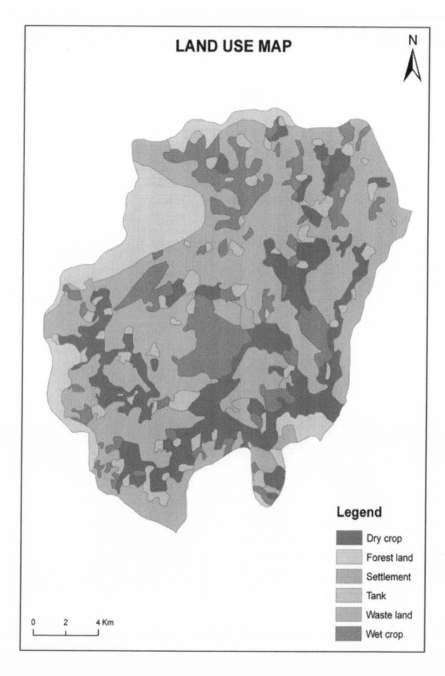

Figure 9.7. Land-use map.

Fault/Lineament

Among the 127 minor basins of 17 major river basins of Tamil Nadu, Thurinjalar minor basin is highly tectonically disturbed. Numerous lineaments are interpreted in this watershed. Confirmation was made by field hydrogeological investigation and geophysical survey. North to south, north-west to south-east, north-east to south-west trending fault zones are identified in the field. In the intersection of lineaments and along the fault planes, groundwater potential is found to be more (Figure 9.8).

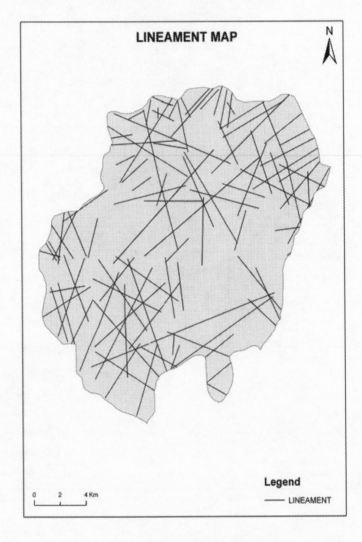

Figure 9.8. Lineament map.

METHODOLOGY

Enumeration of Tanks

The number of tanks was identified village-wise from the following sources:

1. toposheet of 1972 (1:63,360)
2. aerial photographs of 1978 (1:50,000)
3. the satellite imagery of IRS 1D 1998
4. resource satellite IRS P6 LISS-4.

The number of tanks that have disappeared and newly found were taken into account. As to date, the existing number of tanks is 115, and they are verified in the field by GPS surveying 2012. During 1998 the number of tanks was 109. During 1978 the number of tanks was 101.

In other minor basins, there was a decrease in the number of tanks, but in this watershed, the number of tanks is in increasing trend as PWD, Agricultural Engineering Department, and Revenue Department have formed new tanks.

RESULT AND DISCUSSION

As tanks are favourable for artificial recharge, they have to be desilted and modernized. Hence, prioritization was made based on scientific findings.

Depth to Bedrock

The tank layer was superimposed on depth to bedrock layer using overlay analysis of GIS techniques (Figure 9.9). The contours above 50–70 m are favourable fractured zones. Contours between 70 and 90 are highly favourable fractured zones from the overlay analysis. The following village tanks are lying in favourable zones.

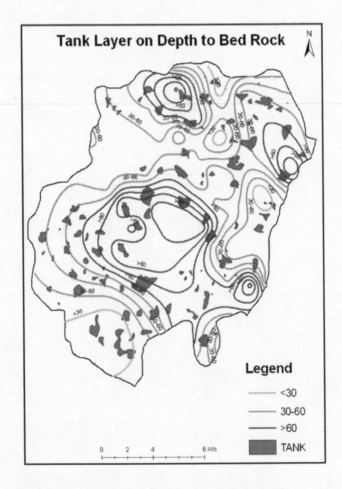

Figure 9.9. Tank layer on depth to bedrock.

Favourable zones	Highly favourable zones
1. Samudram	Adaiyur
2. Nallavanpallyam	Devanandal
3. Sanipudi	Kosalai
4. Ayyampalayam	Adiannamalai
5. Ayyampalayam	Athiyandal
6. Aswanagasuranai	Vengikkal
7. Athiyandal	Andapattu
8. Kalasthmbadi	Sorandai
9. Kariyandal	Mallavadi
10. Kunammurinji.	Karindurambadi
	Nukkambady
	Nambiyandal.

Geomorphology

Tanks lie in among six geomorphic zones, moderately buried plain is the best favourable zone for recharge, and hence tanks located in the zone are selected for recharge (Figure 9.10).

1. Meyyur
2. Meltikkan
3. Meiputtiyandal
4. Savalpundi
5. Nallavanpalyam
6. Arasudaiyanpattu
7. Manjampundi
8. Samudram
9. Kanandampundi
10. Ayyampalyam
11. Aswanathasuranai
12. Kilkachirapattu
13. Nochimalai
14. Kilyapattu
15. Vengikkal
16. Adaiyur
17. Kalasthambadi
18. Karimbalur
19. Samanandal
20. So Nambianda.

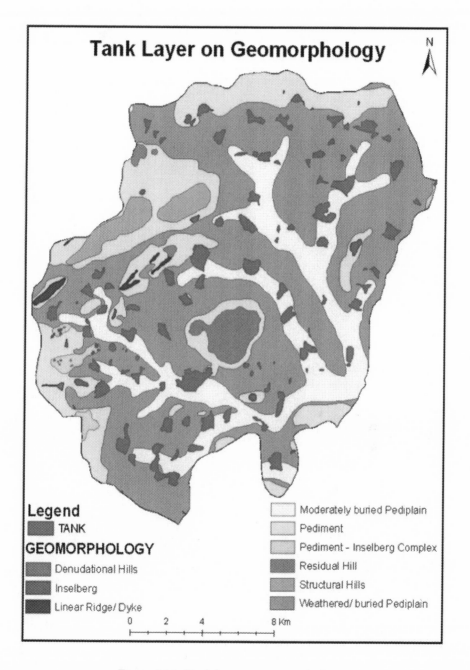

Figure 9.10. Tank layer on geomorphology.

Fault/Lineament

Intersection of lineaments and lineament passing through are considered for selection of tanks for desilting and modernization (Figure 9.11).

1. Thenmattur
2. Samudram
3. Kilnachipattu
4. Kilkachirapettu
5. Meltikkan
6. Nallavanpallyam
7. Arasduyainpattu
8. Melsirupakkam
9. Perumbakkam
10. Periyakolapaddi
11. Chinnakolapddi
12. Adaiyur
13. Kosalai
14. Adiannamalai
15. Nukkambadi
16. Madalambadi
17. Koothalavadi
18. Sorandai
19. Mallavadi.

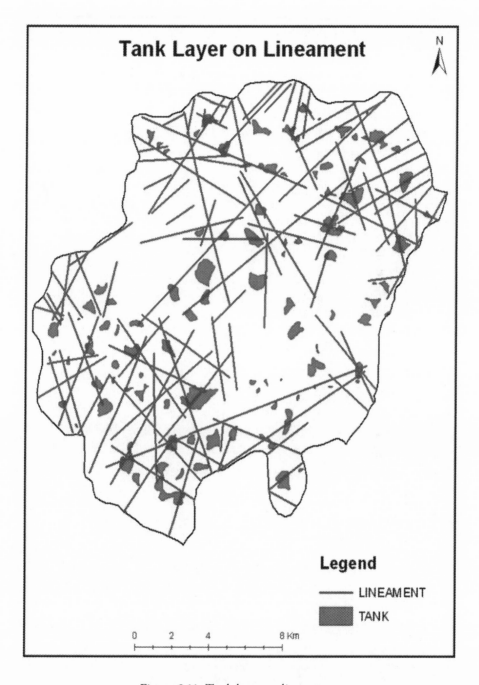

Figure 9.11. Tank layer on lineament.

Prioritization of Tanks for Desilting and Modernization

GIS overlay analysis is very useful in prioritizing irrigation tanks for desilting and modernization. When tank layer was superimposed on death to bedrock map, 22 tanks were selected. While tank layer was overlaid on geomorphology layer, 20 favourable tanks have been selected. When the tank layer was superimposed on the lineament map, 18 tanks have been selected.

In the depth to bed-rock, geomorphology and lineament categories, the following 11 tanks found place in two or three categories:. the :

1. Samudram
2. Nallavanpalyam
3. Adaiyur
4. Ayyampalayam
5. Aswanagsurnai
6. Kosalai
7. Adiannamalai
8. Sorandai
9. Mallvadi
10. Nambiandal
11. Nukkambadi.

All these 11 tanks are highly suitable in Upper Thurinjalar watershed for desilting and modernization. In the same manner, in all river basins of Tamil Nadu, prioritization of tanks can be carried out successfully.

CONCLUSIONS

Among the 115 tanks which lie in the watershed, 11 tanks are in the top list to be prioritized as all scientific analyses found them highly favourable. This watershed is a model to verify that tanks which are alive are actually in the field with the help of GPS. The same methodology can be applied for all the watersheds of 127 minor basins of 17 major river basins in Tamil Nadu so that the exact number of existing irrigation tanks can be determined.

REFERENCES

Climate change and water supplies options for sustaining tank irrigation potential in India, Dr K. Palanisamy, Paper in Economical and political weekly June 26, 2010.

Integrated resources of Ponnaiyar basin Tamilnadu report Dr Ramley. FAO Expert World Bank Report, 1987.

Irrigation tanks in Thiruvannamalai District Tank Memoir, PWD (Irrigation), Govt of Tamilnadu June 1981.

Productivity improvement of wasteland through artificial recharging of tank water, The case of Thurinjallar minor basin in Tamilnadu. DST Project Report, Centre for Water Research, Sathyabama University, Chennai.

Rejuvenating Irrigation tanks through local institutions, Dr R. Sakthivadivel, Paper in Economical and Political weekly July 31.

Remote Sensing—GIS applications in Tank Management Studies—by Vinay Rangari—Circle Water Management Engineering, Maharastra.

Water planning report of Ponnaiyar River basin Tamilnadu, State Frame Work Institute for Water Sluices WRO, PWD, Chennai, Tamilnadu.

10 DOWN-CORE VARIATION OF TEXTURAL CHARACTERISTICS AND TRACE ELEMENT GEOCHEMISTRY OF KORAIYARU RIVER ESTUARINE SEDIMENT, NEAR MULLIPALLAM CREEK, TAMIL NADU, SOUTH-EAST COAST OF INDIA

S. Muralidharan[1], S. Ramasamy[1], and N. Rajeshwara Rao[2]
[1]Department of Geology, University of Madras Guindy Campus, Chennai 600 025
[2]Department of Applied Geology, University of Madras Guindy Campus, Chennai 600 025
Email: mangrovemurali@gmail.com

ABSTRACT

A 120 cm long core was collected from the mangroves in the Mullipallam Creek near the mouth of Korayar River (10° 21' 46" N, 79° 31' 96" E), Tiruvarur District (tributary of the River Cauvery). GPS was used for fixing the sample locations. It was subsampled at the intervals of 3 cm, and 40 subsamples were obtained in total. Down-core variations in sediment texture, $CaCO_3$, and organic matter contents are discussed in detail. Based on the textural studies, four types of sediments are identified: clayey sand, silty sand, sand, and sandy silt. Among these, clayey silt is found to be the dominant lithology. Similarly, an increasing trend of the organic matter and calcium carbonate is noticed in the subsamples. The environmental implications of the trace elements are discussed in detail for the Koraiyaru estuarine sediments of Mullipallam creek.

Keywords: Koraiyaru estuary, mangroves, down-core variations, sediment texture, trace element, geochemistry, anthropogenic activity.

INTRODUCTION

It has been recognized for many years that the concentrations of metals found in rivers, estuaries, and offshore coastal areas, whether they are in the dissolved or particulate phase, may be derived from a variety of anthropogenic and natural sources. In most circumstances, the major part of the anthropogenic metal load in the sea and seabed sediments has a terrestrial source, from mining and industrial developments along major rivers and estuaries. Metals with an anthropogenic origin must be distinguished from naturally occurring metals if contamination is to be properly assessed, monitored, and controlled. The presence of mineralization in a river catchment can give rise to a substantial proportion of the metal concentration present and is not amenable to control. It can also account for major differences between river basins in both concentration and distribution of the metallic elements.

STUDY AREA

The Mullipallam Creek area is located near Muthupet, spreading into the coastal segments of Nagapattinam and Thiruvarur districts of Tamil Nadu. The area of investigation is a marshy mangrove wetland located in the southernmost end of the Cauvery delta along the coastal zone of Palk Strait in the Bay of Bengal. The dominant species in the Muthupet mangrove wetland is *Avicennia marina* (95%) and the rest are *Acanthus ilicifolius, Aegiceras corniculatum, Excoecaria agallocha*, and *Rhizophora mucronata* (Selvam 2003). Other mangrove species colonized in the study area are *Acanthus ilicifolius, Aegiceras corniculatum, Excoecaria agallocha*, and *Rhizophora mucronata*. It is a typical arcuate delta and the alignment of the arc passes through Thiruthuraipoondi. It is part of large coastal wetland complex called the Great Vedaranyam Swamp. This area is drained by the distributaries of the Cauvery, viz. Paminiyar, Koraiyar, Kandankurichanar, Kilathangiyar, and Marakkakoraiyar. The Muthupet wetland system is spread over an area of 68.03 km^2 and is fed by minor rivers Paminiyar, Koraiyar, Kandankurichanar, Kilaithangiyar, and Marakkakoraiyar, which form part of the distributaries of the Cauvery delta (Figure 10.1). Some 10% of which is thick forest while 20% of the area is submerged underwater.

MATERIALS AND METHODS

Core sampling was done at one selected location (10° 21' 46" N, 79° 31' 96" E) during April 2013. This location was selected to decipher the influence of the coastal region, as it is very close to the mouth of the Koraiyaru River. Collection of core sample was accomplished using a PVC coring tube of 1.20 m length and 2.5 cm diameter, and the water depth at the coring site was 2 m. The core location was selected by the following criteria: low water level and undisturbed by human activities. The core sample was transported to the CIBA (Central Institute of Brackishwater Aquaculture) Laboratory in Chennai and stored at –20° C in the deep freezer for a week's time. The core sample was further subsampled at 3 cm interval, and 40 subsamples in total have been retrieved. The subsamples are kept in the sunlight for a week for drying and later packed and preserved in tightly packed polythene covers.

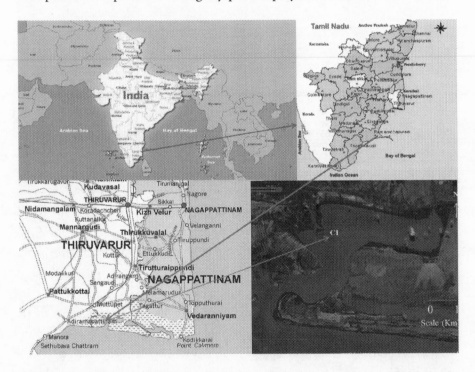

Figure 10.1. Location map of the study area (Koraiyaru river estuary, Muthupet).

During the first stage of work, textural studies for sand, silt, and clay were carried out by the Krumbein and Pettijohn (1938) method. Loring and Rantala (1992) method was followed to determine the calcium carbonate content (CaCO$_3$), and organic carbon (OC) was determined following the procedure of Gaudette et al. (1974). Trace elements (Mn, Cr, Cu, Ni, Co, Pb, and Zn) were determined after preliminary treatment and total decomposition of sediments following the procedure of Loring and Rantala (1992). The final solution was analysed using AAS.

RESULTS AND DISCUSSION

Sand-Silt-Clay Ratio

The analysis on sand, silt, clay is followed by the pipette method in accordance with the procedure adopted by the Krumbein and Pettijohn (1938), and one of the methods is used to identify the sand-silt-clay ratio for Muthupet core sample. This result (Table 10.1) is used to plot the trilinear diagram (Figure 10.2). It is clearly illustrated that four types of sediments are observed. Clayey sand, silty sand, sand, and sandy silt types of sediments were observed (Figure 10.3).

Table 10.1 Sand, silt, clay, OM, and CaCO$_3$ percentage for Muthupet core sample

Sand,Silt,Clay,CaCO3 and Organic Matter percentage for Muthupet Core					
Core length	Sand %	Silt %	Clay %	CaCO3 %	Organic Matter %
0	67.7	16.7	15.6	5.5	3.1
3	79.5	6.3	14.2	16.5	0.9
6	68.7	12.5	18.8	11.5	1.9
9	67.2	14.8	18	11.0	1.9
12	61.5	32.0	6.5	11.0	2.0
15	64.0	19.6	10.1	10.5	2.2
18	85.0	17.9	16	20.0	1.9
21	70.0	16.2	10.3	14.0	2.0
24	71.7	16.0	7.3	4.0	2.5
27	77.5	5.8	16.7	12.0	2.3
30	78.5	3.2	18.3	7.5	2.1
33	60.3	22.8	16.9	12.5	2.2
36	72.2	10.4	17.4	10.5	2.1
39	78.0	5.1	16.9	9.5	1.5
42	78.5	3.2	18.3	13.5	2.6
45	76.2	4.0	19.8	14.0	1.2
48	69.0	10.9	20.1	11.0	0.5
51	68.6	11.1	20.3	13.5	2.4
54	60.7	42.6	16.7	18.0	1.3
57	91.1	5.0	3.9	11.5	2.6
60	85.8	5.9	8.27	4.0	1.8
63	72.3	9.6	18.1	10.0	0.7
66	86.8	7.7	5.5	12.0	1.8
69	73.7	9.0	17.3	6.0	1.3
72	69.1	14.7	16.2	4.0	1.8
75	84.6	14.0	1.4	19.0	2.0
78	75.0	3.4	21.6	13.5	2.0
81	71.7	14.0	14.3	19.5	1.8
84	72.1	21.8	6.1	6.0	2.6
87	81.5	17.8	0.7	3.5	0.7
90	67.0	8.8	24.2	4.0	0.9
93	74.7	11.6	13.7	3.5	0.4
96	78.6	16.9	4.5	4.5	0.3
99	46.6	48.0	5.4	24.5	0.4
102	66.3	10.4	23.3	26.0	0.3
105	47.1	37.8	15.1	20.0	0.3
108	69.6	13.6	16.8	40.0	0.7
111	77.3	13.3	9.4	29.5	0.3
114	71.6	21.6	6.8	3.5	1.1
117	79.0	14.4	6.6	5.0	0.2
Maximum	91.1	48.0	24.2	40.0	3.1
Minimum	46.6	3.2	0.7	3.5	0.2
Average	72.2	15.3	13.3874	12.8	1.5

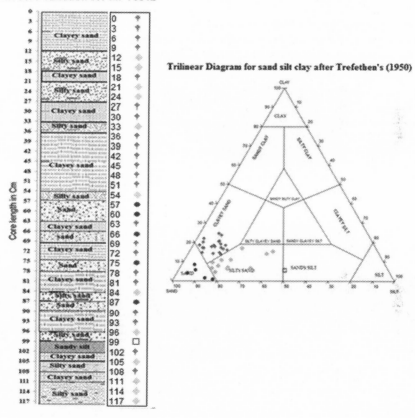

Figure 10.2. Trilinear plot for the Muthupet core sample (Trefethen 1950).

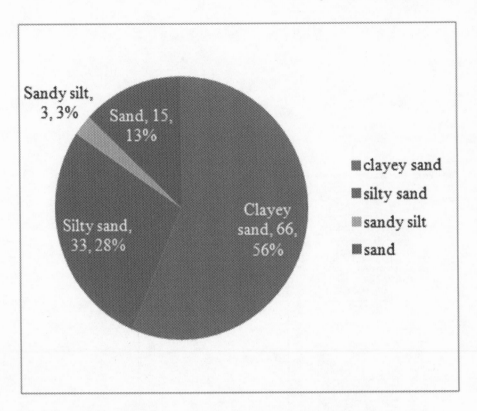

Figure 10.3. Pie chart for sand, silt, and clay of Muthupet core sample.

Sand-silt-clay ratio is compared, with down-core variation total of 120 cm core. Clayey sand dominates 66 cm (56%), silty sand dominates 33 cm (28%), sand dominates 15 cm (13%), and sandy silt dominates 3 cm (3%) (Figure 10.4). The observation of sand-silt-clay ratio results indicates that sand has the maximum percentage at a depth of 54 to 57 cm. Major part of silt is observed at a depth of 99 to 102 cm, and clay has a higher proportion at a depth of 90 to 93 cm.

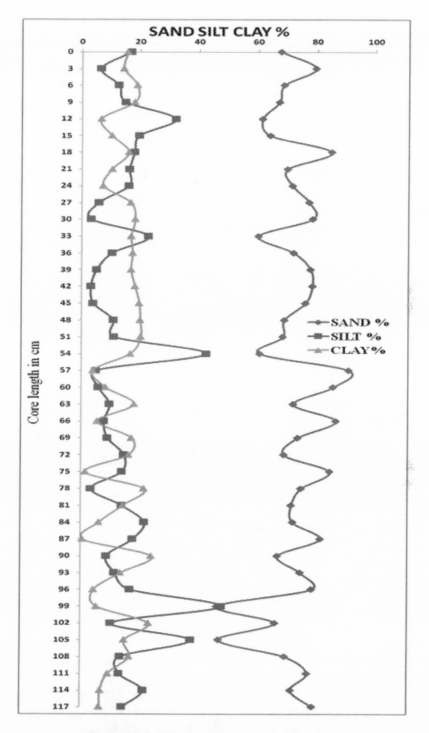

Figure 10.4. Sand-silt-clay ratio for the Muthupet core sample.

Calcium Carbonate

Calcium carbonate content ranges from 3.5% to 40% (Figure 10.5). Higher amount of calcium carbonate content is noticed at deeper depth of 108–111 cm. The average concentration of calcium carbonate is 12.8% in the core. Down-core variations of $CaCO_3$ are shown in Figure 10.5. From the top portion of the core to a depth of 96 cm, the $CaCO_3$ content does not vary much. It varies from 5.5 to 3.5%. From 96 to 111 cm, increasing trend is noticed. Between 111 and 117 cm, the $CaCO_3$ content is decreased gradually from 40 to 3.5%.

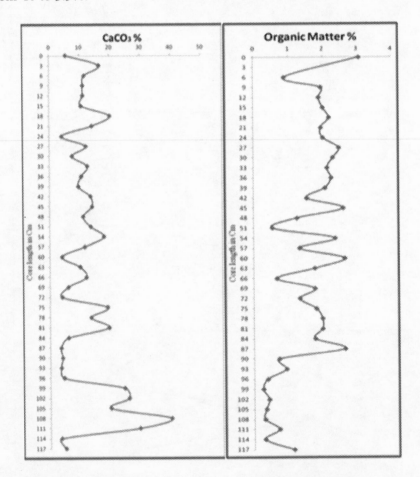

Figure 10.5. Calcium carbonate percentage for Muthupet core sample.

Figure 10.6. Organic matter percentage for Muthupet core sample.

Organic Matter

Organic matter content ranges between 0.2 and 3.1% at a depth of 114 and 0 cm respectively (Figure 10.6). At the top (first 3 cm) surface region, the organic matter is at a maximum amount, and it decreases with the increase in depth. The percentage has been fluctuating between 42 and 60 cm after it gradually decreased. The $CaCO_3$ and organic matter results were matched; they indicate that both percentages were nearly inversely proportional.

Trace Element

Trace metal enrichment in sediments started with the industrial revolution in the Indian subcontinent at the end of the nineteenth century. As a result, the fluxes of trace metals from terrestrial areas (especially aquatic regions) have increased significantly in developing countries. Down-core trace metal distribution of Muthupet is given in Table 10.2. It is clearly indicated that the down-core maximum percentage of Fe is 34,830 and the minimum is 25,440 ppm at a depth of 48 and 84 cm respectively. Mn has a maximum of 510 and a minimum of 195 ppm at a depth of 0 and 72 cm respectively. Cr dominates with a maximum of 648.4 and a minimum of 50 ppm at a depth of 36 and 42 cm respectively. Cu has a maximum of 83.8 and a minimum of 24.4 ppm at a depth of 12 and 48 cm respectively. Ni has a maximum of 47.1 and a minimum of 1.9 ppm at a depth of 0 and 72 cm respectively. Pb has a maximum of 31 and a minimum of 0.7 ppm at a depth of 108 and 114 cm respectively. Zn has a maximum of 87.1 and a minimum of 42 ppm at a depth of 0 and 90 cm respectively. Cd has a maximum of 6.6 and a minimum of 0.2 ppm at a depth of 54 and 24 cm respectively. Co has a maximum of 31.8 and a minimum of 4.7 ppm at a depth of 18 and 60 cm respectively (Figure 10.7).

Figure 10.8 indicates increasing and decreasing trend of trace element. The arrows from left to right side indicate higher concentration of trace element, and the arrows from right to left side indicate lower concentration. The comparative study of trace element concentration of the Marakkanam (Table 10.3), Thamirabarani (Punnakayal) (Table 10.4), and Muthupet (Koraiyaru) (Table 10.5) reveals that Muthupet trace element concentration is not high in amount. However, compared with UCC data (except Mn), Fe, Co, Ni, Pb, and Zn are considered very high in concentration (Table 10.6). From top to 30 and

66 cm, Fe, Cr, Cu, and Ni are observed to be of very high concentration, and they are low concentration at a depth of 84 and 114 cm. Pb, Co, Cd, Mn are considered to be rich at a depth of 18, 46, and 96 cm, and low concentration is observed at a depth of 60 cm.

Table 10.2 Trace element concentration of the Muthupet core sample

	Depth in cm	Fe %	Mn ppm	Cr ppm	Cu ppm	Ni ppm	Pb ppm	Zn ppm	Cd ppm	Co ppm
1	0	29900	510	62.9	61.5	47.1	13	87.1	4.6	25.6
2	6	32370	413	380.6	59.7	46.6	11.7	67.7	6.3	15.8
3	12	33660	362	356.2	83.8	42.8	16.1	78.6	2.6	23.8
4	18	27710	470	88.3	64.8	37.4	18.6	65.4	4.6	31.8
5	24	27790	394	66.3	68.7	27.1	24	74.8	0.2	21.9
6	30	30620	343	179.3	80.1	42.7	25.9	66.6	1.8	20.4
7	36	28170	421	452	74.8	27.1	14.6	72.4	1.4	23.4
8	42	27690	295	50	59.1	23.6	16.9	68.4	5.1	17.8
9	48	34830	212	268.1	24.4	16.8	27.6	80.8	3.4	16.2
10	54	31480	226	294.3	31.9	10.3	1.5	51.3	6.6	18.2
11	60	30580	247	133.8	41.7	18	12	46.6	0.8	4.7
12	66	31250	397	321.3	65	25	1.1	73.5	5.5	17.4
13	72	33911	195	180.8	42.6	1.9	6.6	60.7	4.8	9
14	78	27580	384	64.7	51.4	12.4	15.8	67.6	1.7	18.8
15	84	25440	383	166.7	32.9	12.3	29.5	73.3	1.3	22.3
16	90	29879	338	160.4	29.1	32.2	17.4	42	0.5	5.4
17	96	29342	338	350.4	63.3	16.8	12.3	59.3	6.4	25.4
18	102	31280	349	162.8	66.7	28	6.1	46.6	0.4	16.9
19	108	29459	302	222.3	44.3	39.5	31	63.3	4.6	9
20	114	29835	250	367.3	39.6	32.4	0.7	46.9	4.8	9.2
	Maximum	34830	510	452	83.8	47.1	31	87.1	6.6	31.8
	Minimum	25440	195	50	24.4	1.9	0.7	42	0.2	4.7
	Average	30138.5	342.455	219.568	54.2545	26.7727	15.1864	64.6364	3.37273	17.7045

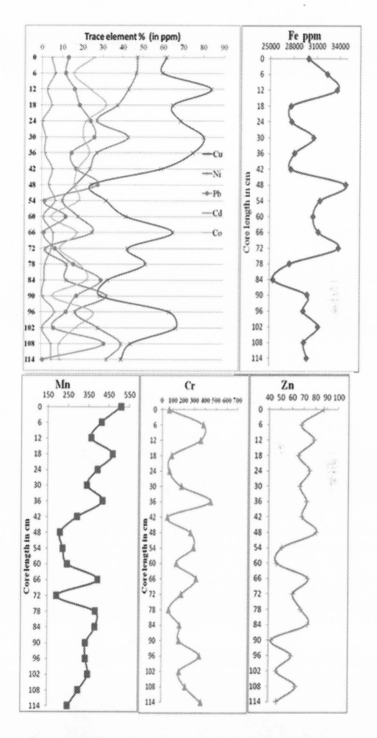

Figure 10.7. Trace element concentration for Muthupet core.

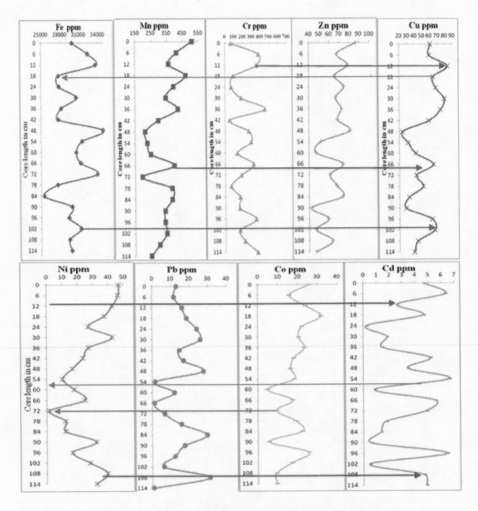

Figure 10.8. Increasing and decreasing trend of trace
element concentration of Muthupet core sample.

Table 10.3 Trace element concentration of Marakkanam (Hema Achyuthan et al. 2002)

Trace elements concentration of Marakkanam							
Elements	Mn ppm	Fe%	Cr ppm	Pb ppm	Ni ppm	Zn ppm	Co ppm
Maximum	498	1.5	61	15	23	94	9
Minimum	59	0	24	0	0	56	2
Average	332.69	1.0429	41.615	8.8462	12.615	75.308	7

Table 10.4 Trace element concentration of Thamirabarani (unpublished data, Muralidharan et.al)

Trace elements concentration of Thamiraparani									
Element	Fe %	Mn ppm	Cr ppm	Pb ppm	Ni ppm	Zn ppm	Cu ppm	Co ppm	Cd ppm
Maximum	69180	1077	852.9	148.2	126.5	111.3	78.5	59.2	13.5
Minimum	5509	339	216.9	4.4	38.7	50.1	35.6	12.4	8.1
Average	26482.176	660.6471	471.5765	43	85.82941	82.34118	54.59412	37.78235	10.25294

Table 10.5 Trace element concentration of Muthupet (Koraiyaru estuary) (present data)

Trace elements concentration of Muthupet									
Elements	Fe %	Mn(ppm)	Cr(ppm)	Cu(ppm)	Ni(ppm)	Pb(ppm)	Zn(ppm)	Cd(ppm)	Co(ppm)
Maximum	34830	510	648.4	83.8	47.1	31	87.1	6.6	31.8
minimum	25440	195	50	24.4	1.9	0.7	42	0.2	4.7
Average	30138	342.455	237.42	54.255	26.773	15.186	64.636	3.37273	17.70455

Table 10.6 Core trace elements compared with UCC (Hema Achyuthan et al 2002)

Elements	UCC	Present study
Mn(ppm)	600	510
Fe(%)	3.5	34830
Co(ppm)	10	31.8
Ni(ppm)	20	47.1
Pb(ppm)	20	31
Zn(ppm)	71	87.1

CONCLUSION

The lower values of calcium carbonate from the depth of 0 to 96 cm (from top to bottom of the core sample) may be due to greater dilution from terrigenous sediments. However, high $CaCO_3$ content is observed at the bottom depth (100 to 115 cm) due to shell fragments. The textural analysis indicates (clayey sand and silty sand) low-energy environment. The high organic matter is observed at 0–3 cm due to redox condition and dense mangrove in the Muthupet. In the comparative studies of Marakkanam, Punnakkayal, and Muthupet, the trace metal percentage and pollution are also very low, indicating that the Koraiyaru river of Muthupet is not under threat.

ACKNOWLEDGEMENTS

This study is fully supported by the CPEPA-UGC Project (F. No. 8-2/2008 NS/PE) dated 14/12/2011 in New Delhi. We thank the professor and head of the Department of Geology, University of Madras, Chennai, for providing the necessary facilities. We thank Dr Rajeshwara Rao and Dr M. Jayaprakash of the Department of Applied Geology, University of Madras, Chennai, for the trace element analysis and valuable suggestions during the research work. And thanks to the director of Central Institute of Brackishwater Aquaculture (CIBA) in Chennai for providing cold room for the deep-freezing of the core sample.

REFERENCES

Antonio Cobelo-Garcia and Ricardo Prego (2003), Heavy metal sedimentary records in Galician Ria (NW Spain) Background values and recent contamination; *Marine Pollution Bulletin* 46 1253–1262.

Forstner, U., and Wittmann, G. T. W. (1981), Metal pollution in the aquatic environment (Berlin: Springer) 486 p.

Forstner, U., and G. T. W. Whitman (1979), Metal pollution in the aquatic environment, springer-Berlin ; New York: Springer-Verlag, 1979 xvi, 486 p.: ill.verlag, berlin.

Gaudette, H. E., Flight, W. R., Toner, L., Folger. D. W. (1974), An inexpensive titration method for the determination of organic carbon in recent sediments. J. Sediment Petrol 44:249–253.

Goncalves G. O. (1993), Instrucao Tecnica, IT 003, Biblioteca CETEM, Rio de Janeiro, 6 p.

GSI (1969) District resource map Tirunelveli district Goverment of india 2005.

Harbison P. (1986), Mangrove muds: a sink and a source for trace metals. Mar Pollut Bull 17:246–250.

Hema achyuthan and D. Richardmohan (2002), Indian journal of marine sciences, pp. 141–149.

Janaki-Raman, D., Jonathan, M. P., Srinivasalu, S., Armstrong-Altrin, J. S., Mohan, S. P., Ram-Mohan, V. (2007), Trace metal enrichments in core sediments in Muthupet mangroves, SE coast of India: application of acid leachable technique. Environ Poll 145:245–257.

Jonathan, M. P., Ram-Mohan, V. (2003), Heavy metals in sediments of the innershelf off Gulf of Mannar, south-east coast of India. Mar Pollut Bull 46:263–268.

Jonathan, M. P., Ram-Mohan, V., Srinivasalu, S. (2004), Geochemical variations of major and trace elements in recent sediments, off   the Gulf of Mannar, the south-east coast of India. Environ Geo l45:466–480.

Krumbein and Pettijohn (1938), Manual of Sedimentary Petrography. 166. 168.

Loring D. H. (1991), Normalization of heavy-metal data from estuarine and coastal sediments. ICES J Mar Sci 48:101–115.

Loring, D. H., Rantala, R. T. T. (1992), Manual for the geochemical analyses of marine sediments and suspended particulate matter. Earth Sci Rev 32:235–283.

Madras consultancy group, Chennai Thoothukudi vision 2025 (April 2008) CII.

Mason, B., and Moore, C. R. (1982), Principles of geochemistry. Wiley New York, 344 p.

11 ASSESSMENT OF HEAVY METAL IN THE SEDIMENTS OF THAMIRABARANI RIVER, EAST COAST OF TAMIL NADU, INDIA

A. Chandrasekaran, M. V. Mukesh, S. R. Singarasubramanian, H. M. Sabeen[1], R. Muthukumarasamy, M. Tamilselvi

Department of Earth Sciences, Annamalai University, Annamalainagar, Tamil Nadu, India

[1] Department of Geology, Government College, Kariavattam, Thiruvananthapuram, Kerala, India

Email: geochandru@gmail.com, mukeshearthsciences@gmail.com

ABSTRACT

The present study aims to investigate the concentration and spatial distribution of trace metals in Thamirabarani River, located in the southeast coast of India. Sediment samples collected from sixteen locations were analysed using flame atomic absorption spectrophotometer. The concentration of pollution in sediments like cadmium, lead, copper, zinc, chromium, and nickel along with geochemical normalization and sediment quality are assessed using respective enrichment factor (EF) and geoaccumulation index (I_{geo}). The results indicate significant upward concentration of contamination in Cd and low in Cu, Zn, and Cr. The geoaccumulation index of Cu, Zn, and Cr is classified as unpolluted except that of Cd, which is classified as highly polluted. It is evident that the sediment and water of the river area altered due to the entry of sewage and other domestic wastes into the aquatic system, which leads to a serious threat to the entire estuarine environment.

Keywords: Thamirabarani River, sediments, heavy metals, enrichment factors, geoaccumulation.

INTRODUCTION

Heavy metal pollution of aquatic ecosystem has become a potential global problem. These heavy metals are among the most common environmental pollutants, and their occurrence in waters and sediments highlights the presence of natural or anthropogenic sources. Trace amount of heavy metals are always present in fresh waters from terrigenous sources such as weathering of rocks, which may be recycled via chemical and biological contaminates in sediments in these ecosystems (Muwanga 1997, Zvinowanda et al. 2009, Harikumar et al. 2010, Sekabira et al. 2010). Heavy metal contamination in sediments could affect the quality and bioassimilation and bioaccumulation of metals in aquatic ecosystem, and these sediments are immobilized within the sediments and, thus, might be involved in absorption, co-precipitation, and complex creation (Okafor and Opuene 2007, Mohiuddin et al. 2010, Sekabira. K. et al. 2010). These elements accumulate in the sediments through heterogeneous physical and chemical adsorption mechanisms, depending upon the nature of the sediment matrix into other elements as oxides, hydroxides, Fe, Mn, and in another form (Awofolu et al. 2005, Mwiganga and Kanisiime 2005, Rabee et al. 2011). Elements like Cd and As show signs of extreme toxicity even at trace level (Nicolau et al. 2006 and Harikumar et al. 2010). In natural waters, the suspended sediments during their transport undergo numerous changes which affect the behaviour and bioavailability (Akcay, H. et al 2003, Abdel Ghani et al. 2007, Harikumar et al. 2009, Harikumar et al. 2010).

The occurrence of metal contamination in fluvial ecosystems is commonly due to urban and mining activities occurring in its watershed (Guasch et al. 2009, Ferreira da Silva et al. 2009, Sierra and Gómez 2010). Trace metals may produce toxic effects on aquatic organisms, depending on metal speciation, which, in turn, determines bioavailability, toxicity, and metal accumulation in accordance with this environmental problem (Tessier and Turner 1995, Meylan et al. 2004).

The effect of heavy metals on soil depends upon the series of physical and chemical characteristics, such as texture, organic matter, pH, and redox potential, and the amount of trace metals in sediments is usually low. Other than that, this clay and colloidal materials are active in the surface and contain organic matter, and they can act as a shield in controlling the deposition of trace metals in sediments from an estuary to a coastal region (Harikumar et al. 2010). The absorption of heavy metal in sediments can be a good sign of man-induced pollution rather than natural enrichment of the sediment by weathering. Human activities transformed the geochemical cycle of trace metals, which bring environmental contamination (Nriagu, J. O. 1988). Heavy metals may enter into the ecosystems from anthropogenic sources, such as industrial wastewater discharges, sewage wastewater, fossil fuel combustion, and atmospheric deposition (Linnik and Zubenko 2000, Campbell 2001, Lwanga et al. 2003, El Diwani and El Rafie 2008, Idrees 2009, Sekabira 2010).

The accumulation of heavy metals which contaminate into the environment is a serious problem to the society. Therefore, heavy-metal concentration in sediment unravels out the history and intensity of local and regional pollution (Nyangababo et al. 2005a, Sekabira 2010).

Mainly, the rivers are dominant pathway for the transport of metals (Miller et al. 2003), and trace elements may become significant pollutants of many small riverine systems (Dassenakis et al. 1998). The behaviour of metals in nature waters is a function of the substrate sediment composition, the suspended sediment composition, and the water chemistry. During transport, the trace elements undergo numerous changes in their specification due to dissolution, precipitation, sorption, and complex phenomena, which affect their behaviour and bioavailability (Dassenakis et al. 1998, Akcay et al. 2003, Nicolau et al. 2006).

The objective of this work is to assess the geochemistry of Thamirabarani River's sediments to establish the prospects of secondary pollution in sediments. The significant amount of waste drained, which contain toxic metals, help us to determine the effects of heavy metal due to natural and anthropogenic activity, which affects the tributaries and estuaries in Thamirabarani sediments.

MATERIALS AND METHODS

Study Area

Thamirabarani River originates from Western Ghats hills in the study area and confluences in the east coast of Bay of Bengal. Thamirabarani River discharges falls in the part of Tirunelveli and Thoothukudi districts, east coast of Tamil Nadu state, India. It falls in the Geological Survey of India survey sheets Nos. 58 L/2 and located between 8° 25' to 9° 10' N and 77° 10' to 78°

15' E (Figure 11.1). The study area is blessed with deltaic system with different active and inactive distributaries. The western part is dominated by active river and tide and distributaries are along the coast (Figure 11.2) (Magesh et al. 2011).

Sediment Sampling and Analysis

In the study area, sixteen sediment samples were collected at the river mouth and tributaries. Each sampling location identified and recorded using a hand-held GPS (Magellan). Subsurface sediment samples were also collected for geochemical analysis and packed in thick polyethylene bags. In the laboratory, the collected samples were deep-frozen at $-4°$ to avoid soil contamination and dried in a hot-air oven at 40 °C and, after homogenization using pestle and mortar, sieved and stored in polyethylene bags for further analysis (Praveena 1997, Shetye et al. 2009). The sediment samples were digested and subjected to the assessment of trace metals using AAS (atomic absorption spectrometer, Elico make) with specific flame and wavelength using a series of solution over the range 2–10mg/l.

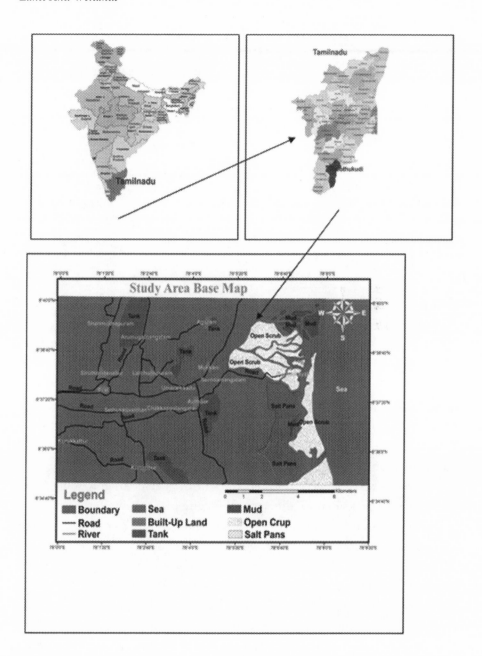

Figure 11.1. Study area base map.

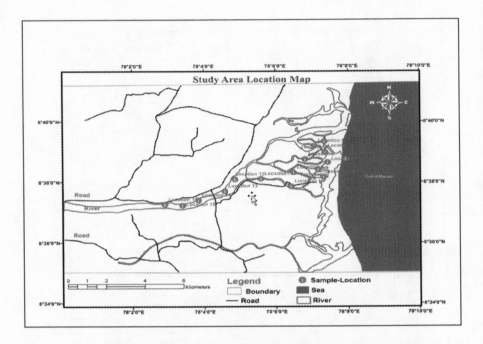

Figure 11.2. Study area location map.

Determination of Enrichment Factor (*EF*)

Enrichment factor (*EF*) is the proportional abundance of the chemical elements that helps to assess the degree of contamination and to understand the distribution among the elements of anthropogenic origin from sites by individual elements in the sediments. *EF* is computed relative to the abundance of species in source material to that found in the earth's crust and is found to be a better method to measure geochemical trends (Simex and Helz 1981, Praveena 2007, Harikumar and Jisha 2010, Sekabira et al. 2010).

Enrichment factor = *(Cn/Fe) sample / (Cn/Fe) background*

Cn is the concentration of element *n*. The background value is that of average shale (Turekian and Wedepohl 1961). The calculated *EF* values of the samples are given in Table 11.1. Deely and Fergusson (1994) proposed Fe as an acceptable normalization element to be used in the calculation of the enrichment factor since they considered that the Fe distribution was not related to other heavy metals. Fe usually has a high natural concentration, and therefore, it is not substantially enriched from anthropogenic sources in estuarine sediments (Niencheski et al. 1994). An element qualifies as a reference if it is of low occurrence variability and is present throughout the environment in trace amounts (Loska et al. 2003, Sekabira et al. 2010). Naturally derived elements have an EF value of near identity while elements of anthropogenic origin have EF values of several orders of magnitude.

Based on this, four categories are recognized: <1 (background concentration), 1–2 (depletion to minimal enrichment), 2–5 (moderate enrichment), 5–20 (significant enrichment), 20–40 (very high enrichment), and >40 (extremely high enrichment) (Sekabira et al. 2010, Harikumar and Jisha 2010, Sutherland 2000). Different enrichment calculation methods and reference material have been reported by many researchers, like Ogusola et al. (1994), Gaiero et al. (1997), Sutherland et al. (2000), Kamau (2002), Valdés et al. (2005), Ghrefat and Yusuf (2006), Abrahim and Parker (2008), Akoto et al. (2008), Dragović et al. (2008), Charkravarty and Patgiri (2009), Harikumar and Jisha (2010), Sekabira (2010), Olubunmi and Olorunsola (2010), and Mmolawa (2011).

Determination of Contamination Factor

The levels of contamination of sediment by a metal are frequently expressed in terms of a contamination factor calculated as follows:

Contamination factor (CF) = metal content in the sediment.

Background Level of Metal

CF < 1 means to low contamination, $1 \geq CF \geq 3$ means moderate contamination, $3 \geq CF \geq 6$ indicates considerable contamination, and CF > 6 indicates very high contamination. The calculated CF values for the samples were given in Table 11.2.

Geoaccumulation Index (I_{geo})

Enrichment of metal absorption was calculated using the method suggested by Muller (1969), termed the geoaccumulation index (I_{geo}). This method concludes the metal pollution in terms of seven (0 to 6) enrichment classes, ranging from background concentration to very heavily polluted, as follows:

$$I_{geo} = \log_2 (Cn / 1.5 \times Bn)$$

Table 11.1 Enrichment factor (EF)

S. No.	Cu	Cr	Zn	Cd
1	0.532	0.534	0.534	0.534
2	0.459	-	0.460	0.460
3	0.421	0.421	-	0.417
4	0.524	-	0.524	0.524
5	0.468	-	0.468	0.466
6	0.488	0.488	0.488	0.489
7	0.460	-	0.460	0.458
8	0.455	0.455	0.455	0.452
9	0.437	0.437	0.437	0.434
10	0.452	0.453	0.453	0.453
11	-	0.517	0.517	0.515
12	0.605	-	0.605	0.605
13	0.894	-	0.895	0.896
14	0.741	-	0.741	0.739
15	-	0.925	0.925	0.923
16	0.787	-	0.789	-

Table 11.2 Contamination factor for studied heavy metals in sediments of Thamirabarani River

Cu	0.014	Low contamination
Cr	0.485	Low contamination
Zn	0.368	Low contamination
Cd	12.234	Very high contamination

Where Cn = measured concentration of heavy metal in the Tigris sediment. Bn = geochemical background value in average shale of element n (Turekian and Wedepohl 1961).

The factor 1.5 is used for the possible variations of the background data due to lithological variations. Different geoaccumulation index classes along with associated qualities based on Muller's (1969 and 1981) seven grades or classes of the I_{geo} values are given in Table 11.3.

Table 11.3 I_{geo} classes with respect to sediment quality standard

I_{geo} value	I_{geo} class	Designation of soil quality
>5	6	Extremely contaminated
4–5	5	Strongly to extremely contaminated
3–4	4	Strongly contaminated
2–3	3	Moderately to strongly contaminated
1–2	2	Moderately contaminated
0–1	1	Uncontaminated to moderately contaminated
0	0	Uncontaminated

The I_{geo} class 0 suggests the lack of contamination while the I_{geo} class 6 highlights the upper limit of the contamination. The highest class 6 (extremely contaminated) shows the extreme enrichment of the metals relative to their background values (Harikumar et al. 2010, Sekabira 2010, Riyadi 2012). The geoaccumulation index for heavy metals in sediment of Thamirabarani River is given in Table 11.4.

Table 11.4 Geoaccumulation index for studied heavy metals in sediment of Thamirabarani River

Geoaccumulation (I_{geo})		
Cu	–3.4102	Unpolluted
Cr	–1.6226	Unpolluted
Zn	–2.0243	Unpolluted
Cd	3.0274	Highly polluted

RESULT AND DISCUSSION

The total trace metal concentrations for each sampling site found in sediments of Thamirabarani River's estuary sediments are depicted in Table 11.5.

Table 11.5 Sediments sample for copper, chromium, zinc, and cadmium in parts per million

S. No.	Cu	Cr	Zn	Cd
1	2.2	58.6	18.6	4.21
2	3.92	BDL	9.3	4.92
3	3.74	94.5	BDL	1.42
4	5.44	BDL	20.27	2.81
5	15.85	BDL	29.17	1.45
6	13.86	112.3	24.1	4.22
7	9.78	BDL	12.66	2.88
8	2.18	58.3	74	1.41
9	15.84	120.4	30	2.11
10	7.92	103.3	16.07	1.46
11	BDL	145.5	39.74	2.88
12	17.82	BDL	30.86	2.78
13	10.85	BDL	16.1	2.9
14	10.78	BDL	47.77	2.22
15	BDL	84.4	26.63	1.48
16	3.96	BDL	17.75	BDL
Mean	7.758	97.162	27.534	2.61
Max	17.82	145.5	39.74	4.92
Min	2.2	58.3	9.3	1.41

The metal content ranges at an interval: Cd, 4.92–1.41 ppm; Cr, 145.5–58.3 ppm; Cu, 17.82–2.2 ppm; Zn, 39.74–9.3 ppm (dry weight). The mean concentrations of metals are as follows: Cd, 2.61; Cr, 97.162; Cu, 7.758; Zn, 27.534. The metals are arranged from higher to lower mean content in this area as Cr < Zn < Cu < Cd, which are calculated from the enrichment factors of the elements in the sediment samples of Thamirabarani River (Figure 11.3).

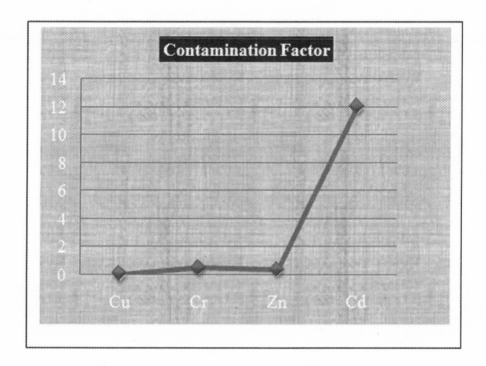

Figure 11.3. Ratio of contamination factor in Thamirabarani sediments.

The output from the available data for a comprehensive study highlights the background and toxicological reference values of the sediments, along with the average values obtained for trace metals of Thamirabarani. It is apparent that the average total metal concentration of cadmium in the sediment samples exceeded the geochemical background (shale standard and continental crust). The table demonstrates that the concentration of Cd varies from the average shale values. The major change in arrangements between the values highlights that the elements have not originated from lithogenic sources but from anthropogenic sources. The element's contribution and enrichment of metals compared with the toxological levels shows that Thamirabarani estuary and river sediments are moderately polluted.

The trace metal concentration of Thamirabarani sediments showed a moderately higher amount of metal presence than the prescribed limits by TEC (US DOE), ISQG (Canadian EQG), US EPA, and Ontario MOE (Japan) for the trace metal standards studied all over the world. The results specify that the levels of trace metals found in the sediments of study area are hazardous to the aquatic system and public health (Figure 11.4).

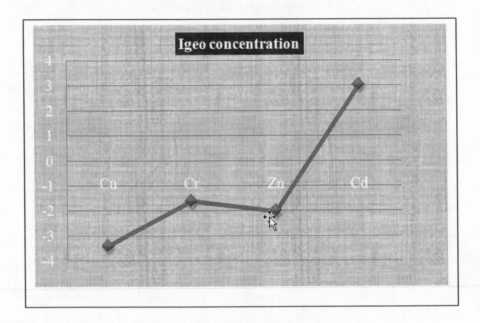

Figure 11.4. The trend of I_{geo} concentration of elements.

CONCLUSION

A quantitative geochemical analysis of the sediments in Thamirabarani River revealed that the higher amount of absorption concentration of trace metals to the sediments is due to anthropogenic influences. The pollution intensity combined with the distribution pattern of trace metals in the sediments according to enrichment factor shows Cd with very high contamination and Cu, Cr, and Zn with low contamination. The Cd concentration is found throughout the estuary sediment, and its I_{geo} value is determined as highly polluted while the other elements are shown as unpolluted (Magesh et al. 2011). The Thamirabarani River requires compulsory monitoring and remediation strategy to avoid potential ecological risk in the study area.

ACKNOWLEDGEMENTS

The authors wish to express their sincere thanks to the university authorities for undertaking this project work. We are also thankful to the Ministry of Earth Sciences (MOES/MRDF-11/1/25/P/09-PC-III) for the financial grant given for this work. Thanks are as well due to the technical staffs of CIRT laboratory and geochemical laboratory for the analysis work undertaken and to our scholars for assisting in the field. We also appreciate our colleagues for their constant support and valuable suggestions.

REFERENCE

Abrahim, G. M. S., Parker, R. J. (2008), Assessment of heavy metal enrichment factors and the degree of contamination in marine sediments from Tamaki Estuary, Aukland, New Zealand. Envron Monit. Assess. 136: 227–238.

Adel Mashaan Rabee, Yaaroub Faleh Al-Fatlawy, Abd-Al-Husain Najim Abd own and Mustafa Nameer December (2011), Using Pollution Load Index (PLI) and Geoaccumulation Index (I_{geo}) for the Assessment of Heavy Metals Pollution in Tigris River Sediment in Baghdad Region Journal of Al-Nahrain University Vol. 14, pp. 108–114.

Adi Slamet RIYADI, Takaaki ITAI, Tomohiko ISOBE1, Muhammad ILYAS, Agus SUDARYANTO, Iwan Eka SETIAWAN, Shin TAKAHASHI and Shinsuke TANABE Spatial Profile of Trace Elements in Marine Sediments from Jakarta Bay, Indonesia Interdisciplinary Studies on Environmental Chemistry Environmental Pollution and Ecotoxicology, Eds., M. Kawaguchi, K. Misaki, H. Sato, T. Yokokawa, T. Itai, T. M. Nguyen, J. Ono and S. Tanabe, pp. 141–150.

Akcay, H., Oguz, A., Karapire, C. (2003), Study of heavy metal pollution and speciation in Buyak Menderes and Gediz river sediments. Water Res., 37 (4), 813–822 (10).

Akoto, O., Ephraim, J. H., Darko, G. (2008), Heavy metal pollution in surface soils in the vicinity of abundant raiway servicing workshop in Kumasi, Ghana. Int. J. Environ. Res. 2 (4): 359–364.

Awofolu, O. R., Mbolekwa, Z., Mtshemla, V., Fatoki, O. S. (2005), Levels of trace metals in water and sediments from Tyume River and its effects on an irrigated farmland. Water SA., 31 (1), 87–94.

Campbell, L. M. (2001), Mercury in Lake Victoria (East Africa): Another emerging issue for a Beleaguered Lake PhD dissertation, Waterloo, Ontario, Canada.

Chakravarty, M., Patgiri, A. D. (2009), Metal pollution assessment in sediments of the Dikrong River, NE India. J, Hum Ecol., 27 (1), 63–67.

Dassenakis, M., Scoullos, M., Foufa, E., Krasakopoulou, E., Pavlidou, A., Kloukiniotou, M. (1998), Effects of multiple source pollution on a small Mediterranean river. Appl. Geochem., 13 (2), 197–211 (15).

Deely, J. M., Fergusson, J. E. (1994), Heavy metal and organic matter concentration and distribution in dated sediments of a small estuary adjacent to a small urban area. The science of the Total Environment, 153, 97–111.

Diwani, G., El Rafie, Sh. (2008), Modification of thermal and oxidative properties of biodiesel produced from vegetable oils. Int. J. Environ. Sci. Tech., 5 (3), 391–400.

Dragović, S., Mihailović, N., Gajić, B. (2008), Heavy metals in soils: distribution, relationship with soil characteristics and radionuclides and multivariate assessment of contamination sources. Chemosphere 74: 491–495.

Ferreira da Silva, E., Almeida, S. F. P., Nunes, M. L., Luis, A. T., Borg, F., Hedlund, M., Marques de Sá, C., Patinha, C., Teixeira, P. (2009), Heavy metal pollution downstream the abandoned Coval da Mó mine (Portugal) and associated effects on epilithic diatom communities. Sci. Total Environ. 407, 5620–5636.

Ghrefat, H., Yusuf, N. (2006), Assessing Mn, Fe, Cu, Zn and Cd pollution in bottom sediments of Wadi Al-Arab Dam, Jordan. Chemosphere 65: 2114–2121.

Guasch, H., Leira, M., Montuelle, B., Geiszinger, A., Roulier, J. L., Tornés, E., Serra, A. (2009), Use of multivariate analyses to investigate the contribution of metal pollution to diatom species composition: search for the most appropriate cases and explanatory variables. Hydrobiologia 627, 143–158.

Harikumar, P. S., Nasir, U. P., Mujeebu Rahman, M. P. (2010), Distribution of heavy metals in the core sediments of a tropical wetland system, Int. J. Environ. Sci. Tech., 6 (2), 225–23.

Idrees, F. A. (2009), Assessment of trace metal distribution and contamination in surface soils of Amman. Jordan J, Chem., 4 (1), 77–87.

Kamau, J. N. (2002), Heavy metal distribution and enrichment at Port–Reitz creek, Mombasa. Western Indian Ocean J., Mar. Sci. 1 (1): 65– 70.

Linnik, P. M., Zubenko, I. B. (2000), Role of bottom sediments in the secondary pollution of aquatic environments by heavy metal compounds, lakes and reservoirs. Res. Manage, 5 (1), 11–21.

Loska, K., Wiechula, D., Barska, B., Cebula, E., Chojnecka, A. (2003), Assessment of arsenic enrichment of cultivated soils in Southern Poland. Pol. J. Environ. Stud., 12 (2), 187–192.

Magesh, N. S. (2011), Spatial analysis of trace element contamination in sediments of Tamirabarani estuary, south-east coast of India Estuarine, Coastal and Shelf Science 92 618–628.

Meylan, S., Behra, R., Sigg, L. (2004), Influence of metal speciation in natural fresh water on accumulation of copper and zinc in periphyton: a microcosm study. Environ. Sci. Technol. 38, 3104–3111.

Miller, C. V., Foster, G. D., Majedi, B. F. (2003), Baseflow and stormflow metal fluxes from two small agricultural catchments in the coastal plain of Chesapeake Bay Basin, United States. Appl. Geochem., 18 (4), 483–501 (19)

Mmolawa, K. B., Likuku, A. S., and Gaboutloeloe, G. K. (March 2011), Assessment of heavy metal pollution in soils along major roadside areas in Botswana, African Journal of Environmental Science and Technology Vol. 5 (3), pp. 186–196.

Mohiuddin, K. M., Zakir, H. M., Otomo, K., Sharmin, S., Shikazono, N. (2010), Geochemical distribution of trace metal pollutants in water and sediments of downstream of an urban river. Int. J. Environ. Sci. Tech., 7 (1), 17–28.

Muller, G. (1969), Index of geoaccumulation in sediments of the Rhine River. Geo. J., 2 (3), 108–118.

Muwanga, A. (1997), Environmental impacts of copper mining at Kilembe, Uganda: A geochemical investigation of heavy metal pollution of drainage waters, stream, sediments and soils in the Kilembe valley in relation to mine waste disposal. PhD dissertation. Universitat Braunschweig, Germany.

Mwiganga, M., Kanisiime, F. (2005), Impact of Mpererwe Landfill in Kampala Uganda, on the surrounding environment. Phys. Chem. Earth, 30 (11–16) 744–750.

Nicolau, R., Galera-Cunha, A., Lucas, Y. (2006), Transfer of nutrients and labile metals from the continent to the sea by a small Mediterranean river. Chemosphere, 63 (3), 469–476.

Niencheski, L. F., Windom, H. L., and Smith, R. (1994), Distribution of particular trace metal in patos lagoon Estuary (Brazil). Marine pollution Bulletin, 28, 96–102.

Nriagu, J. O., Pacyna, J. (1988), Quantitative Assessment of Worldwide Contamination of Air, Water and Soil by Trace Metals, Nature, 333: 134–139.

Nyangababo, J. T. (2003), Heavy metal in the contour feathers of marabou stork (Leptoptilos crumeniferus) from Kampala City and its surrounding areas. Bull. Environ. Contam. Toxicol. 70, 792–79.

Nyangababo, J. T., Henry, E., Omutange, E. (2005), Lead, cadmium, copper, manganese and zinc in wetland waters of Victoria Lake Basin, East Africa. Bull. Environ. Contam. Toxicol. 74 (5), 1003–1010.

Ogusola, O. J., Oluwole, A. F., Asubiojo, O. I., Olaniyi, H. B., Akeredolu, F. A., Akanle, O. A., Spyrou, N. M., Ward, N. I., Ruck, W. (1994), Traffic pollution: preliminary elemental characterization of roadside dust in Lagos, Nigeria. Sci. Total Environ. 146/147: 175–184.

Okafor, E. Ch., Opuene, K. (2007), Preliminary assessment of trace metals and polycyclic aromatic hydrocarbons in the sediments. Int. J. Environ. Sci. Tech., 4 (2), 233–240.

Olubunmi, F. E., Olorunsola, O. E. (2010), Evaluation of the status of heavy metal pollution of sediment of Agbabu bitumen deposits area, Nigeria. Eur. J. Sci. Res. 41 (3):373–382.

Praveena, S. M., Ahmed, A., Radojevic, M., Abdullah, M. H., Aris, A. Z. (2007) Factor-cluster analysis and enrichment study of mangrove sediments-an example from Mengkabong, Sabah. Malaysian J., Anal. Sci., 11 (2), 421–43.

Sekabira, K., Origa, H. O., Basamba, T. A., Mutumba, G., Kakulidi, E. (2010) Assessment of heavy metal pollution in the urban stream sediments and its tributaries. Int. J. Sci. Tec. 7 (3):435–446.

Sekabira, K., PhD candidate, lecturer, Department of Environment, Faculty of Science and Engineering, Kampala International University PO box (20000), Kampala, Uganda. Turekian KK, Wedepohl KH (1961) Distribution of the elements in some major units of the earth's crust. Geo. Soc. Am. Bull., 72 (2), 175–192.

Sierra, M. V., Gómez, N. (2010), Assessing the disturbance caused by and industrial discharge using field transfer of epipelic biofilm. Sci. Total Environ. 408, 2696–2705.

Simex, S. A., Helz, G. R. (1981), Regional geochemistry of trace elements in Chesapeake Bay. Environ. Geo. 3, 315–323.

Sutherland, R. A. (2000), Bed sediment associated trace metals in an urban stream Oahu. Hawaii. Environ. Geo. 39 (6), 611–627.

Taylore, S. R., McLennan, S. M., Armstrong, R. L., Tarney, J. (1981), The composition and Evolution of the continental crust; Rare Earth elements evidence from Sedimentary rock and discussion. Royal Society Publication, Physical Sciences vol. 301 pp. 381–399.

Tessier, A., Turner, D. R. (1995), Metal Speciation and Bioavailability in Aquatic Systems. John Wiley and Sons, Chichester.

Thomilson, D. C., Wilson, D. J., Harris, C. R., Jeffrey, D. W. (1980), Problem in heavy metals in estuaries and the formation of pollution index. Helgol. Wiss. Meeresunlter. 33, 566–575.

Turekian, K. K., Wedepohl, K. H. (1961), Distribution of the elements in some major units of the earth's crust. Geol. Soc. Am. Bull., 72, 175–182.

Valdés, J., Vargas, G., Sifeddine, A., Orttlieb, L., Guiñez, M. (2005), Distribution and enrichment evaluation of heavy metals in Mejillones bay (23° S), Northern Chile: geochemical and statistical approach. Mar. Pollut. Bull. 50: 1558–1568.

12 FLUVIO-PARALIC ENVIRONMENTS OF COASTAL CRETACEOUS-PLANT SIGNATURES

A. Rajanikanth, C. H. Chinnappa, and S. Vasudevan[1]
Birbal Sahni Institute of Palaeobotany 53 University Road, Lucknow 226 007, UP, India
[1] Department of Earth Sciences, Annamalai University, Tamil Nadu
Email: rajanikanth.annamraju@gmail.com, chinnabsip@gmail.com.

ABSTRACT

The coastal sedimentary basins of India hold a long geological history and are known for rich palaeontological records. Tectonic activity dictated initiation of sedimentation in the coastal basins attributable to separation of Indian continent from Antarctica and Australia during the Early Cretaceous. The sedimentation during the Cretaceous heralded fluvio-paralic deposition and culminated into a huge marine sequence in the east coast, distributed in a number of unconnected outcrops often referred to as coastal Gondwanas. Continental rock sequences with thin marine intercalations of paralic and lagoonal realms in the coastal environments distributed in intracratonic Pranhita–Godavari (PG) and pericratonic Krishna–Godavari (KG) basins provide excellent tools to delineate palaeoecology. Cretaceous plant signatures of PG and KG basins have been evaluated for ecological inferences. Differential preservation of leaf, spore, pollen, axes, wood, cone, and seed of different groups of plants exemplify varied depositional environments.

Each basin contains signatures of plants represented by mixed floral components comprising many cosmopolitan taxa along with endemic forms. Ecologically significant members of algae, bryophytes, pteridophytes, pteridosperms, cycadales, bennettitales, ginkgoales, taxales, coniferales, and angiosperms preserved in the form of micro- and macro-components in Pranhita– Godavari and Krishna–Godavari basins provide clue to reconstruct past environments. These signatures indicate upland, near basinal, and marginal floral components along the passive east coast. A holistic panorama of intra- and pericratonic depositional settings with floral evidences in conjunction with faunal evidences has been offered. The abundance of spores of cryptogams in each basin and also the overall representation of spores exhibit prevalence of moist–humid conditions near the depositional site.

The rich composition of Bennettito–Conifero association in the KG basin indicates that the flora was probably growing on relatively dry slopes gently descending towards the sea. Further evidences of marine fauna and phytoplankton suggest prevalence of marginal marine conditions. Besides relative distribution of spores, saccate–non-saccate pollen and phytoplankton indicate prevalence of swampy/nearshore brackish conditions in the KG basin. Likewise, abundance of pollen of upland habitat in the PG basin is suggestive of uplifted terrain and gradual descend towards coastal regions.

Furthermore, less abundance and diversity of cycadophytes, scarcity of broad-leaved members, and presence of conifers with narrow and scaly leaves indicate prevalence of dry and humid conditions in the intracratonic PG basin, supported by lack of faunal evidences.

Keywords: cretaceous, east coast, palaeoenvironment, ecology, evolution.

INTRODUCTION

The peninsular India preserved thick sedimentary deposits spanning over a period of nearly 200 million years from latest Carboniferous to Early Cretaceous. These deposits, which are traditionally considered as continental freshwater deposits, are often referred under Gondwana. These sequences are characterized by various depositional realms, like glacial, glacio-fluvial, glacio-marine, fluvial, lacustrine, to shallow marine, over a prolonged period. In the east coast, the marine deposits are often subjected to marine influence. The Cretaceous sedimentation was triggered by the separation of India from Antarctica and Australia. Significant palaeontological signatures were left in the sediments during the northward journey of India during the Cretaceous (Acharyya 2000, Acharyya and Lahiri 1991, Biswas et al. 1993, Metcalfe 1996, Mukhopadhyay et al. 2010, Veevers 2004, Veevers and Tiwari 1995, Yoshida et al. 1992, Ziegler et al. 1983).

It is also suggested that the change over from continental Gondwana to coastal Gondwana had occurred over a time span of about 70 million years between late Jurassic to Cretaceous and controlled by phase-wise upliftment of the basement as a corollary to the Gondwana continental breakup (Yoshida et al. 1992, Rao 1993, 1994, Veevers 2004). Paralic-marginal marine sequences in various pericratonic basins along the eastern coast also coincided with associated fluvial deposits in intracratonic basins.

Geological history of east coast basins offers valuable information regarding biotic signatures utilized to understand evolution and also the environment under which they thrived (Baksi 1977; Bhalla 1969; Bose et al. 1990; Das and Ayyasami 1994; Datta et al. 1983; Dutta and Laha 1977; Sastri et al. 1963, 1973, 1981; Spath 1933; Venkatachala and Sinha 1986; Rajanikanth 1992, 1996a, b; Rajanikanth et al. 2000; Tewari 1999).

The east coast basins of India are well known for their fossiliferous rocks of upper Gondwana age (Early Cretaceous) and are distributed in three states, represented by seven formations, namely Sriperumbudur of Palar basin and Sivaganga formation of Cauvery basin in Tamil Nadu, Vemavaram, Gollapalli, and Raghavapuram of Krishna–Godavari basins (KG) and Gangapur of Pranhita-Godavari basin (PG) in Andhra Pradesh, Athgarh, in Orissa state (Rajanikanth et al. 2000, Venkatachala 1977, Venkatachala and Rajanikanth 1988). Evidences from the Early Cretaceous sequence of KG and PG basins have been evaluated to understand plant evolution and environmental changes. The plant fossil records, both macro and micro, from KG and PG basins which show rich floral diversity and contributed to the formation of hydrocarbons are also reliable palaeoecological tools.

East Coast

Evolution of east coast sedimentary basins was correlated with intense tectonism related to the breakup of the Gondwanic greater Indian continent, which resulted in the development of pericratonic basins and shelves and a few narrow intracratonic rift basins. Interestingly, both peri- and intracratonic sedimentary basins share a common floral bondage.

KG Basin

The KG basin is one of India's most promising petroliferous areas located on the continental margin of east coast of India covering an area of about 15,000 km² on land. The major geomorphologic units of the KG basin are upland plains, coastal plains, recent floodplains, and delta plains. The basin is a pericratonic passive margin basin initiated through rift tectonics. The basin is also characterized by lagoonal to fluvial to occasionally brackish water sediments.

Palaeontological evidences suggest a period of slow sedimentation and subsidence, but there are changes in water depth during deposition. Tilting of the basin occurred during Cretaceous, leading to widespread marine transgression and deposition of marine shale sequence. This was followed by the onset of overall regressive phase during late Cretaceous, represented by a deltaic sequence (Baksi 1966, 1967c, 1972, 1977; Raju and Misra 1996; Rao 1993, 1994, 2001; Swamy and Kapoor 1999; Vasudeva Rao and Krishna Rao 1977; Venkatarangan and Ray 1993).

The Cretaceous sedimentary units are exposed towards the west and north-west of KG basin and are represented by Gollapalli, Raghavapuram, Tirupathi (Godavari depression), Budavada, Vemavaram, Pavalur (Krishna Depression) litho units. The Gollapalli formation represents rift-fill sediments characterized by micaceous sandstone with conglomeratic bands. Macroflora chiefly contains *Taeniopteris*, *Cladophlebis* and *Onychiopsis*, and the microflora belong to *Cicatricosisporites australiensis–Aequitriradites spinulosus* palyno zone, suggesting an Early Cretaceous (Neocomian) age (tables 12.1 and 12.2).

Deposition of the Raghavapuram shale corresponds to the Barremian–Aptian marine transgression, which took place during the rift–drift phase represented essentially by carbonaceous shale. The intervening sands possibly represent brief regressive phase. Overall, sedimentological inputs demonstrated occurrence of delta plain distributaries with interdistributor swamps and fossiliferous white clay, a mix of *Ptilophyllum* flora and invertebrate fauna of prodelta/shallow marine environment during the deposition of Raghavapuram shale (Rao 1994, 2001). The sequence yielded invertebrate fossils of ammonite, lamellibranch, brachiopod, and foraminifera along with macro–micro plant remains (tables 12.1 and 12.2) (Baksi 1967a, b; Bhalla 1969; Govindan 1980; Prasad and Pundir 1999; Mehrotra et al. 2005, 2010; Rajanikanth 2009;

Sahni 1928, 1931; Sukh Dev 1987). Macroflora is characterized by megafossils of *Ptilophyllum, Elatocladus, Ginkgoites,* and the microflora represented by spores, pollens, and dinoflagellate cysts assignable to Barremian–Aptian to early Albian age.

The Tirupati sandstone deposited during post-rift phase in the late Cretaceous time is characterized by haematitic hard-to-compact sandstone with conglomerate. Macroflora is poorly known except some petrified woods, and the microflora is represented by *Retistephanocolpites* spp., *Erdtmanipollis, Tricolporites apoxyexinus, Racemonocolpites* spp., *Phyllocladidites mawsonii.* Plant evidences considered in toto along with marine fossils indicate freshwater paralic transitional to marginal marine, inner shelf, and marginal marine environments to the Cretaceous sequence of Godavari depression (Rawat and Berry 1999; Rajanikanth 2009; Prasad and Pundir 1999; Mehrotra et al. 2005, 2010) (see tables 12.1 and 12.2, figures 12.1and 12.2). The Vemavaram (Ommevaram) formation (Krishna depression) is characterized by light greyish purple shales intercalated by sandstones and pebble conglomerates These hard variegated grey-purple argillaceous shales are known for both faunal and floral remains (Bose 1974, Bose and Jain 1967, Bose and Bano 1978, Feistmental 1879, Foote 1879, Jain 1968, Seward and Sahni 1920, Sahni 1928 and 1931, Spath 1933, Suryanarayana 1954, Bose and Kasat 1972, Vagyani 1984 and 1985, Vagyani and Zutting 1986; see Chinnappa et al. in this book). Palynological studies were carried out by Ramanujam (1957) and Kar and Sah (1970), and they suggested an Early Cretaceous age to the formation based on their palynological data (Chinnappa et al. 2014). Faunal remains of Vemavaram formation were described by Spath (1933) and are represented by ammonites, brachiopods, lamellibranchs, fish scales, and mammalian ribs. The Budavada and Pavalur litho units are little known for plant relics.

Table 12.1 Relative distribution of microflora in KG and PG basins

Basin name	KG			PG
Formation name	Vem	Rag	Gol	Gan
Plant group				
Bryophytes				
Foraminisporis assymetricus	−	−	−	+
Foraminisporis dailyi	−	−	+	−
Foraminisporis wonthaggiensis	−	−	+	+
Coronatispora sp.	−	+	−	−
Aequitriradites spinulosus	−	−	−	+
Aequitriradites verrucosus	−	−	−	+
Coptospora cauveriana	−	+	−	−
Coptospora cutchensis	−	−	−	+
Coptospora sp.	−	−	−	+
Cooksonites minor	−	−	−	+
Cooksonites variabilis	−	+	+	+
Staplinisporites caminus	−	−	−	+
Pteridophytes				
Lycopodiaceae				
Lycopodiacidites asperatus	−	−	−	+
Lycopodiumsporites austroclavidites	−	−	−	+
Lycopodiumsporites crassimacerius	−	−	−	+
Lycopodiumsporites reticulumsporites	−	−	−	+
Lycopodiumsporites sp.	+	+	−	−
Reticulatazonalesporites sp.	+	−	−	−
Reticulatisporites sp.	+	−	−	−
Retitriletes austroclavatidites	−	−	+	−
Retitriletes circolumenus	−	−	+	−
Retitriletes eminulus	−	−	+	−
Sestrosporites pseudoalveolatus	−	−	+	+

Selaginellaceae				
Ceratosporites couliensis	–	–	–	+
Ceratosporites equalis	–	–	+	+
Densoisporites microregulatus	–	–	+	–
Densoisporites sp.	–	–	–	+
Densoisporites velatus	–	+	+	–
Neoraistrickia neozealandica	–	–	–	+
Neoraistrickia rallapetensis	–	–	–	+
Neoraistrickia truncatus	+	–	–	+
Steriosporites antiquasporites	-	-	-	+
Ophioglossaceae				
Foveosporites sahnii	-	-	-	+
Osmundaceae				
Baculatisporites comaumensis	–	+	+	+
Baculatisporites rotundus	–	–	–	+
Biformaesporites sp.	–	–	–	+
Biretisporites potoniae	–	+	–	–
Biretisporites spectabilis	–	–	–	+
Osmundacidites wellmanii	+	–	–	+
Todisporites minor	–	–	+	–
Gleicheniaceae				
Concavisporites sp.	–	–	–	+
Gleichinidites circinidites	–	–	+	–
Gleichinidites senonicus	–	–	–	+
Gleichinidites sp.	–	–	–	+
Ornamentifera echinata	–	–	–	+
Ornamentifera sp.	–	+	–	+
Plicifera senonicus	–	+	+	–
Plicifera sp.	–	–	–	+
Matoniaceae				
Dictyophyllidites harrisii	–	+	–	–
Dictyophyllidites sp.	–	–	–	+
Matonisporites phlebopteroides	–	–	–	+

Matonisporites sp.	–	+	–	–
Schizaeaceae				
Appendicisporites sellingii	–	+	–	–
Cicatricosisporites augustus	–	–	–	+
Cicatricosisporites australiensis	–	+	+	+
Cicatricosisporites dorogensis	–	–	–	+
Cicatricosisporites gangapurensis	–	–	–	+
Cicatricosisporites hallei	–	–	–	+
Cicatricosisporites hughesii	–	+	+	+
Cicatricosisporites imbricatus	–	–	–	+
Cicatricosisporites lodbrokiae	–	+	–	+
Cicatricosisporites mohrioides	–	–	–	+
Cicatricosisporites sp.	–	+	–	+
Cicatricosisporites verrumuratus	–	–	–	+
Contignisporites cooksoniae	–	–	+	+
Contignisporites glebulentus	–	+	+	+
Contignisporites multimuratus	–	–	–	+
Contignisporites psilatus	–	–	–	+
Contignisporites sp.	–	+	–	–
Impardecispora adilabadensis	–	–	–	+
Impardecispora apiverrucata	–	–	–	+
Impardecispora croassus	–	–	–	+
Impardecispora purverulenta	–	+	–	–
Impardecispora sp.	–	+	–	–
Ischyosporites createris	–	–	–	+
Ischyosporites punctatus	–	–	+	+
Ischyosporites pusillus	–	–	–	+
Ischyosporites sp.	+	–	–	–
Klukisporites foveolatus	–	–	+	+
Klukisporites scaberis	–	–	+	+
Klukisporites areolatus	–	–	–	+
Schizosporis regulatus	–	–	–	+

Marsileaceae				
Crybelosporites sp.	–	+	–	–
Crybelosporites punctatus	–	–	–	+
Crybelosporites striatus	–	+	–	–
Crybelosporites stylosus	–	+	–	–
Cyatheaceae/Dicksoniaceae				
Kuylisporites lunaris	–	–	–	+
Kuylisporites sp.	–	–	–	+
Alsophyllidites grandis	–	–	+	–
Concavissimisporites punctatus	–	–	+	+
Concavissimisporites sp.	–	+	–	–
Concavissimisporites variverrucatus	–	+	+	+
Cyatheacidites tectifera	–	+	–	–
Cyathidites asper	+	–	–	+
Cyathidites australis	–	+	+	+
Cyathidites cutchensis	+	–	–	–
Cyathidites ghuneriensis	–	–	–	+
Cyathidites jurassicus	+	–	–	–
Cyathidites pseudopunctatus	+	–	–	–
Cyathidites punctatus	+	–	–	–
Cyathidites rajmahalensis	+	–	–	–
Cyathidites sp.	+	+	–	–
Cyathidites minor	+	–	–	–
Cyathidites trilobatus	+	–	–	–
Deltoidospora diaphana	–	–	+	–
Deltoidospora juncta	–	–	–	+
Leptolepidites major	–	–	–	+
Leptolepidites verrucatus	–	–	+	–
Triletes sp.	–	+	–	–
Triletes tuberculiformis	–	–	–	+
Triletes verrucosus	–	+	–	–

Polypodiaceae				
Laevigataletes sp.	+	–	–	–
Laevigatazonaletes sp.	+	–	–	–
Laevigatimonoletes sp.	+	–	–	–
Laevigatisporites sp.	+	–	–	–
Metamonoletes haradensis	–	–	–	+
Metamonoletes sp.	–	–	–	+
Monolites indicus	–	–	–	+
Polypodiisporites multiverrucosus	–	–	–	+
IPT				
Liratosporites sp.	+	–	–	–
Lygestepollenites balmei	–	+	–	–
Striatella balmei	–	–	+	–
Polycingulatisporites clavus	–	–	–	+
Polycingulatisporites reduncus	–	–	–	+
Polycingulatisporites sp.	–	–	–	–
Polycingulatisporites reduncus	–	–	+	+
Taurocusporites segmentatus	–	–	+	–
Undulatisporites venkatachalai	–	–	–	+
Gymnosperms				
Cycadophytes				
Cycadopites couperi	–	–	–	+
Cycadopites fragilis	–	–	–	+
Cycadopites gracilis	–	–	–	+
Cycadopites nitidus	–	–	–	+
Monosulcites ellipticus	–	–	–	+
Ginkgoaceae				
Ginkgocycadophytus srivastavae	+	–	–	–
Ginkgocycadophytus vitidus	–	+	–	–
Araucariaceae				
Araucariacites australis	+	–	–	+
Araucariacites ghuneriensis	–	–	–	+
Araucariacites indicus	–	+	+	–

Cheirolepidiaceae				
Classoidites glandis	–	–	–	+
Classoidites glanris	–	–	–	+
Classopollis belloyensis	–	–	–	+
Classopollis classoides	–	+	–	+
Classopollis obidesensis	–	–	–	+
Classopollis pflugii	–	–	–	+
Classopollis torosus	+	–	–	–
Podocarpaceae				
Callialasporites enigmaticus	–	–	–	+
Callialasporites radisaccus	–	–	–	+
Callialasporites crassimarginatus	–	–	–	+
Callialasporites dampieri	+	+	–	+
Callialasporites discoidalis	–	–	–	+
Callialasporites doeringii	–	–	–	+
Callialasporites monoalasporus	+	–	–	–
Callialasporites reticulatus	–	–	–	+
Callialasporites segmentatus	+	+	–	+
Callialasporites sp.	–	+	–	–
Callialasporites triletus	–	–	–	+
Callialasporites trilobatus	+	–	+	+
Microcachryidites antarcticus	–	+	+	+
Platysaccus bhardwajii	–	–	–	+
Platysaccus densus	–	–	–	+
Platysaccus indicus	–	–	–	+
Platysaccus sp.	+	–	–	+
Podocarpidites alareticulosus	+	–	–	–
Podocarpidites cristiexinus	+	–	–	–
Podocarpidites ellipticus	–	–	–	+
Podocarpidites grandis	+	–	–	–
Podocarpidites major	–	–	–	+
Podocarpidites minisulcus	–	–	–	+
Podocarpidites multisimus	+	–	–	–

Podocarpidites rarus	+	–	–	–
Podocarpidites sp.	+	+	–	–
Podocarpidites typicus	+	–	–	–
Podosporites raoi	+	–	–	–
Podosporites tripakshii	–	+	+	+
Podosporites sp.	+	–	–	–
IGY				
Alisporites grandis	+	–	–	+
Alisporites ovalis	–	–	–	+
Alisporites rotundus	–	–	–	+
Alisporites sp.	+	+	–	–
Abietineaepollenites ellipticus	+	–	–	–
Abietineaepollenites robustus	+	–	–	–
Dacrycarpites australiensis	–	–	–	+
Entylissa sp.	+	–	–	–
Florinites sp.	+	–	–	–
Granuloperculatipollis flavatus	+	–	–	–
Granuloperculatipollis mundus	–	–	–	+
Granuloperculatipollis subcircularis	+	–	–	–
Granuloperculatipollis triletus	+	–	–	–
Indusiisporites microsaccatus	+	–	–	–
Pityosporites sp.	+	–	–	–
Vitreisporites pallidus	-	–	–	+
Cedripites cretaceus	+	–	–	–
Cedripites nudis	+	–	–	+
Laricoidites indicus	+	–	–	+
Laricoidites sp.	–	–	–	+
Psilospora lata	–	–	–	+
Angiosperms				
Asteropollis asteroides	–	+	–	–
Cearipites nudis	–	-	–	+
Clavatipollenites hughesii	–	+	–	–
Clavatricolporites leticiae	–	+	–	–

liliacidites reticulatus	–	+	–	–
Polybrevicolpites sp.	–	+	–	–
Polycolpites sp.	–	+	–	–
Racemonocolpites facilis	–	+	–	–
Racemonocolpites ramonus	–	+	–	–
Rousea georgensis	–	+	–	–
Spinizonocolpites echinatus	–	+	–	–
Tricolpites georgensis	–	+	–	–
Tubulifloridites lilleie	–	+	–	–
Turonipollis helmegii	–	+	–	–
Incertae sedis				
Abiespollenites triangularis	–	–	–	+
Apiculatasporites sp.	+	–	–	–
Apiculatimonoletes sp.	+	–	–	–
Apicultaletes sp.	+	–	–	–
Bhujiasporites sp.	–	+	–	–
Complexiopollis complicatus	–	+	–	–
Complexiopollis sp.	–	+	–	–
Coniatisporites telata	–	+	–	–
Coniavisporites minimolivisus	–	–	–	+
Crassimonoletes surangei	–	–	–	+
Dictyotosporites complex	–	–	+	–
Dictyotosporites ilosus	–	–	–	+
Erdtmannipollis sp.	–	+	–	–
Odontochitina operculata	–	+	–	+
Periplecosporites sp.	+	–	–	–
Ramanujamiaspora reticulata	+	–	–	–
Regulatisporites sp.	–	+	–	–
Setosisporites sp.	+	–	–	–
Singhipollis rudis	+	–	–	–
Singhipollis triletus	+	–	–	–
Striatotuberculatisporites sp.	+	–	–	–

Table 12.2 Relative distribution of macroflora in KG and PG basins

Basin name	KG			PG
Formation	Vem	Gol	Rag	Gan
Plant group				
Pteridophytes				
Actinopteris sp.	–	–	–	+
Cladophlebis denticulata	–	–	–	+
C. indica	–	–	–	+
C. medlicottiana	–	–	+	–
Cladophlebis cf. *longipennis*	–	+	–	–
Cladophlebis sp.	+	+	+	+
Equisetites sp.	–	–	–	+
Gleichenia bosahii	–	+	–	+
G. nordenskioldii	–	–	+	+
Gleichenia sp.	–	–	–	+
Marattiopsis macrocarpa	–	+	+	–
Neocalamites sp.	–	–	–	+
Onychiopsis psilotoides	–	–	+	+
Todites indicus	–	+	–	–
Sphenopteris specifica	–	+	–	–
Sphenopteris sp.	+	+	–	+
Gymnosperms				
Pteridosperms				
Thinnfeldia feistmantelii	+	–	+	–
Thinnfeldia sp.	+	–	–	+
Pachypteris gangapurensis	–	–	–	+
Pachypteris indica	+	+	+	+
Cycadales				
Morrisia dentata	+	–	+	–
Nilsoniopteris sp.	–	–	–	+
Taeniopteris kutchensis	–	–	–	+
Taeniopteris longifolium	–	–	–	+

Taeniopteris spatulata	+	+	+	+
Bennettitales				
Anomozamites amarjolense	+	–	–	–
A. fissus	+	–	–	–
A. jungens	+	–	–	–
Anomozamites sp.	–	–	–	+
Bucklandia sp.	–	+	+	+
Cycadolepis sp.	+	–	–	–
Cycadites sp.	–	–	–	+
Dicyozamites falcatus	+	–	+	–
D. feistmantelii	+	+	+	–
D. gondwanensis	–	–	–	+
D. indicus	+	+	–	–
D. ommevaramensis	+	–	–	–
D. sahnii	–	–	+	+
Dictyozamites sp.	–	–	–	+
Otozamites acutifolius	+	–	–	–
O. bengalensis	+	–	+	+
O. exhislopi	+	–	–	–
O. goldlaei	–	–	–	+
O. gondwanensis	+	–	–	–
O. imbricatus	+	–	–	–
O. vemavaramensis	+	–	+	+
Otozamites sp.	+	–	+	+
Pterophyllum braunianum	–	+	–	–
P. distans	+	–	+	+
P. footeanum	+	–	–	–
P. incisum	+	–	–	–
P. kingianum	–	+	–	–
P. medlicottianum	–	–	–	+
P. morrisianum	–	+	–	–
Pterophyllum sp.	+	+	–	–
Ptilophyllum acutifolium	+	+	+	+

P. cutchense	+	+	+	+
P. deodikarii	–	+	–	–
P. heterophylla	+	–	–	–
Ptilophyllum cf. *distans*	+	–	+	+
Ptilophyllum cf. *institacallum*	–	+	–	–
Ptilophyllum cf. *amarjolense*	–	+	–	–
Ptilophyllum cf. *gladiatum*	–	+	–	–
Ptilophyllum cf. *horridum*	–	+	–	+
Ptilophyllum cf. *jabalpurense*	–	+	–	–
P. rarinervis	+	–	+	+
P. tenerrimum	–	+	–	–
Ptilophyllum sp.	**–**	**–**	**–**	**+**
Williamsonia blandfordii	–	+	–	–
W. indica	–	+	–	–
Zamites sp.	+	–	–	+
Ginkgoales				
Ginkgocycadophytus deterius var. *majus*	+	–	+	–
Ginkgo crassipes	–	–	+	–
G. feistmantelii	–	–	+	–
Coniferales				
Allocladus bansaensis	–	–	–	+
Araucarites cutchensis	+	+	+	+
A. fibrosa	–	+	–	–
A. macropteris	–	+	+	–
A. minutus	+	–	–	–
Araucarites sp.	–	–	–	+
Brachyphyllum expansum	+	+	–	–
B. feistmantelii	+	–	+	–
B. regularis	–	+	–	–
B. rhombicum	–	–	+	–
B. sehoraensis	–	–	–	+
Brachyphyllum sp.	+	+	+	+
Cheirolepis cf. *muensterii*	–	+	–	–

Coniferocaulon rajmahalense	–	–	–	+
Conites sessilis	+	–	+	–
Conites sriperumaturensis	–	–	–	+
Conites sp.	+	–	+	+
Desmiophyllum indicum	+	–	–	–
Echinostrobus sp.	–	+	–	–
Elatocladus andhrii	–	–	–	+
Elatocladus bosei	–	–	–	+
Elatocladus confertus	–	+	+	+
E. heterophylla	–	–	–	+
E. jabalpurensis	+	–	–	+
E. kingianus	–	–	–	+
E. loyolii	+	–	–	–
E. plana	+	+	+	+
E. sehoraensis	–	–	–	+
E. vemavaramensis	+	–	–	–
Elatocladus sp.	+	–	–	–
Pagiophyllum feistmantelii	+	–	–	–
P. gollapallensis	–	+	–	–
Pagiophyllum cf. *grantii*	–	+	–	–
Pagiophyllum marwarensis	–	–	–	+
Pagiophyllum cf. *marwarensis*	–	–	+	+
P. ommevaramensis	+	–	–	–
P. rewaensis	–	–	–	+
P. peregrinum	–	–	–	+
Pagiophyllum sp.	+	–	–	–
Torreyites constricta	+	–	–	–
Woods				
Araucarioxylon amraparense	–	–	–	+
Baieroxylon cicatricum	–	–	–	+
Platyspiroxylon parenchymatosum	–	–	–	+
Podocarpoxylon parthasarathyi	–	–	–	+
Cupressinoxylon coromandelinum	–	–	+	–

Figure 12.1. Paralic sequence of KG basin.

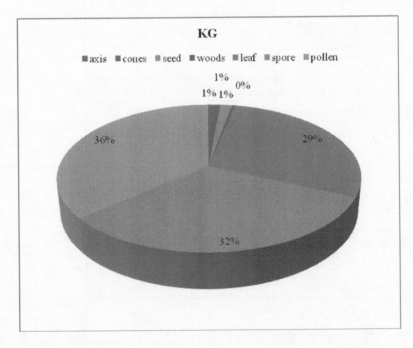

Figure 12.2. Relative distribution of plant parts in KG basin.

PG Basin

The Pranhita–Godavari basin (PG) is an intracratonic east coast basin, and its geological history is closely related with pericratonic KG basin. It encompasses a sequence corresponding to Permian to Early Cretaceous along a narrow belt of outcrops in the states of Andhra Pradesh and Maharashtra. The basin plunges into the adjoining KG basin, and exposures of Cretaceous sedimentary rocks demarcate the basin margin where the north-west–south-east trending Pranhita–Godavari sequence abuts the KG basin. Geological and stratigraphic study has established its close affinity with evolution of other east coast pericratonic basins and adjoining Antarctic Enderby Land (Bandhopadhyay and Rudra 1985, Biswas et al. 1993, King 1880, Kutty 1969, Lakshminarayana 1996, Lakshminarayana and Murti 1990, Lakshminarayana et al. 1995, Raiverman 1986). Macrofloral evidences of Early Cretaceous (Gangapur formation) have been studied by Bose, Kutty, and Maheshwari (1982), Manik and Srivastava (1991), Muralidhara Rao and Ramakrishna (1988), Ramakrishna and Muralidhara Rao (1986, 1991), Sahni (1928, 1931), Sukh-Dev and Rajanikanth (1989), Lakshminarayana and Kutumba Rao (1988) and Rajanikanth (1996a) (Table 12.2). Microflora has been known through the studies of Rajeshwar Rao and Ramanujam (1979), Ramanujam and Rajeshwar Rao (1979, 1980), Bose et al. (1982), Ramakrishna and Ramanujam (1987), Ramakrishna et al. (1985, 1986), Rajeshwar Rao et al. (1983) and Ramanujam et al. (1987) (Table 12.1). The Gangapur formation, which was named after the village of Gangapur, Adilabad District, Andhra Pradesh, is characterized by pebbly sandstone, white argillaceous sandstone, buff-siltstone, carbonaceous clay, and claystone (Figure 12.3). Faunal evidences are not known. Coeval Chikiala litho unit is less known.

Palaeoecology

The relationship between plants and the environment in past times is a subject of curiosity, and the distribution pattern of plant parts and their anatomy are often used to infer palaeoecology (Behrensmeyer and Hook 1992, DiMichele and Gastaldo 2008). Relying on plant relics, reconstruction of vegetal landscape of a region has been suggested. The nature of sedimentary layers, such as volcanic, continental, marine, fluvial, and lacustrine layers, is interpreted based on fossil content and sediment characters (DiMichele and

Wing 1988, DiMichele et al. 2004, Lyons and Darrah 1989, Pfefferkorn 1980, Spicer 1980, Sellwood et al. 1993). Relative distribution of plant parts and their quantitative and qualitative analyses present a holistic panorama. The type of sediment in fresh water and marine and embedded plant signatures help to reconstruct past environments (Table 12.3 and Figure 12.5).

Plant fossils only constitute a miniscule subset of life that lived in the past. Resource alterations, like temperature variations, water availability, nutrient supply, gas exchange, and light capture, are reflected in various plant organs/ tissue structures, which reflect environmental stresses placed upon plants thriving under different ecological realms. Both morphology and anatomy of fossil plants give a clue to the then existed micro- and mega-environmental parameters. Nature and composition of floral components preserved in various sedimentary environments help to build taphocoenosis of a particular selected geographic province. Characters exemplified by cuticles, wood, leaf morphology, palynodebris, and associated preserved organic contents should be carefully studied for signatures of micro- and mega-environmental changes that occurred in the geological past.

The micro and macro plant fossil evidences of KG and PG coastal basins suggest existence of plant ecosystem occupied by mosses, liverworts, horsetails, ferns, water ferns, pteridosperms, cycadophytes, ginkgoales, conifers, and aquatic flowering plants (tables 12.1 and 12.2, figures 12.2 and 12.4). Similarly, preponderance of spore (Figure 12.5) indicates growth of cryptogams occupying shade areas and near water bodies. Leaf and pollen distributions indicate good growth of terrestrial plants. Good representation of pteridophytes, especially the ferns, indicates near-brackish water conditions (Page 2002). Presence of ginkgoales suggests wetland condition (Greb et al. 2006, Royer et al. 2003). Representatives of *Podocarpaceae* and *Araucariaceae* (gymnosperms) constituted the main canopy-forming trees in the depositional basin (Krassailov 1978, Lyons and Darrah 1989, Ramanujam 1980, Rao 1963).

Since PG basin is intracratonic, closely associated with pericratonic KG basin, and exhibits similar flora (tables 12.1 and 12.2), the 'upland' components came from the raised terrain of PG basin. Upland vegetation is also marked by saccate pollen, and similar ecological inferences in Cretaceous assemblages are well known (Pfefferkorn 1980, Parmesan 2006, McLoughlin et al. 2002). Fossil woods also indicate seasonal factors and Cretaceous woods of east coast (Phillippe et al. 2004, Falcon-Lang 2005, Rajanikanth and Tewari 2004,

Jefferson 1982). The Benettito–Conifer association reflect marginal coast conditions (Pole and Douglas 1999). Whether the flora is indigenous or existed as a result of migration from the adjoining countries needs investigation. Gondwanan elements of *Araucariaceae* and *Podcarpaceae* also favour such presumption (Vakhrameev 1991). Was evolution a function of environmental stimuli, or was it a direct result of the pace of biological diversification? That is still a mute point to ponder! Ecological factors bear a direct link to evolution, and plants discovered many strategies to evolve (Sahni 1936).

Table 12.3 Showing some ecologically sensitive taxa

	Family	Habitat
1	Reillaceae(*Rousea*)	Wet condition
2	Lycopodiaceae(*Lycopodiumsporites*)	Swamp
3	Selaginellaceae(*Densoisporites*)	Brackish
4	Equisetaceae(*Equisetites*)	Wet condition
5	Cyathiaceae(*Cyatheacidites*)	Stream margin
6	Gleicheniaceae(*Ornamentifera*)	Aquatic/Semi Aquatic
7	Matoniaceae(*Matonisporites*)	Marginal marine
8	Osmundaceae(*Biretisporites*)	Stream banks
9	Schizaeceae(*Contignisporites*)	Swamp
10	Marsiliaceae(*Crybelosporites*)	Aquatic
11	Corystospermaceae (*Pachypteris*)	Brackish
12	Bennettitales(*Ptilophyllum*)	Coastal margins
13	Ginkgoales(*Ginkgoites*)	Wetland
14	Cheirolepidiaceae(*Classopollis*)	Brackish
15	Potamogetonaceae(*Potamogeton*)	Aquatic
16	Trapaceae(*Trapa*)	Aquatic

Figure 12.3. Fluvial deposit PG basin.

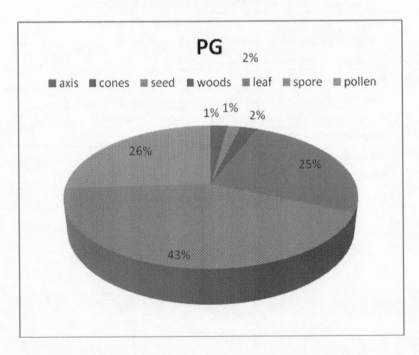

Figure 12.4. Relative distribution of plant parts in PG basin.

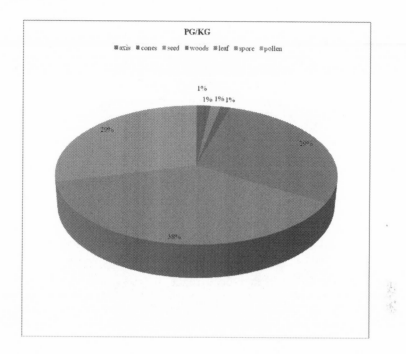

Figure 12.5. Composite distribution of plant parts in KG–PG basins.

ACKNOWLEDGEMENTS

The authors are thankful to Prof Sunil Bajpai, director of Birbal Sahni Institute of Palaeobotany, Lucknow, for the guidance and infrastructural facilities.

Abbrevations: KG (Krishna–Godavari basin), PG (Pranhita Godavari basin), IGY (*incertae sedis* gymnosperms), IPT (*incertae sedis* pteridophytes), Vem (Vemavaram formation), Gol (Gollapalli formation), Rag (Raghavapuram formation), Gan (Gangapur formation).

REFERENCES

Acharyya, S., K. (2000), Break-up of Australia-India-Madagaskar block, opening of the Indian Ocean and continental accretion in south-east Asia with special reference to the characteristics of the peri-Indian collision zones. Gondwana Research., 3: 425–443.

Acharyya, S. K., and Lahiri, T. C. (1991), Cretaceous palaeogeography of the Indian sub-continent: a review. Cretaceous Research, 12: 3–26.

Baksi, S. K. (1966), On the foraminifera from Raghavapuram mudstone, west Godavari district, Andhra Pradesh. Bulletin Geological Mining. Society India, 37: 1–19.

Baksi, S. K. (1967a), Fossil plants from Raghavapuram mudstone, west Godavari district, Andhra Pradesh, India. Palaeobotanist, 16: 206–216.

Baksi, S. K. (1967b), On new occurrence of *Gingoites feistmantelii* Bose and Sukh Dev (1958) from the coastal Gondwana of South India. Current Science, 36: 580.

Baksi, S. K. (1967c), Depositional environment of the Raghavapuram Mudstone of the east coast Gondwana of India UNESCO Gondwana Stratigraphy. Proceedings International Union of Geological Sciences Symposium Buenous Aires Argentine: 681–700.

Baksi, S. K. (1972), Fossil fish remains from coastal Gondwana Raghavaputram Mudstone West Godavari District Andhra Pradesh. Proceedings of National Science Academy, 38:3 2–44.

Baksi, S. K. (1977), Marine transgression, sedimentation and tectonics of the West Godavari coastal rocks of Andhra Pradesh. Indian Journal of Earth Sciences (S. Ray Volume), 67 94.

Bandopadhyay, S., and Rudra, D. K. (1985), Upper Gondwana stratigraphy, north of the Pranhita–Godavari Valley confluence, southern India. Journal of the Geological Society of India, 26: 261–266.

Behrensmeyer, A. K., and Hook, R. W. (1992), Paleoenvironmental contexts and taphonomic modes in the terrestrial fossil record. *In:* Behrensmeyer, A. K., Damuth, J., DiMichele, W. A., Potts, R. H., Sues, D., and Wing, S. L. (eds.) Terrestrial Ecosystems through Time. The University of Chicago Press, Chicago: 15–138.

Bhalla, S. N. (1969), Foraminifera from the type Raghavapuram shale, east coast Gondwanas, India. Micropalaentology, 15: 61–84.

Biswas, S. K., Bhasin, A. L., and Ram, J. (1993), Classification of Indian Sedimentary basins in the framework of plate tectonics. *In* Biswas, S. K. et al. (eds.) Proceedings. II Seminar Petroliferous basins of India Dehradun I: 1–46.

Bose, M. N. (1974), The genus *Otozamites* Braun from the Mesozoic rocks of India. Palaeontographica, 147B: 100–106.

Bose, M. N., and Bano, Z. (1978), The genus *Dictyozamites* Oldham from India. Palaeobotanist, 25: 79–99.

Bose, M. N., and Jain, K. P. (1967), *Otozamites vemavaramensis* sp. nov. from the Upper Gondwana of the East Coast of India. Palaeobotanist, 15: 314–315.

Bose, M. N., and Kasat, M. L. (1972), The genus *Ptilophyllum* in India. Palaeobotanist, 19: 115–145.

Bose, M. N., Kutty, T. S., and Maheshwari, H. K. (1982), Plant fossils from the Gangapur Formation. Palaeobotanist, 30: 121–125.

Bose, M. N., Taylor, E. L., and Taylor, T. N. (1990), Gondwana floras of India and Antarctica: A survey and appraisal *In*: Taylor, E. L., and Taylor, T. N. (eds.), Antarctic Palaeobiology: 118–148.

Chinnappa, C. H., Rajanikanth (2014), The Face of Climate Change. Manibarathi Publishers, Tamil Nadu. Eds. Vasudevan, S., Ramkumra, T., Rajanikanth and Ramesh, G.

Das, S. N., and Ayyasami, K. (1994), Biological diversity of fossil fauna and flora of the coastal Gondwanas of India and Sri Lanka. Gondwana Nine, volume 1: 31–44.

Datta, N. R., Mitra, N. D., and Bandyopadhyay, S. K. (1983), Recent trends in the study of Gondwana basins of peninsular and extra-peninsular India, Petroleum Asia Journal: 159–169.

DiMichele, W. A., Behrensmeyer, A. K., Olszewski, T. D., Labandeira, C. C., Pandolfi, J. M., Wing, S. L., and Bobe, R. (2004), Long-term stasis in ecological assemblages: Evidence from the fossil record. Annual Review of Ecology Evolution and Systematics, 35: 285–322.

DiMichele, W. A., and Gastaldo, R. A. (2008), Plant Paleoecology in Deep Time, Annals of the Missouri Botanical Garden, March: 144–198.

DiMichele, W. A., and Wing, S. L. (1988), Methods and Applications of Plant Paleoecology Paleontological Society Special Publication No. 3.

Dutta, P. K., and Laha, C. (1977), Climatic and tectonic influence on Mesozoic sedimentation in Peninsular India. Proceedings of the 4ᵗʰ International Gondwana Symposium, Kolkata, 2: 563–580. Hindustan Publ. Co. New Delhi.

Falcon-Lang, H. J. (2005), Global climate analysis of growth rings in woods, and its implications for deep-time paleoclimate studies. Paleobiology, 31: 434–444.

Feistmantel, O. (1879), The fossil flora of the upper Gondwana, outliers on the Madras coast. Memoirs of the Geological Survey of India. Palaeontologia Indica, 2: 1191–1224.

Foote, R. B. (1879), Geological structure of the Eastern Coast from Lat. 15° N. to Masulipatam. Memoirs of the Geological Survey of India, 16: 1–66.

Govindan, A. (1980), Cretaceous foraminifera from the eastern part of Indian peninsula and their paleo-climatological significance. Bulletin of Oil and Natural Gas Corporation, 17: 35–43.

Greb, S. F., DiMichele, W. A., and Gastaldo, R. A. (2006), Evolution of wetland types and the importance of wetlands in earth history. *In*: Greb, S., and DiMichele, W. A. (eds.) Wetlands through Time Geological Society of America Special Papers: 1–40.

Jain, K. P. (1968), Some plant remains from the Upper Gondwana of East-Coast of India Palaeobotanist, 16: 151–154.

Jefferson, T. H. (1982), Fossil forests from the lower Cretaceous of Alexander Island. Antarctica. Palaeontology, 25: 681–708.

Kar, R. K., and Sah, S. C. D. (1970), Palynological investigation of the Gondwana outcrop from Vemavaram with remarks on the age of the Beds. Palaeobotanist, 18: 103–117.

King, W. (1881), The Geology of the Pranhita-Godavari Valley. Memoirs of the Geological Survey of India, 18: 1–150.

Krassilov, V. A. (1978) Araucariaceae as indicator of climate and environment. Review of Palaeobotany and Palynology, 26: 113–124.

Kutty, T. S. (1969), Some contributions to the stratigraphy of the Upper Gondwana formations of the Pranhita-Godavari Valley Central India. Journal of the Geological Society of India, 10: 33–48.

Lakshminarayana, G. (1996), Stratigraphy and structural framework of the Gondwana sediments in the Pranhita-Godavari Valley, Andhra Pradesh. Gondwana Nine (1): 311–330.

Lakshminarayana, G., and Kutumba Rao (1988), A note on the occurrence of Ptiliphyllum flora from the Chintalapudi Sub-Basin, Pranhita-Godavari valley, Khammam district, Andhra Pradesh. Journal of the Geological Society of India, 32 (2): 137–142.

Lakshminarayana, G., and Murti, K. S. (1990), Stratigraphy of the Gondwana formations in the Chintalapudi Sub-Basin Godavari Valley Andhra Pradesh. Journal of the Geological Society of India, 36: 13–26.

Lakshminarayana, G., Rao, A. T., and Yoshida, M. (1995), Sediment dispersal pattern in the Chintalpudi Sub-Basin and its bearing on the reconstruction of intercontinental Gondwana palaeodrinage. *In:* Yoshida, M., Santosh, M., and Rao, A. T. (eds.) Gondwana Research Group Memoir. 2 India as a fragment of East Gondwana: 73–85.

Lyons, P. C., and Darrah, W. C. (1989), Earliest conifers in North America: Upland and/or paleoecological indicators. Palaios, 4: 480–486.

Manik, S. R., and Srivastava, S. C. (1991), Conifer woods from new sites of Gangapur Formation India. Acta Biol Szeged: 45–55.

McLoughlin, S. Tosolini, M. P. Nagalingum, N., and Drinnan, A. N. (2002), The Early Cretaceous (Neocomian) flora and fauna of the lower Strzelecki Group, Gippsland Basin, Victoria, Australia. Memoir Association Australasian Palaeontollogy, 26:1–144.

Mehrotra, N. C., Venkatachala, B. S., and Kapoor, P. N. (2005), Palynology in Hydrocarbon Exploration part II: Spatial and temporal distribution of significant spores/pollen and dinoflagellate cyst taxa from the Mesozoic Tertiary sediments. Memoirs of the Geological Society of India, 61: 1–128.

Mehrotra, N. C., Venkatachala, B. S., and Kapoor, P. N. (2010), Palynology in hydrocarbon Exploration: high Impact Palynological studies in western Offshore and Krishna Godavari basins. Journal of the Geological Society of India, 75:364–379.

Metcalfe, I. (1996), Gondwana land dispersion, Asian accretion and evolution of eastern Tethys. Australian Journal Earth Sciences, 43: 605–623.

Mukhopadhyay, G., Mukhopadhyay, K., Roychowdhury, M., and Parui, P. K. (2010), Stratigraphic correlation between different gondwana basins of India. Journal of the Geological Society of India, 76: 251–266.

Muralidhara Rao, G., and Ramakrishna, H. (1988), *Torreyites sitholeyi*, a new record from the Gangapur Formation of Andhra Pradesh. Curret. Science, 57: 203–204.

Page, C. N. (2002), Ecological strategies in fern evolution: A neopteridological overview. Review Palaeobotany Palynology, 119: 1–34.

Parmesan, C. (2006), Ecological and evolutionary responses to climate change. Review Ecology. Evolution and Systematics, 37: 637–669.

Pfefferkorn, H. W. (1980), A note on the term 'upland flora'. Review Palaeobotany Palynology, 30: 157–158.

Philippe, M., Bamford, M., McLoughlis, S., Da Rosa, Alves, L. S., Falcon-Lang, H. J., Gnaedinger, S., Ottone, E., Pole, M., Rajanikanth, A., Shoemaker, R. E., Torres, T., and Zamuner, A. (2004), Biogeographic analysis of Jurassic–early Cretaceous wood assemblages from Gondwana. Review of Palaeobotany and Palynology, 129: 141–173.

Pole, M., and Douglas, J. G. (1999), Bennettitales, Cycadales and Ginkgoales from the mid Cretaceous of the Eromanga Basin, Queensland, Australia. Cretaceus Research, 20: 523–538.

Prasad, B., and Pundir, B. S. (1999), Biostratigraphy of the exposed Gondwana and Cretaceous rocks of Krishna–Godavari basin, India. Journal Palaeontogical Society India, 44: 91–117.

Raiverman, V. (1986), Depositional model of Gondwana sediments in Pranhita Godavari Graben South India. Bulletin Geological Metallurgical Society India, 54:69–90.

Rajanikanth, A. (1992), Rock building Cretaceous-Tertiary algae from India: an ecological perspective. Palaeobotanist, 40: 399–412.

Rajanikanth, A. (1996a), Palaeobotany and stratigraphic implication of Mesozoic Gondwana sediments of Pranhita-Godavari Graben. Gondwana Nine, 1: 425–439.

Rajanikanth, A. (1996b), Diversification and evolution of early Cretaceous east coast flora of India. Palaeobotanist, 45: 121–131.

Rajanikanth, A. (2009), Status of Coastal Gondwana, A floristic perspective. *In*: Jayappa, K. S., and Narayana, A. C., eds., (2007), Coastal environments: Problems and Perspectives I. K. International, New Delhi: 264–275.

Rajanikanth, A., and Tewari, R. (2004), Environmental implications of Gondwana Wood Studies in India. Palaeobotanist, 53: 69–82.

Rajanikanth, A., Venkatachala, B. S., and Ashok Kumar (2000), Geological age of the Ptilophyllum flora in India: a critical reassessment. Memoirs of the Geological Society of India, 46: 245–256.

Rajeswara Rao, P. V., and Ramanujam, C. G. K. (1979), The genus *Contignisporites* from the Lower Cretaceous Gangapur beds, Pranhita Godavari Basin. Geophytology, 9: 139–143.

Rajeswara Rao, P. V., Ramanujam, C. G. K., and Verma, Y. N. R. (1983), Palynology of the Gangapur beds Pranhita Godavari Basin Andhra Pradesh. Geophytology, 13: 22–45.

Raju, D. S. N., and Misra, P. K. (1996), Cretaceous Stratigraphy of India-A review. Memoirs of the Geological Society of India, 37: 1–33.

Ramakrishna, H., and Muralidhra Rao, G. (1986), *Pterophyllum medlicottianum* from the Gangapur Formation of Andhra Pradesh. Current Science, 55: 1199–1200.

Ramakrishna, H., and Muralidhara Rao, G. (1991), *Conites sripermaturensis* from the Gangapur Formation A. P. Journal Swamy Botanical Club, 8: 113–114.

Ramakrishna, H., Prabhakar, M., and Muralidhara Rao, G. (1986), Reworked Permian palynotaxa in the Lower Cretaceous Gangapur Formation of Adilabad District Andhra Pradesh Journal Palynology, 22: 125–132.

Ramakrishna, H., and Ramanujam, C. G. K. (1987), Palynoflora from Gangapur beds at Moar in Adilabad District, Andhra Pradesh India Journal Earth Sciences, 14: 64–72.

Ramakrishna, H., Ramanujam, C. G. K., and Prabhakar, M. (1985), Palyno assemblage of the Upper Gondwana deposits of Balhanpur area Adilabad District, Andhra Pradesh, Journal Palynology, 21: 126–132.

Ramanujam, C. J. K. (1957), Microfossils from carbonaceous shale near Vemavaram (Jurassic) in the East Coast Gondwanas of India. Journal of Indian Botanical Society, 36: 181–197.

Ramanujam, C. G. K. (1980), Geological history of Araucariaceae in India. Botanique, 9: 1–2.

Ramanujam, C. G. K., and Rajeswara Rao, P. V. (1980), Polynological approach to the study of some Upper Gondwana clays at Ralpeta near Asifabad in Adilabad district of Andhra Pradesh. Geological survey of India. Miscellaneous Publication: 45–60.

Ramanujam, C. G. K., and Rajeswara Rao, P. V. (1980), Palynological approach to the study of some Upper Gondwana clays at Ralapet near Asifabad in Adilabad district Andhra Pradesh. Proceedings International. Palynological Conference: 386–391 BSIP Lucknow.

Ramanujam, C. G. K. Muralidhara Rao and Ramakrishna, H. (1987), Floristic and Stratigraphic significance of the assemblage of Gangapur Formation in Andhra Pradesh. Gondwana Geological Magazine, 2: 1–5.

Rao, G. N. (1993), Geology and hydrocarbon prospects of East Coast sedimentary basins of India with special reference to Krishna–Godavari Basin: Journal of Geological Society of India., 41: 444–454.

Rao, G. N. (1994), Sedimentation and strati-structural control for hydrocarbon accumulations in Krishna Godavari Basin: Indian Journal of Earth Sciences, 21: 153–163.

Rao, G. N. (2001), Sedimentation, stratigraphy and petroleum potential of Krishna–Godavari Basin, east coast of India Bulletin AAPG, 8: 623–1643.

Rao, A. R. (1963), The Podocarpaceae in India. Memoirs of Indian Botanical Society India, 4: 50–157.

Rawat, M. S., and Berry, C. M. (1990), Palynofacies maturation and source rock potential in Krishna–Godavari Basin Palaeobotanist, 38: 180–187.

Royer, D. L., Hickey, L. J., and Wing, S. L. (2003), Ecological conservatism in the "living fossil" Ginkgo. Paleobiology, 29: 84–104.

Sahni, B. (1928), Revision of Indian fossil plants Part I Coniferales (a) impressions and incrustations. Memoirs Geological Survey India, Palaeontologia Indica, 11: 1–49.

Sahni, B. (1931), Revision of Indian fossil plants. Part II Coniferales (b) petrifactions. Memoirs Geological Survey India, Palaeontologia Indica, 11: 54–124.

Sahni, B. (1936), Revolutions in the plant world Proceedings of the National Academy of Sciences India, 7: 46–60.

Seward, A. C., and Sahni, B. (1920), Indian Gondwana plants: a revision. Memoirs of the Geological Survey of India, 7: 1–41.

Sukh Dev and Rajanikanth, A (1989), The Gangapur Formation: Fossil flora and Stratigraphy. Geophytology, 18: 1–27.

Sastry, V. V., Chandra, A., and Pant, S. C. (1963), Foraminifera from Raghavapuram shale near Tirupati Andhra Pradesh, India. Records of the Geological Survey of India, 92: 311–314.

Sastry, V. V., Raju, A. T. R., Singh, R. N., and Venkatachala, B. S. (1973), Evolution of the Mesozoic sedimentary basins on the east-coast of India. APEA Journal: 29–41.

Sastry, V. V., Venkatachala, B. S., and Narayanan, V. (1981): The evolution of the east coast of India. Palaeogeography, Palaeoclimatology, Palaeoecology, 36 (1): 23–54.

Sellwood, B. W., and Price, G. D. (1993), Sedimentary facies as indicators of Mesozoic palaeoclimate. Philosophical Transactions, 341B: 225–233.

Spath, I. F. (1933), Revision of the Jurassic Cephalopod fauna of Cutch (Kutch). Memoirs Geolological Survey India, Palaeontologia Indica, 9: 1–945.

Spicer, R. A. (1980), Physiological characteristics of land plants in relation to environment through time. Transactions of the Royal Society of Edinburgh: Earth Sciences, 80: 321–329.

Swamy, S. N., and Kapoor, P. N. (1999), Source rock palynological model for exploration of fossil fuels in Krishna: Godavari Basin. Journal of the Geological Society of India, 53: 549–560.

Sukh Dev (1987), Floristic zones in the Mesozoic formations and their relative age. Palaeobotanist, 36: 161–167.

Suryanarayana, K. (1954), Fossil plants from the Jurassic rocks of the Madras Coast, India. Palaeobotanist, 4: 87–90.

Tiwari, R. S. (1999), The palynological succession and spatial relationship of the Indian Gondwana sequence. Proceedings Indian National Science Academy, 65: 329–375.

Vagyani, B. A. (1984), On the occurrence of *Desmiophyllum indicum* Sahni from Vemavaram: *In* Tiwari, R. S. et al. (eds.), Proceedings of 5th Indian Geophytological Conference, Paleobotanical Society, Lucknow: 362.

Vagyani, B. A. (1985), Occurrence of *Ginkgoites crassipes* (Feistmental) Seward from the Jurassic of Andhra Pradesh. Current Science, 54: 705–706.

Vagyani, B. A., and Zutting, M. P. (1986), Occurrence of *Pterophyllum distans* Morris from Uppugunduru, Andhra Pradesh. Geophytology, 16: 133.

Vakhrameev, V. A. (1991), Jurassic and Cretaceous floras and climates of the Earth. Cambridge University Press, Cambridge.

Vasudeva Rao, P., and Krishna Rao, V. V. (1977), Stratigraphy, basin framework, sedimentation structures and petroleum prospects of the Gondwanas of Godavari Graben: Proceedings of IV Gondwana: 25–30.

Veevers, J. J. (2004), Gondwanaland from 650–500 Ma assembly through 320 Ma merger in Pangea to 185–100 Ma breakup: supercontinental tectonics via stratigraphy and radiometric dating. Earth Science Review, 68: 1–132.

Veevers, J. J., and Tiwari, R. C. (1995), Gondwana master basin of peninsular India between Tethys and the interior of the Gondwanaland province of Pangea. Memoirs Geological Society America, 187: 1 73.

Venkatachala, B. S. (1977), Fossil floral assemblages in the east coast Gondwana: a critical review. Journal of the Geological Society of India, 18: 378–397.

Venkatachala, B. S., and Rajanikanth, A. (1988), Stratigraphic implication of 'Late Gondwana' floras in the east coast of India. Palaeobotanist, 36: 183–196.

Venkatachala, B. S., and Sinha, R. N. (1986), Stratigraphy, age and palaeoecology of upper Gondwana equivalents of the Krishna Godavari Basin, India. Palaeobotanist, 35: 22–31.

Venkatarangan, R., and Ray, D. (1993), Geology and petroleum systems-Krishna-Godavari basins. *In:* Biswas, S. K. et al. (eds.) Proceedings of the second Seminar on petroliferous basins of India 1:331–354 Indian Petroleum Publishers Dehradun.

Yoshida, M., Funaki, M., and Vitannage, P. W. (1992), Proterozoic to Mesozoic East Gondwana: The juxtaposition of India Sri Lanka and Antarctica. Tectonics, 11: 381–391.

Ziegler, A. M., Scotese, C. R., and Barrett, S. F. (1983), Mesozoic and Cenozoic paleogeographic maps *In*: Brosche, P., and Sundermann, J. (eds.) Tidal Friction and the Earth's Rotation II. Springer Berlin, 240–252.

13 ENVIRONMENTAL IMPACT ASSESSMENT (EIA) OF CAUVERY RIVER IN PARTS OF TAMIL NADU WITH REFERENCE TO DIATOM INDICES AND WATER QUALITY INDEX

P. Karthikeyan and R. Venkatachalapathy
Department of Geology, Periyar University, Salem 636 011, Tamil Nadu, India
Email: pkarthikeyangold@gmail.com

ABSTRACT

Diatoms are used as bioindicators to assess the water quality of surface waters. The diatom assemblage of Cauvery River was analysed and evaluated for its applicability to assess the water quality of Cauvery River in part of Tamil Nadu, India. There are 60 species belonging to 21 genera that are recorded from Cauvery River. Water samples are assessed by analysing the various physico-chemical parameters, such as pH, electrical conductivity, dissolved solid, biochemical oxygen demand (BOD), calcium (Ca), magnesium (Mg), sodium (Na), potassium (K), chloride (Cl), bicarbonate (HCO_3) and sulphate (SO_4). These 11 parameters are considered to compute the water quality index (WQI). The results of the present study on diatom assemblages in Cauvery River at Siluvampalayam and Koneripatti indicate moderate pollution while at Peramachipalayam, Kottampatti, Sanyasipatti, and Bhavani, results show high level of pollution. The water quality index (WQI) reveals that the water of Cauvery River is unpolluted in the upstream of the city and unfit for human consumption towards the downstream. The values of DO and BOD levels indicate the absence of major organic pollution sources.

The averages of plant nutrients like phosphate, nitrates, potassium, and also sulphates at drain outfalls and mixing zones were not showing any significant variation in their concentration and indicate no sign of problems like eutrophication, which is generally due to agricultural and sewage wastes.

The river water is not polluted in Mettur area, and the Bhavani region experiences highly polluted status, and all results are compared with national river water quality standards. In the present study, an attempt has been made to evaluate the applicability of diatom-based indices for water quality assessment in Cauvery River in part of Tamil Nadu.

Keywords: Cauvery River, diatom indices, diatom assemblages, water quality index.

INTRODUCTION

Diatoms are the main producers in rivers and are present in all aquatic environments. Diatoms can be easily collected and preserved. Due to their rapid response to environmental changes, deterioration of water quality, especially from impacts such as nutrient enrichment, acidification, and metal contamination, diatoms have been used widely for biomonitoring of aquatic ecosystems (Kelly and Whitton 1995, Stoerme and Smol 1999). The shape, size, and pattern of silica frustules form the basis for classification and identification of diatom taxa. According to Kelly et al. (2008), diatoms are one of the basic components of river biomonitoring and assessment of its ecological status. They have also established many diatom indices for water quality assessment of rivers and lakes. Recent studies have shown that the diatom-based indices vary in their capacity to ionic composition and organic pollution in rivers (Gómez and Licursi 2001, Taylor et al. 2007). Diatoms are sensitive to environmental changes and can be used as an important tool in monitoring environmental conditions of surface waters (Venkatachalapathy and Karthikeyan 2012). Benthic diatoms can be used in identification of the river sites affected/influenced by urban pollution (Venkatachalapathy and Karthikeyan 2013a, b, c, d, f, and g). There are more than a hundred small, medium, and large industries, including dying factories and foundries, in Mettur and Bhavani towns which provide employment to 50% of the population. These towns do not have facilities for treatment of industrial, municipal, and domestic wastes, and the river has been used for disposal of wastes. Natural drainage networks have been converted to storm water drains for letting the sewerage into wetlands without any treatment.

Surface water constitutes water sources intended for household, commercial, and irrigation functions. The surface water quality is largely determined equally because of the natural techniques (precipitation rate, weathering process, land erosion) and the anthropogenic influences, viz. domestic, urban, commercial, and agricultural pursuits (Nouri et al. 2008). Seasonal variations in precipitation, surface run-off, groundwater flow, and water interception and abstraction possess a sturdy effect on river discharge and eventually for the focus of contaminants within river water (Vega et al. 1998, Shrestha and Kazama 2007).

STUDY AREA

The Cauvery River is one of the major rivers of South India. It originates in the Western Ghats and flows in an eastwardly direction, passing through the states of Karnataka, Tamil Nadu, Kerala, and Pondicherry before it drains into the Bay of Bengal. The total length of the river from its source to merger into the Bay of Bengal is about 800 km, and it extends over an area of 81,155 km^2. The shape of the basin is somewhat rectangular with a maximum length and breadth of 360 km and 200 km respectively. The study area lies at 77° 40' to 77° 42' E and 11° 25' to 11° 27' N with an area of 41.1 km^2 (Figure 13.1).

METHODS AND MATERIALS

The WQI synthesizes difficult facts regarding multiple water quality parameters that could be respected as well as noticed. The WQI has a scale of 0 to 100, wherein a greater number signifies better water quality.

Calculation of Water Quality Index (WQI)

WQI is a dimensionless quantity that brings together many water-quality ingredients through normalizing valuations (Miller et al. 1986). Factors which are part of WQI design might vary based on the specified water utilizes in addition to local inclinations. A few of these factors include DO, pH, BOD, COD, total coliform bacteria, temperature, and nutrients (nitrogen and phosphorus), and many others. Most of these parameters take place in several ranges and are stated in different units. The WQI takes the difficult methodical information on these kinds of variables and synthesizes them into a single number. Various researchers enjoyed these kinds of ideas in addition to these effective concepts and models, together with circumstance cases (Bolton et al. 1978, Bhargava 1983, House 1989, Mitchell and Stapp 1996, Pesce and Wunderlin 2000, Cude 2001, Liou et al. 2004, Said et al. 2004, Nasiri et al. 2007). The present study includes water quality index parameters, such as pH, change in temperature (°C), DO, BOD, turbidity, total phosphorus, nitrate nitrogen, faecal coliforms, involving river water quality from Cauvery River. The model for calculation is shown in Table 13.1.

Table 13.1 Model for water quality index calculator

Parameter	Test result	Units	Q-value	Weighting factor	Weighting factor	Subtotal
pH		pH units	NM	0.12	NM	NM
Change in temp		°C	NM	0.11	NM	NM
DO		saturation (%)	NM	0.18	NM	NM
BOD		mg/l	NM	0.12	NM	NM
Turbidity		NTU	NM	0.09	NM	NM
Total phosphorus		mg/l P	NM	0.11	NM	NM
Nitrate nitrogen		mg/l NO_3-N	NM	0.10	NM	NM
Faecal coliforms*		CFU/100 ml	NM	0.17	NM	NM
*Only use one microorganism, not faecal coliforms.			Totals	0.00	0.00	
			Water quality index		NM	
			Water quality rating		NM	

Diatom Sample Collection and Preparation

Macrophyte samples are collected from ten (10) different locations in Cauvery River at Mettur Dam, Navappatti, Nerunjipettai, Ammapettai, Siluvampalayam, Koneripatti, Peramachipalayam, Kottampatti, Sanyasipatti, and Bhavani (Figure 13.1) for water quality assessment using diatom indices.

The samples are collected in polythene bottles from all obtainable habitats such as plants (epiphytic) and stones (epilithic), following the methods suggested by Taylor et al. (2007) and Karthick et al. (2010). In Table 13.2, diatoms are sampled by brushing stones with a toothbrush, following the recommendations of Kelly et al. (1998). At least five, pebble- to cobble-sized (5–15 cm) stones are collected from the river bottom. They are brushed, and the diatom suspension was put in a small plastic bottle. Epilithic and epipelic diatoms are sampled at five sampling stations during May 2013. Epiphytic samples were taken by brushing the undersurfaces and petioles of at least 20 plant leaves and roots. In all studies, diatom samples were preserved in formaldehyde (4%). For polarizing microscopy analysis, a 10 ml epiphytic and epilithic subsamples were extracted and cleaned using 30% H_2O_2 and concentrated HNO_3 (Stoermer et al. 1995). Identification of diatoms was carried out using taxonomic guides (Gandhi 1957 1959a, 1959b, 1961, 1962, 1967, 1998; Karthick et al. 2008). The diatom species are identified and photographed using Euromex (Holland) polarizing microscope.

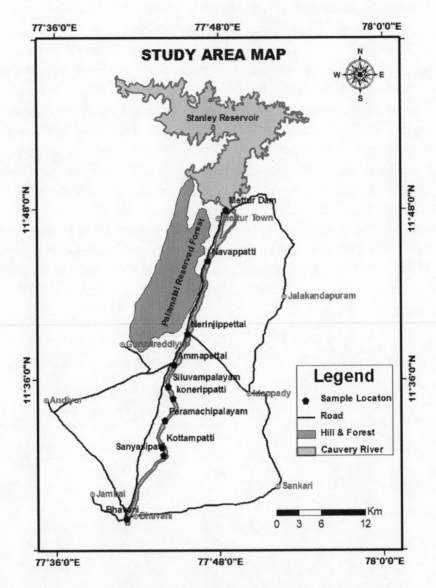

Figure 13.1. Sample locations in Cauvery River, parts of Tamil Nadu.

Sample Collection and Analytical Procedures

Water samples from 10 sites are collected (a depth representative of the mixed water columns) during on 2013 on the Cauvery River from Mettur to Bhavani town, for a period (pre- to post-monsoon 2013). The samples are kept in 2 l polyethylene plastic bottles, which had been previously cleaned with metal-free soap, rinsed repeatedly with distilled water, soaked in 10% nitric acid for 24 h, and finally rinsed with ultrapure water. All water samples are maintained at 4 °C first during transportation to the laboratory and then later for processing and analysis.

There are 17 parameters are determined in 10 sampling sites throughout the Cauvery River. The water samples are generally compiled upon sampling, preservation, and transportation, which are then analysed by the effective method (APHA 2005). This biological samples are analysed with regard to 17 parameters, such as pH, change in temperature, turbidity, electrical conductivity, dissolved oxygen, dissolved solid, biochemical oxygen demand (BOD), calcium (Ca), magnesium (Mg), sodium (Na), potassium (K), chloride (Cl), bicarbonate (HCO_3), sulphate (SO_4), total phosphorus, nitrate nitrogen and faecal coliforms.

Most water samples usually are studied for distinct physico-chemical parameters within 48 h of collection, with chemical oxygen demand (COD) determined on the same sampling day while biological oxygen demand (BOD) can be established instantly to stop time-induced adjustments within the microbial concentration. The BOD usually is dependent on the dilution and also the seeding technique. SO_4 is determined spectrophotometrically with the barium sulphate turbidity technique. NO_3-N can be studied by means of phenol disulphonic acid calorimetry. The particular acid-treated water samples usually are analysed for the determination of major cations. Ca, Na, and K are measured by flame photometry while Mg is determined by the flame atomic absorption spectrometer (FAAS).

RESULT AND DISCUSSION

Diatom Distributions

A total number of 60 diatoms belonging to 21 genera species are identified in Cauvery River. The diatom species reported in the present study are: *Achnanthes brevipes, A. inflata, Achnanthidium binodis, A. minutissima, Amphora holsatica, A. ovalis, Anomoeoneis sphaerophora, Caloneis pulchra, C. silicula, Cocconeis placentula, Ctenophora pulchella, Cyclotella catenata, C. meneghiniana, Cymbella aspera, C. cymbiformis, C. lanceolata, C. tumida, C. tumidula, C. turgida, C. ventricosa, Eunotia curvata, E. fallax, E. pectinalis, Fragilaria intermedia, Gomphonema affine, G. clavatum, G. gracile, G. lanceolatum, G. parvulum, G. olivaceum, G. truncatum, G. undulatum, G. undulatum, Mastogloia braunii, Melosira granulata, M. moniliformis, M. varians, Navicula mutica, N. radiosa, N. symmetrica, N. virudila, N. acicularis, N. linearis, N. microcephala, N. palea, N. pseudofonticola, N. recta, N. thermalis, N. sigma, Tabellaria flocculos, Pinnularia acrosphaeria, Pleurosira indica, Pleurosigma salinarum, Stauroneis anceps, Surirella linearis, S. robusta, S. splendida, S. tenera, Synedra rumpens, S. ulna.*

Dominance

Dominance is the total of a particular species with respect to different species in an ecological community predominate, ranging from 0 (all taxa are equally present) to 1 (a taxon dominates the community completely). The dominance analysis shows that the Nerunjipettai locality in Cauvery River has 10 species with *Cyclotella meneghiniana* as dominant species (dominance: 0.14) while *Aulacoseira granulata* (19.86%) dominated Koneripatti (dominance: 0.11) and *Sellaphora pupula* (23.17%) and *Gomphonema parvulum* (18.48%). Remaining sites showed dominance index value between 0.1 and 0.4 (Table 13.3).

Evenness

Evenness is the measure of biodiversity which quantifies how equal the community is numerically. *Sellaphora pupula* constitute more than 23.17% of the total population accounted for low evenness in Koneripatti (tables 13.3 and 13.4).

Shannon Index

Shannon diversity index (H'), computed as per Equation 2 (Table 13.2), takes into account the number of individuals as well as number of taxa. This varies from 0 for communities with only a single taxon to high values for communities with many taxa, each with few individuals. Low H' was recorded in Nerunjipettai (2.03, *C. meneghiniana* representing 92%) (tables 13.3 and 13.4).

Fisher's Alpha Diversity Index

High Fisher's alpha diversity index computed (Equation 6, Table 13.2) was noticed in Sanyasipatti (11.67), Koneripatti (9.55), and Ammapettai (8.28). Nerunjipettai (1.8) has less number of taxa and shows low index value (Table 13.3 and 13.4).

Table 13.2 Diversity parameters and indices (following Karthick, B. 2009)

Index	Equation	Remarks	References	Eq. No.
Abundance	$\dfrac{\text{No. of Individuals of a Species X 100}}{\text{No. of Sampling Units}}$			1
Shannon Weiner's (H')	$-\displaystyle\sum_{I=1}^{S} \text{pi ln pi}$ Pi: proportion of individuals of ith species.	The value ranges between 1.5 and 3.5 and rarely surpasses 4.5	Ludwig and Renolds (1998), Legendre and Legendre (1998)	2
Simpson's (D)	$D = \dfrac{\sum_{I=1}^{S} \text{ni (ni} - 1)}{N(N-1)}$	The value varies from 0 to 1. A value of 0 indicates the presence of only one species while 1 means that all species are equally represented.	Ludwig and Reynolds (1998)	3
Dominance	$D = \text{sum}\left(\dfrac{ni}{n}\right)^{2}$ Where ni is the number of individuals of taxon i.	It is the occupancy of a species over an area. It ranges from 0 (all taxa are equally present) to 1 (one taxon dominates the community completely).		4

214

	Formula	Description	Author	No.
Evenness	$$H' = -\sum_{I=1}^{s} pl \ In \ pi$$	It is the measure of biodiversity which quantifies how equal the community is.		5
Fisher's alpha	$$S = a \times In\left(\frac{1+n}{a}\right)$$ Where S is the number of taxa, n is the number of individuals, and a is the Fisher's alpha.	It is a mathematical model used to measure diversity.		6
Berger–Parker	$$d = \frac{Nmax}{N}$$ Where *Nmax* is the number of individuals in the most abundant species and *N* is the total number of individuals in the sample.	It is the number of individuals in the dominant taxon relative to n, where n is the total number of species.	Berger and Parker (1970)	7

Sivaprakasam Vasudevan et. al.,

Table 13.3 Diatom indices values for the Cauvery River

Sampling site	IPS	SLAD	DESCY	L and M	SHE	WAT	TDI	EPI-D	ROTT	GDI	CEE	IBD	IDAP
Mettur dam	16.5	14.8	17.4	15.0	16.4	18.1	31.7	12.7	16.1	16.7	19.4	16.2	19.0
Navappatti	14.9	14.4	17.4	14.7	15.5	16.8	45.2	12.4	15.0	15.5	17.3	15.6	16.0
Nerunjipettai	15.9	14.9	16.3	14.5	16.1	19.4	33.6	12.7	14.6	15.9	17.0	16.5	18.1
Ammapettai	15.1	14.3	16.3	14.7	14.5	17.5	38.0	12.6	14.3	15.3	16.4	14.7	18.0
Siluvampalayam	15.2	14.4	15.1	13.6	15.2	18.0	32.8	12.4	13.2	12.2	16.4	15.0	16.0
Koneripatti	12.2	14.3	14.6	13.1	9.8	9.7	31.5	11.5	11.1	12.6	16.0	10.6	12.3
Peramachipalayam	8.1	13.4	16.5	13.8	13.6	13.2	63.7	10.3	13.6	7.2	13.4	11.0	12.8
Kottampatti	7.2	13.9	15.0	14.9	13.6	14.0	26.6	13.3	14.5	7.2	16.8	13.3	16.3
Sanyasipatti	7.1	14.7	15.3	14.5	16.4	18.8	28.4	12.4	14.9	7.4	16.6	16.5	18.2
Bhavani	7.2	15.0	14.7	14.5	15.8	19.0	29.9	12.5	14.8	7.1	16.0	16.7	17.9

Table 13.4 Diversity indices for Cauvery River

	No. of. Species	Domi-nance	Simpson	Shan-non H	Evenness	Margalef	Equita-bility	Fisher	Berger-Parker
Mettur dam	16	0.07	0.93	2.7	0.93	2.61	0.97	3.56	0.1
Navappatti	22	0.05	0.95	3.02	0.93	3.5	0.98	4.99	0.08
Nerunjipettai	8	0.14	0.86	2.03	0.95	1.4	0.97	1.81	0.19
Ammapettai	36	0.03	0.97	3.5	0.92	5.43	0.98	8.28	0.05
Siluvampalayam	21	0.05	0.95	3	0.95	3.39	0.98	4.85	0.09
Koneripatti	12	0.11	0.89	2.34	0.86	3.46	0.94	9.55	0.21
Peramachipalayam	15	0.07	0.93	2.64	0.93	3.41	0.97	6.35	0.08
Kottampatti	19	0.05	0.95	2.92	0.98	4.09	0.99	7.76	0.06
Sanyasipatti	51	0.02	0.98	3.88	0.95	7.34	0.99	11.67	0.04
Bhavani	23	0.05	0.95	3.08	0.94	3.64	0.98	5.22	0.08

Berger–Parker Index

Berger–Parker is calculated (Equation 7, Table 13.2) from the number of individuals in the dominant taxon relative to the total number of species. *Cyclotella meneghiniana* is the dominant species (with 92% abundance) showing a high index value in Koneripatti. In Nerunjipettai, *Aulacoseira granulata*, *Cyclotella meneghiniana*, and *Nitzschia obtuse* represent 23% of the population from a macrophytic habitat. *Gomphonema parvulum* represents 32% in Bhavani. *Nitzschia palea* (45%) and *Navicula* sp. (32%) characterize the Mettur dam (tables 13.3 and 13.4).

Diatom Assemblages and Trophic Condition

In Bhavani cosmopolitan, extreme pollution-resistant species, such as *Achnanthes minutissima*, *Achnanthidium Plonensis*, *Aulacoseira distans*, *Cymbella turgida*, *Cymbella ventricosa*, *Fragilaria intermedia* var. *robusta*, *Gomponema lanceolatum*, *Nitzschia sigma*, *Synedra rumpens*, *S. ulna*, were the most abundant species dominant among the 23 species, highlighting eutrophic status of water with higher electrolyte. *Aulacoseira granulata* and *Cyclotella meneghiniana* are dominant among 16 species in the epilithic substrata of Mettur. Epiphytic substratum sample is represented by *Gomphonema parvulum* and *G. affine*, which are tolerant to extreme pollution and occur in water with elevated electrolyte. *Cyclotella meneghiniana*, a cosmopolitan species resistant to extreme pollution, with wide range of distribution including eutrophic, electrolyte-rich water, accounts for more than 90% of 10 species in Bhavani.

Diatom Indices

Diatom-specific indices, like the generic diatom index or GDI (Coste and Ayphassorho 1991), the specific pollution-sensitivity index or SPI (Indice de Polluo-Sensibilité Spécifique or IPS) (Coste in Cemagref 1982), the biological diatom index or BDI (Lenoir and Coste 1996), the Artois-Picardie diatom index or APDI (Prygiel et al.1996), the Sládeček's index or SLA (Sládeček 1986), the eutrophication/pollution index or EPI (Dell'Uomo 1996), the Rott's index or ROT (Rott 1991), the Leclercq and Maquet's index or LMI (Leclercq and Maquet 1987), the Commission of Economical Community index or CEC (Descy and Coste 1991), Schiefele and Schreiner's index or SHE (Schiefele and

Schreiner 1991), the trophic diatom index or TDI (Kelly and Whitton 1995), and the Watanabe index or WAT (Watanabe et al. 1986), were also computed and listed in Table 13.4. All the diatom indices were calculated using Equation 8 (Zelinka and Marvan 1961) except for the CEC, SHE, TDI, and WAT. And all the above indices, except TDI (maximum value of 100), the maximum value of 20 indicates pristine water.

$$index = \frac{\sum_{j=1}^{n} a_j s_j v_j}{\sum_{j=1}^{n} a_j v_j} \qquad \text{Equation 8}$$

Where a_j = abundance (proportion) of species j in sample, v_j = indicator value, and s_j = pollution sensitivity of species j.

The performance of the indices depends on the values given to the constants s and v for each taxon, and the values of the index ranges from 1 to an upper limit equal to the highest value of s. Each diatom species used in the calculation/equation is assigned two values; the first value reflects the tolerance or affinity of the diatom to a certain water quality (good or bad) while the second value indicates how strong (or weak) the relationship is. Abundance and weighted average were computed. This would indicate how many of the particular diatoms in the sample occur in relation to the total number counted. The class limit values for diatom indices are shown in Table 13.5.

Table 13.5 Class limit values for diatom indices (Eloranta and Soininen 2002)

Index score	Class	Trophy
>17	High quality	Oligotrophy
15 to 17	Good quality	Oligo-mesotrophy
12 to 15	Moderate quality	Mesotrophy
9 to 12	Poor quality	Meso-eutrophy
<9	Bad quality	Eutrophy

This study elaborates the WQI concepts as well as various WQI types through the literary works. Additionally, it exhibits in case scenario of figuring out WQI, making use of different types with an instance data set. Each one of these WQI types is actually formulated for flowing or standing water resources such as rivers, streams, and lakes.

Physico-Chemical Characteristics of Water in Cauvery River Pre-Monsoon (2013)

The physico-chemical characteristics of water from 10 different locations were given in tables 13.6a to 13.6j. In Mettur (Table 13.6a), water quality index is determined, and the calculated values are as follows: pH (8.4), change in temperature (24.1 °C), DO (8.5), BOD (1.06), turbidity (2.57), total phosphorus (0.03), nitrate nitrogen (0.28), faecal coliforms (170). The values fall within the limit of CPCB (2008). The water quality index is 57.16, and the water quality rating is medium in pre-monsoon, 2013 (Table 13.6a).

Table 13.6a Physico-chemical characteristics of water in Cauvery River in Mettur (pre-monsoon 2013)

Parameter	Test result	Units	Q-value	Weighting factor	Weighting factor	Subtotal
pH	7.9	pH units	87	0.12	0.12	10.46
Change in temp	20	°C	19	0.11	0.11	2.11
DO	3.6	saturation (%)	4	0.18	0.18	0.66
BOD	1.08	mg/l	89	0.12	0.12	10.68
Turbidity	3.62	NTU	88	0.09	0.09	7.96
Total phosphorus	0.02	mg/l P	97	0.11	0.11	10.67
Nitrate nitrogen	1.3	mg/l NO_3-N	66	0.10	0.10	6.62
Faecal coliforms*	110	CFU/100 ml	42	0.17	0.17	7.19
*Only use one microorganism, not faecal coliforms and *E. coli*.				Totals	1.00	56.35
				Water quality index		56.35
				Water quality rating		Medium

The water quality index of Navappatti (Table 13.6b)is calculated, and the values are as follows: pH (8.3), change in temp (24 °C), DO (0.78), BOD (0.78), turbidity (3.08), total phosphorus (0.02), nitrate nitrogen (0.4), faecal coliforms (170). They are all within the limit of CPCB (2008). The water quality index is 57.28, and the water quality rating is medium in pre-monsoon (2013).

Table 13.6b Physico-chemical characteristics of water in Cauvery River in Navappatti (pre-monsoon 2013)

Parameter	Test result	Units	Q-value	Weighting factor	Weighting factor	Subtotal
pH	8.3	pH units	79	0.12	0.12	9.42
Change in temp	24	°C	14	0.11	0.11	1.57
DO	7.2	saturation (%)	6	0.18	0.18	1.09
BOD	0.78	mg/l	91	0.12	0.12	10.97
Turbidity	3.08	NTU	90	0.09	0.09	8.07
Total phosphorus	0.02	mg/l P	97	0.11	0.11	10.65
Nitrate nitrogen	0.4	mg/l NO_3-N	92	0.10	0.10	9.20
Faecal coliforms*	170	CFU/100 ml	37	0.17	0.17	6.31
*Only use one microorganism, not faecal coliforms and *E. coli*.				Totals 1.00		57.28
				Water quality index		57.28
				Water quality rating		Medium

The water quality index of Nerunjipettai (Table 13.6c) is calculated and the values are as follows: pH (7.8), Change in temperature (22 °C), DO (8.2), BOD (1.06), turbidity (5.36), total phosphorus (0.02), nitrate nitrogen (0.3), faecal coliforms (260). The values are within the limit of CPCB (2008). The water quality index is 57.65 and water quality rating is medium in pre-monsoon (2013).

Table 13.6c Physico-chemical characteristics of water in Cauvery River in Nerunjipettai (pre-monsoon 2013)

Parameter	Test Result	Units	Q-value	Weighting factor	Weighting factor	Subtotal
pH	7.8	pH units	89	0.12	0.12	10.65
Change in temp	22	°C	16	0.11	0.11	1.81
DO	8.2	saturation (%)	7	0.18	0.18	1.20
BOD	1.06	mg/l	89	0.12	0.12	10.70
Turbidity	5.36	NTU	85	0.09	0.09	7.63
Total phosphorus	0.02	mg/l P	98	0.11	0.11	10.76
Nitrate nitrogen	0.3	mg/l NO_3-N	95	0.10	0.10	9.46
Faecal coliforms*	260	CFU/100 ml	32	0.17	0.17	5.44
*Only use one microorganism, not faecal coliforms.				Totals	1.00	57.65
				Water quality index		57.65
				Water quality rating		Medium

The water quality index of Ammapettai (Table 13.6d) is calculated, and the values are as follows: pH (8.1), change in temperature (24 °C), DO (5.1), BOD (1.08), turbidity (6.57), total phosphorus (0.04), nitrate nitrogen (0.6), faecal coliforms (170). The values are within the limit of CPCB (2008). The water quality index is 55.73, and the water quality rating is medium in pre-monsoon (2013).

Table 13.6d Physico-chemical characteristics of water in Cauvery River in Ammapettai (pre-monsoon 2013)

Parameter	Test result	Units	Q-value	Weighting factor	Weighting factor	Subtotal
pH	8.1	pH units	83	0.12	0.12	9.99
Change in temp	24	°C	14	0.11	0.11	1.57
DO	5.1	saturation (%)	5	0.18	0.18	0.84
BOD	1.08	mg/l	89	0.12	0.12	10.68
Turbidity	6.57	NTU	82	0.09	0.09	7.41
Total phosphorus	0.04	mg/l P	94	0.11	0.11	10.37
Nitrate nitrogen	0.6	mg/l NO_3-N	86	0.10	0.10	8.56
Faecal coliforms*	170	CFU/100 ml	37	0.17	0.17	6.31
*Only use one microorganism, not faecal coliforms.				Totals	1.00	55.73
				Water quality index		55.73
				Water quality rating		Medium

The water quality index of Siluvampalayam (Table 13.6e) is calculated, and the values are as follows: pH (8.6), change in temperature (23 °C), DO (7.2), BOD (5.21), turbidity (8.25), total phosphorus (0.006), nitrate nitrogen (1.1), and faecal coliforms (110). The values are within the limit of CPCB (2008). The water quality index is 55.73, and water quality rating is medium in pre-monsoon (2013).

Table 13.6e Physico-chemical characteristics of water in Cauvery River in Siluvampalayam (pre-monsoon 2013)

Parameter	Test result	Units	Q-value	Weighting factor	Weighting factor	Subtotal
pH	8.6	pH units	70	0.12	0.12	8.36
Change in temp	23	°C	15	0.11	0.11	1.68
DO	7.2	saturation (%)	6	0.18	0.18	1.09
BOD	5.21	mg/l	56	0.12	0.12	6.76
Turbidity	8.25	NTU	79	0.09	0.09	7.12
Total phosphorus	0.0055	mg/l P	98	0.11	0.11	10.81
Nitrate nitrogen	1.1	mg/l NO_3-N	70	0.10	0.10	7.04
Faecal coliforms*	110	CFU/100 ml	42	0.17	0.17	7.19
*Only use one microorganism, not faecal coliforms.				Totals	1.00	50.07
				Water quality index		50.07
				Water quality rating		Medium

The water quality index of Koneripatti (Table 13.6f) is calculated, and the values are as follows: pH (8.4), change in temperature (23 °C), DO (7.8), BOD (4.21), turbidity (8.94), total phosphorus (0.018), nitrate nitrogen (0.6), faecal coliforms (130). The values are within the limit of CPCB (2008). The water quality index is 52.72, and the water quality rating is medium in pre-monsoon (2013).

Table 136f. Physico-chemical characteristics of water in Cauvery River in Koneripatti (pre-monsoon 2013)

Parameter	Test result	Units	Q-value	Weighting factor	Weighting factor	Subtotal
pH	8.4	pH units	76	0.12	0.12	9.10
Change in temp	23	°C	15	0.11	0.11	1.68
DO	7.8	saturation (%)	6	0.18	0.18	1.15
BOD	4.21	mg/l	63	0.12	0.12	7.62
Turbidity	8.94	NTU	78	0.09	0.09	7.01
Total phosphorus	0.018	mg/l P	98	0.11	0.11	10.74
Nitrate nitrogen	0.6	mg/l NO_3-N	86	0.10	0.10	8.56
Faecal coliforms*	130	CFU/100 ml	40	0.17	0.17	6.85
*Only use one microorganism, not faecal coliforms.				Totals	1.00	52.72
				Water quality index		52.72
				Water quality rating		Medium

The water quality index of Peramachipalayam (Table 13.6g) is calculated, and the values are as follows: pH (8.3), Change in temperature (21 °C), DO (8.1), BOD (7.32), turbidity (13), total phosphorus (0.08), nitrate nitrogen (1.1), faecal coliforms (110). The values are within the limit of CPCB (2008). The water quality index is 47.15, and the water quality rating is bad in pre-monsoon (2013).

Table 13.6g. Physico-chemical characteristics of water in Cauvery River in Peramachipalayam (pre-monsoon 2013)

Parameter	Test result	Units	Q-value	Weighting factor	Weighting factor	Subtotal
pH	8.3	pH units	79	0.12	0.12	9.42
Change in temp	21	°C	18	0.11	0.11	1.95
DO	8.1	saturation (%)	7	0.18	0.18	1.19
BOD	7.32	mg/l	44	0.12	0.12	5.27
Turbidity	13	NTU	71	0.09	0.09	6.41
Total phosphorus	0.076	mg/l P	79	0.11	0.11	8.67
Nitrate nitrogen	1.1	mg/l NO_3-N	70	0.10	0.10	7.04
Faecal coliforms*	110	CFU/100 ml	42	0.17	0.17	7.19
*Only use one microorganism, not faecal coliforms.				Totals	1.00	47.15
				Water quality index		47.15
				Water quality rating		Bad

The water quality index of Kottampatti (Table 13.6h) is calculated, and the values are as follows: pH (8.6), change in temperature (23 °C), DO (7.2), BOD (5.21), turbidity (8.25), total phosphorus (0.05), nitrate nitrogen (1.1), faecal coliforms (110). The values are within the limit of CPCB (2008). The water quality index is 44.20, and the water quality rating is bad in pre-monsoon (2013).

Table 13.6h. Physico-chemical characteristics of water in Cauvery River in Kottampatti (pre-monsoon 2013)

Parameter	Test result	Units	Q-value	Weighting factor	Weighting factor	Subtotal
pH	8.6	pH units	70	0.12	0.12	8.36
Change in temp	23	°C	15	0.11	0.11	1.68
DO	7.2	saturation (%)	6	0.18	0.18	1.09
BOD	5.21	mg/l	56	0.12	0.12	6.76
Turbidity	8.25	NTU	79	0.09	0.09	7.12
Total phosphorus	0.05	mg/l P	90	0.11	0.11	9.94
Nitrate nitrogen	1.1	mg/l NO_3-N	70	0.10	0.10	7.04
Faecal coliforms*	110	CFU/100 ml	42	0.17	0.17	7.19
*Only use one microorganism, not faecal coliforms.				Totals	1.00	49.20
				Water quality index		49.20
				Water quality rating		Bad

Water quality index of Sanyasipatti (Table 13.6i) is calculated, and the values are as follows: pH (8.7), change in temperature (25 °C), DO (9.2), BOD (3.2), turbidity (7.9), total phosphorus (0.4), nitrate nitrogen (0.18), faecal coliforms (110). The values are within the limit of CPCB (2008). The water quality index is 45.46, and water quality rating is bad in pre-monsoon (2013).

Table 13.6i. Physico-chemical characteristics of water in Cauvery River in Sanyasipatti (pre-monsoon 2013)

Parameter	Test result	Units	Q-value	Weighting factor	Weighting factor	Subtotal
pH	8.7	pH units	66	0.12	0.12	7.92
Change in temp	25	°C	13	0.11	0.11	1.47
DO	9.2	saturation (%)	7	0.18	0.18	1.31
BOD	3.2	mg/l	71	0.12	0.12	8.56
Turbidity	7.9	NTU	80	0.09	0.09	7.18
Total phosphorus	0.4	mg/l P	37	0.11	0.11	4.03
Nitrate nitrogen	0.18	mg/l NO_3-N	97	0.10	0.10	9.70
Faecal coliforms*	280	CFU/100 ml	31	0.17	0.17	5.29
*Only use one microorganism, not faecal coliforms.				Totals	1.00	45.46
				Water quality index		45.46
				Water quality rating		Bad

Water quality index of Bhavani (Table 13.6j) is calculated, and the values are as follows: pH (8.7), change in temperature (°C) (25), DO (11), BOD (3.7), turbidity (16.8), total phosphorus (0.03), nitrate nitrogen (0.5), faecal coliforms (851). The values are within the limit of CPCB (2008). The water quality index is 45.46, and the water quality rating is bad in pre-monsoon (2013).

Table 13.6j. Physico-chemical characteristics of water in Cauvery River in Bhavani (pre-monsoon 2013)

Parameter	Test result	Units	Q-value	Weighting factor	Weighting factor	Subtotal
pH	8.7	pH units	66	0.12	0.12	7.92
Change in temp	25	°C	13	0.11	0.11	1.47
DO	11	saturation (%)	8	0.18	0.18	1.50
BOD	3.7	mg/l	67	0.12	0.12	8.09
Turbidity	16.8	NTU	66	0.09	0.09	5.93
Total phosphorus	0.03	mg/l P	96	0.11	0.11	10.60
Nitrate nitrogen	0.5	mg/l NO_3-N	89	0.10	0.10	8.89
Faecal coliforms*	851	CFU/100 ml	23	0.17	0.17	3.97
*Only use one microorganism, not faecal coliforms.				Totals 1.00		48.37
				Water quality index		48.37
				Water quality rating		Bad

Physico-Chemical Characteristics of Water in Cauvery River (Post-Monsoon 2013)

The physico-chemical characteristics of water in Cauvery River during post-monsoon are given in tables 13.7a to 13.7j. The water quality index of Mettur (Table 13.7a) is calculated, and the values are as follows: pH (7.9), change in temperature (20 °C), DO (3.6), BOD (1.08), turbidity (3.62), total phosphorus (0.02), nitrate nitrogen (1.3), faecal coliforms (110). The values are within the limit of CPCB (2008). The water quality index is 56.35, and the water quality rating is medium in post-monsoon (2013).

Table 13.7a Physico-chemical characteristics of water in Cauvery River in Mettur (post-monsoon 2013)

Parameter	Test result	Units	Q-value	Weighting factor	Weighting factor	Subtotal
pH	8.4	pH units	76	0.12	0.12	9.10
Change in temp	24.1	°C	14	0.11	0.11	1.56
DO	8.5	saturation (%)	7	0.18	0.18	1.23
BOD	1.06	mg/l	89	0.12	0.12	10.70
Turbidity	2.57	NTU	91	0.09	0.09	8.17
Total phosphorus	0.03	mg/l P	96	0.11	0.11	10.58
Nitrate nitrogen	0.28	mg/l NO_3-N	95	0.10	0.10	9.51
faecal coliforms*	170	CFU/100 ml	37	0.17	0.17	6.31
*Only use one microorganism, not faecal coliforms.				Totals	1.00	57.16
				Water quality index		57.16
				Water quality rating		Medium

The water quality index of Navappatti (Table 13.7b) is calculated, and the values are as follows: pH (8.1), change in temperature (25 °C), DO (6.5), BOD (1.05), turbidity (9.31), total phosphorus (0.03), nitrate nitrogen (0.23), faecal coliforms (790). The values are within the limit of CPCB (2008). The water quality index is 54.36, and the water quality rating is medium in post-monsoon (2013).

Table 13.7b. Physico-chemical characteristics of water in Cauvery River in Navappatti (post-monsoon 2013)

Parameter	Test result	Units	Q-value	Weighting factor	Weighting factor	Subtotal
pH	8.1	pH units	83	0.12	0.12	9.99
Change in temp	25	°C	13	0.11	0.11	1.47
DO	6.3	saturation (%)	5	0.18	0.18	0.98
BOD	1.05	mg/l	89	0.12	0.12	10.71
Turbidity	9.31	NTU	77	0.09	0.09	6.95
Total phosphorus	0.03	mg/l P	96	0.11	0.11	10.60
Nitrate nitrogen	0.23	mg/l NO_3-N	96	0.10	0.10	9.61
faecal coliforms*	790	CFU/100 ml	24	0.17	0.17	4.04
*Only use one microorganism, not faecal coliforms.				Totals	1.00	54.36
				Water quality index		54.36
				Water quality rating		Medium

The water quality index of Nerunjipettai (Table 13.7c) is calculated, and the values are as follows: pH (7.9), change in temperature (25 °C), DO (11), BOD (1.57), turbidity (5.68), total phosphorus (0.06), nitrate nitrogen (0.2), faecal coliforms (3,500). The values are within the limit of CPCB (2008). The water quality index is 52.92, and the water quality rating is medium in post-monsoon (2013).

Table 13.7c. Physico-chemical characteristics of water in Cauvery River in Nerunjipettai (post-monsoon 2013)

Parameter	Test result	Units	Q-value	Weighting factor	Weighting factor	Subtotal
pH	7.9	pH units	87	0.12	0.12	10.46
Change in temp	25	°C	13	0.11	0.11	1.47
DO	11	saturation (%)	8	0.18	0.18	1.50
BOD	1.57	mg/l	85	0.12	0.12	10.19
Turbidity	5.68	NTU	84	0.09	0.09	7.57
Total phosphorus	0.06	mg/l P	86	0.11	0.11	9.42
Nitrate nitrogen	0.2	mg/l NO_3-N	97	0.10	0.10	9.67
faecal coliforms*	3500	CFU/100 ml	16	0.17	0.17	2.65
*Only use one microorganism, not faecal coliforms.				Totals 1.00		52.92
				Water quality index		52.92
				Water quality rating		Medium

The water quality index of Ammapettai (table 13.7d) is calculated, and the values are as follows: pH (8.6), change in temperature (26 °C), DO (8.7), BOD (1.57), turbidity (4.51), total phosphorus (0.78), nitrate nitrogen (0.22), faecal coliforms (1,700). The values are within the limit of CPCB (2008). The water quality index is 52.92, and the water quality rating is bad in post-monsoon (2013).

Table 13.7d. Physico-chemical characteristics of water in Cauvery River in Ammapettai (post-monsoon 2013)

Parameter	Test result	Units	Q-value	Weighting factor	Weighting factor	Subtotal
pH	8.6	pH units	70	0.12	0.12	8.36
Change in temp	26	°C	13	0.11	0.11	1.38
DO	8.7	saturation (%)	7	0.18	0.18	1.25
BOD	1.57	mg/l	85	0.12	0.12	10.19
Turbidity	4.51	NTU	87	0.09	0.09	7.79
Total phosphorus	0.78	mg/l P	23	0.11	0.11	2.57
Nitrate nitrogen	0.22	mg/l NO_3-N	96	0.10	0.10	9.63
faecal coliforms*	1700	CFU/100 ml	20	0.17	0.17	3.33
*Only use one microorganism, not faecal coliforms.				Totals	1.00	44.50
				Water quality index		44.50
				Water quality rating		Bad

The water quality index of Siluvampalayam (table 13.7e) is calculated, and the values are as follows: pH (8.2), change in temperature (26 °C), DO (6.6), BOD (5.21), turbidity (9.25), total phosphorus (0.59), nitrate nitrogen (0.27), faecal coliforms (2,200). The values are within the limit of CPCB (2008). The water quality index is 41.67, and water quality rating is bad in post-monsoon (2013).

Table 13.7e. Physico-chemical characteristics of water in Cauvery River in Siluvampalayam (post-monsoon 2013)

Parameter	Test result	Units	Q-value	Weighting factor	Weighting factor	Subtotal
pH	8.2	pH units	81	0.12	0.12	9.72
Change in temp	26	°C	13	0.11	0.11	1.38
DO	6.6	saturation (%)	6	0.18	0.18	1.02
BOD	5.21	mg/l	56	0.12	0.12	6.76
Turbidity	9.25	NTU	77	0.09	0.09	6.96
Total phosphorus	0.59	mg/l P	29	0.11	0.11	3.20
Nitrate nitrogen	0.27	mg/l NO_3-N	95	0.10	0.10	9.53
faecal coliforms*	2200	CFU/100 ml	18	0.17	0.17	3.09
*Only use one microorganism, not faecal coliforms.				Totals	1.00	41.67
				Water quality index		41.67
				Water quality rating		Bad

The water quality index of Koneripatti (table 13.7f) is calculated, and the values are as follows: pH (8.1), change in temperature (25 °C), DO (14), BOD (12.2), turbidity (29.8), total phosphorus (0.02), nitrate nitrogen (0.48), faecal coliforms (1,100). The values are within the limit of CPCB (2008). The water quality index is 44.59, and water quality rating is bad in post-monsoon (2013).

Table 13.7f. Physico-chemical characteristics of water in Cauvery River in Koneripatti (post-monsoon 2013)

Parameter	Test result	Units	Q-value	Weighting factor	Weighting factor	Subtotal
pH	8.1	pH units	83	0.12	0.12	9.99
Change in temp	25	°C	13	0.11	0.11	1.47
DO	14	saturation (%)	10	0.18	0.18	1.80
BOD	12.2	mg/l	27	0.12	0.12	3.22
Turbidity	29.8	NTU	53	0.09	0.09	4.75
Total phosphorus	0.02	mg/l P	97	0.11	0.11	10.67
Nitrate nitrogen	0.48	mg/l NO_3-N	90	0.10	0.10	8.95
faecal coliforms*	1100	CFU/100 ml	22	0.17	0.17	3.73
*Only use one microorganism, not faecal coliforms.				Totals	1.00	44.59
				Water quality index		44.59
				Water quality rating		Bad

The water quality index of Peramachipalayam (table 13.7g) is calculated, and the values are as follows: pH (8.7), change in temperature (26 °C), DO (7.9), BOD (7.8), turbidity (9.1), total phosphorus (0.31), nitrate nitrogen (0.21), faecal coliforms (2,200). The values are within the limit of CPCB (2008). The water quality index is 39.63, and water quality rating is bad in the post-monsoon (2013).

Table 13.7g. Physico-chemical characteristics of water in Cauvery River in Peramachipalayam (post-monsoon 2013)

Parameter	Test result	Units	Q-value	Weighting factor	Weighting factor	Subtotal
pH	8.7	pH units	66	0.12	0.12	7.92
Change in temp	26	°C	13	0.11	0.11	1.38
DO	7.9	saturation (%)	6	0.18	0.18	1.17
BOD	7.8	mg/l	42	0.12	0.12	4.99
Turbidity	9.1	NTU	78	0.09	0.09	6.98
Total phosphorus	0.31	mg/l P	40	0.11	0.11	4.45
Nitrate nitrogen	0.21	mg/l NO_3-N	97	0.10	0.10	9.65
Faecal coliforms*	2200	CFU/100 ml	18	0.17	0.17	3.09
*Only use one microorganism, not faecal coliforms.				Totals:	1.00	39.63
				Water quality index =		39.63
				Water quality rating =		Bad

The water quality index of Kottampatti (table 13.7h) is calculated, and the values are as follows: pH (8.7), change in temperature (25 °C), DO (8), BOD (7.8), turbidity (12.4), total phosphorus (0.03), nitrate nitrogen (0.58), faecal coliforms (1,100). The values are within the limit of CPCB (2008). The water quality index is 44.97, and water quality rating is bad in post-monsoon (2013).

Table 13.7h. Physico-chemical characteristics of water in Cauvery River in Kottampatti (post-monsoon 2013)

Parameter	Test result	Units	Q-value	Weighting factor	Weighting factor	Subtotal
pH	8.7	pH units	66	0.12	0.12	7.92
Change in temp	25	°C	13	0.11	0.11	1.47
DO	8	saturation (%)	7	0.18	0.18	1.18
BOD	7.8	mg/l	42	0.12	0.12	4.99
Turbidity	12.4	NTU	72	0.09	0.09	6.49
Total phosphorus	0.03	mg/l P	96	0.11	0.11	10.56
Nitrate nitrogen	0.58	mg/l NO_3-N	86	0.10	0.10	8.63
Faecal coliforms*	1100	CFU/100 ml	22	0.17	0.17	3.73
*Only use one microorganism, not faecal coliforms.				**Totals:** 1.00		44.97
				Water quality index =		44.97
				Water quality rating =		**Bad**

The water quality index of Sanyasipatti is calculated, and the values are as follows: pH (8.7), change in temp (25 °C), DO (11), BOD (3.7), turbidity (16.8), total phosphorus (0.03), nitrate nitrogen (0.5), faecal coliforms (851). The values are within the limit of CPCB (2008). The water quality index is 48.37, and water quality rating is bad in post-monsoon (2013).

Table 13.7i. Physico-chemical characteristics of water in Cauvery River in Sanyasipatti (post-monsoon 2013)

Parameter	Test result	Units	Q-value	Weighting factor	Weighting factor	Subtotal
pH	8.7	pH units	66	0.12	0.12	7.92
Change in temp	25	°C	13	0.11	0.11	1.47
DO	11	saturation (%)	8	0.18	0.18	1.50
BOD	3.7	mg/l	67	0.12	0.12	8.09
Turbidity	16.8	NTU	66	0.09	0.09	5.93
Total phosphorus	0.03	mg/l P	96	0.11	0.11	10.60
Nitrate nitrogen	0.5	mg/l NO_3-N	89	0.10	0.10	8.89
Faecal coliforms*	851	CFU/100 ml	23	0.17	0.17	3.97
*Only use one microorganism, not faecal coliforms.				Totals 1.00		48.37
				Water quality index		48.37
				Water quality rating		Bad

The water quality index of Bhavani is calculated, and the values are as follows: pH (8.8), change in temp (26 °C), DO (9.3), BOD (7.3), turbidity (17.9), total phosphorus (0.017), nitrate nitrogen (0.23), faecal coliforms (1,017). The values are within the limit of CPCB (2008). The water quality index is 45.38, and the water quality rating is bad in post-monsoon (2013).

Table 13.7j. Physico-chemical characteristics of water in Cauvery River in Bhavani (post-monsoon 2013)

Parameter	Test result	Units	Q-value	Weighting factor	Weighting factor	Subtotal
pH	8.8	pH units	62	0.12	0.12	7.42
Change in temp	26	°C	13	0.11	0.11	1.38
DO	9.3	saturation (%)	7	0.18	0.18	1.32
BOD	7.3	mg/l	44	0.12	0.12	5.28
Turbidity	17.9	NTU	65	0.09	0.09	5.81
Total phosphorus	0.017	mg/l P	98	0.11	0.11	10.75
Nitrate nitrogen	0.23	mg/l NO_3-N	96	0.10	0.10	9.61
Faecal coliforms*	1017	CFU/100 ml	22	0.17	0.17	3.80
*Only use one microorganism, not faecal coliforms and *E. coli*.			Totals	1.00		45.38
			Water quality index			45.38
			Water quality rating			Bad

CONCLUSION

There are 60 diatom species belonging to 21 genera in Cauvery River in parts of Tamil Nadu which are recorded in this study. Among these, the species such as *Achnanthes minutissima, Achnanthidium Plonensis, Aulacoseira distans, Cymbella turgida, C. ventricosa, Fragilaria intermedia* var. *robusta, Gomponema lanceolatum, Nitzschia sigma, Synedra rumpens,* and *S. Ulna,* are abundant in the all the locations. There is the presence of diatom species, viz. *Cyclotella meneghiniana, Nitzschia sigma, Gomphonema parvulum, Synedra rumpens,* and *S. ulna* in good numbers at the following areas: Mettur dam with IPS (indice de polluosen sibilité) of 16.5 and GDI (generic diatom index) of 16.7, Navappatti with IPS of 14.9 and GDI of 15.5, Nerunjipettai with IPS of 15.9 and GDI of 15.8, Ammapettai with IPS of 15.1 and GDI of 15.3. This indicates good quality class, oligo-mesotrophic conditions of the Cauvery River in these areas. At the same time, the diatom assemblages at Siluvampalayam and Koneripatti, with IPS of 13.2 and GDI of 12.2 and IPS of 12.2 and GDI of 12.6 respectively, indicate moderate quality class and mesotrophic conditions. Peramachipalayam with IPS of 8.1 and GDI of 7.2, Kottampatti with IPS of 7.2 and GDI of 7.1, Sanyasipatti with IPS of 7.1 and 7.4, and Bhavani with IPS of 7.2 and GDI of 7.1 indicate bad quality class and eutrophic conditions.

The studies on diatoms indices reveal that water qualities of the Cauvery River are at good quality (oligo-mesotrophic) at Mettur and heavily polluted (eutrophic) at Bhavani sites.

The indiscriminate dumping and release of pollutants into the rivers might lead to serious environmental deterioration, which could be considered as a potential source of threat to the biotic community in the near future. The results of the present study provide scope for utilization of diatom species and indices for water quality assessment of the rivers in India.

REFERENCES

Berger, W. H., Parker, F. L. (1970), Diversity of planktonic foraminifera in deep-sea.

Bhargave, D. S. (1983), Use of water quality index for river classification and zoning of Ganga River, Environmental Poll. Serv. B: Chem. Phys. 6, 51–76.

Bolton, P. W., Currie, J. C., Tervet, D. J., Welch, W. T. (1978), An index to improve water quality classification. Water Pollution Control. 77, 271–284.

Carpenter, K. D., and Waite, I. R. (2000), 'Relations of habitat-specific algal assemblages to land use and water chemistry in the Willamette Basin, Oregon'. Environmental Monitoring and Assessment, 64, pp. 247–257.

Cemagref (1982), Etude des methods biologiques d'appréciation quantitative de la qualitédes eaux. Rapport Q. E. Lyon, Agence de l'eau Rhöne-Me'diterrane'e- Corse-Cemagref, Lyon, France.

Coste, M., and Ayphassorho, H. (1991), Étude de la qualité deseaux du Bassin Artois-Picardie àl'aide des communautés de diatomées benthiques (application des indices diatomiques). Rapport Cemagref. Bordeaux-Agence de l'Eau Artois- Picardie, Douai.

CPCB (2007–2008), Environmental standards: Water quality criteria. Central Pollution Control Board, New Delhi, India. http://cpcb.nic.in/Water Quality Criteria.php.

Cude C. (2001), Oregon Water Quality Index: a tool for evaluating water quality management effectiveness, J. Am. Water Resour. Assoc. 37 (1) 125–137.

Dell'Uomo, A. (1996), Assessment of water quality of an Apennine river as a pilot study. In Whitton, B. A., and E. Rott (eds), Use of Algae for Monitoring Rivers II. Institut fu¨ r Botanik, Universität Innsbruck, 65–73.

Descy, J. P., and Coste, M. (1991), A test of methods for assessing water quality based on diatoms. Verhandlungen der Internationalen Vereinigung für theoretische und angewandte Limnologie 24: 2112–2116.

Gandhi, H. P. (1998), Freshwater Diatoms of Central Gujarat. Bishen Singh Mahendra Pal Singh. Dehra Dun.

Gandhi, H. P. (1959), Freshwater Diatoms from Sagar in the Mysore State. *Journal of the Indian Botanical Society* 38:305–331.

Gandhi, H. P. (1957), A contribution to our knowledge of the diatom genus Pinnularia. Journal of the Bombay Natural History Society 54: 845–853.

Gandhi, H. P. (1961), Notes on the Diatomaceae of Ahmedabad and its environs. Hydrobiologia 17: 218–236.

Gandhi, H. P. (1962), Notes on the Diatomaceae from Ahmedabad and its environs IV, The diatom communities of some freshwater pools and ditches along Sarkhej Road. Phykos 1: 115–127.

Gandhi, H. P. (1967), Notes on Diatomaceae from Ahmedabad and its environs. VI. On some diatoms from fountain reservoirs of Seth Sarabhai's Garden. Hydrobiologia 30: 248–272.

Gómez, N., and Licursi, M. (2001), The Pampean Diatom Index (IDP) for assessment of rivers and streams in Argentina. Aquatic Ecology 35: 173–181.

House, M. A. (1989), A Water quality index for river management. J. Inst. Water Environ. Manage. 3, 336–344. http://dx.doi.org/10.1007/s10653-005-9001-5.

Jarvie, H. P., Whitton, B. A., Neal, C. (1998), Nitrogen and phosphorus in east coast British rivers: Speciation, sources and biological significance. Sci. Total Environ., 210–211, 79–109 (31 pages).

Karthick, B., Alakananda, B., Ramachandra, T. V. (2009), Diatom Based Pollution Monitoring In Urban Wetlands Of Coimbatore, Tamil Nadu, Envis Technical Report 560012, India.

Karthick, B. Krithika, H., and Alakananda, B. (2008), Short Guide to common freshwater Diatom Genera (Poster). Energy and Wetlands Research Group, CES, IISc, Bangalore.

Karthick, B. Taylor, J. C. Mahesh, M. K, and Ramachandra, T. V. (2010), Protocols for collection, Preservation and Enumeration of Diatoms from Aquatic Habitats for Water Quality Monitoring in India. The IUP Journal of Soil and Water Sciences, 3 (1): 25–60.

Kelly, M. G., and Whitton, B. A. (1995), The Trophic Diatom Index: a new index for monitoring Eutrophication in rivers. Journal of Applied Phycology 7:433–444.

Kelly, M. G., Cazaubon, A., Coring, E., Dell'Uomo, A., Ector, L., Goldsmith, B., Guasch, H. Hürlimann, J. Jarlman, A. Kawecka, B. Kwandrans, J.

Laugaste, R. Lindstrøm, E. A. Leitao, M. Marvan, P. Padisák, J. Pipp, E. Prygiel, J. Rott, E. Sabater, S. Dam, V. H., and Vizinet, J. (1998), Recommendations for the routine sampling of diatoms for water quality assessments in Europe. Journal of Applied Phycology 10: 215–224, 1998.

Leclerq, L., and Maquet, B. (1987), Deux nouveaux indices chimique et diatomique de qualite′ d'eau courante. Application au Samson et àses affluents (bassin de la Meuse belge). Comparaison avec d'autres indices chimiques, bioce′notiques et diatomiques. Institut Royal des Sciences Naturelles de Belgique, documented travail 28.

Lecointe, C., Coste, M., and Prygiel, J. (1993), 'Omnidia': Software for taxonomy, calculation of diatom indices and inventories management. Hydrobiology 269/270: 509–513.

Legendre, P., and Legendre, L. (1998), Numerical Ecology. 2nd English edition. Elsevier, Amsterdam.

Lenoir, A., and Coste, M. (1996), Development of a practical diatom index of overall water quality applicable to the French National Water Board network. In Whitton, B. A., and E. Rott (eds), Use of Algae for Monitoring Rivers II. Institut für Botanik. Universität Innsbruck, 29–43.

Ludwig, John A., and Reynolds, J. F. (1988), Statistical ecology: a primer of methods and computing. Wiley Press, New York, New York. 337 pp. Lavoie, I.

Mitchell, M. K., and Stapp, W. B. (1996), Field Manual for Water Quality Monitoring: An Environmental Educational Program for Schools, Thomson-Shore, Inc., Dextor, MI, pp. 277.

Nasiri, F., Maqsiid, I., Haunf, G. Fuller, N. (2007), Water quality index: a fuzzy river pollution decision support expert system. J. Water Resou. Plan. Manage. 133, 95–105.

Nouri, J., Karbassi, A. R., and Mirkia, S. (2008), Environmental Management of Coastal Regions in the Caspian Sea. Int. J. Environ. Sci. Technol., 5 (5), 43–52.

Pesce, S. F., Wunderlin, D. A. (2000), Use of water quality indices to verify the impact of Cordoba City (Argentina) on Suquira river. Water Res. 34:2915–2926.

Prygiel, J., Leveque, L., and Iserentant, R. (1996), Un nouvel indice diatomique pratique pour l'évaluation de la qualité des eaux en réseau de surveillance. Rev. Sci. Eau 1: 97–113.

Said, A., Stevens, D., Selke, G. (2004), An innovative index for water quality in streams. Environ. Manage. 34, 406–414.

Schiefele, S., and Schreiner, C. (1991), Use of diatoms for monitoring nutrient enrichment acidification and impact salts in Germany and Austria. In Whitton, B. A., E. Rott, and G. Friedrich (eds), Use of Algae for Monitoring Rivers. Institüt für Botanik, Univ. Innsbruk.

Schoeman, F. R., and Archibald, R. E. M. (1976–1980), The Diatom Flora of Southern Africa. National Institute for Water Research, Pretoria.

Shrestha, S., Kazama, F. (2007), Assessment of surface water quality using multivariate statistical techniques: A case study of the Fuji River Basin, Japan. *Environmental Modelling and Software*, **22** (4): 464–475.

Singh, K. P., Malik, A., Sinha, S. (2005), Water quality assessment and apportionment of pollution sources of Gomti river (India) using multivariate statistical techniques: a case study. Anal. Chim. Acta 538, 355–374.

Sládeĉcek, V. (1986), Diatoms as indicators of organic pollution. Acta Hydrochimica et Hydrobiologica 14: 555–566.

Somers, K. M., Lavoie, I., Paterson, A. M., and Dillon, P. J. (2000), Assessing scales of variability in benthic diatom community structure. Journal of Applied Psychology 17: 509–513.

Stoermer, E. F., Pilskaln, C. H., Schelske, C. L., Siliceous microfossil distribution in the surfacial sediments of Lake Baikal. Journal of Paleolimnology 14: 69–82 (1995).

Sundaray, S. K., Panda, U. C., Nayak, B. B., and Bhatta, D. (2006), Multivariate statistical techniques for the evaluation of spatial and temporal variation in water quality of Mahanadi river-estuarine system (India), A case study. Environmental Geochemistry and Health, 28 (4), 317–330.

Taylor, J. C., Harding, W. R., and Archibald, C. G. M. (2007), An Illustrated Guide to Some Common Diatom Species from South Africa. WRC Report TT 282/07. Water Research Commission. Pretoria.

Vega, M., Pardo, R., Barrado, E., Deban, L. (1998), Assessment of seasonal and polluting effects on the quality of river water byex ploratory data analysis. *Water Research*, **32** (12): 3581–3592. [doi:10.1016/S0043-1354 (98) 00138-9].

Venkatachalapathy, R., and Karthikeyan, P. (2013a), Physical, Chemical and Environmental Studies on Cauvery River in Parts of Tamil Nadu (Mettur and Bhavani). Universal Journal of Environmental Research, Vol. 3 (3): 415–422.

Venkatachalapathy, R., and Karthikeyan, P. (2013b), Diatoms Assemblages Distribution in Cauvery Bhavani Rivers, Tamil Nadu in Relation to Chemical and Physiographical Factors, Research Journal of Chemical Sciences, Vol. 3 (11): 55–59.

Venkatachalapathy, R., and Karthikeyan, P. (2013c), A taxonomic and morphological study of freshwater Diatom species Synedra ulna (Nitzsch) Ehrenberg in Cauvery River at Bhavani region, Tamil Nadu, India, International Research Journal of Environmental Sciences, Vol. 2 (11), 18–22.

Venkatachalapathy, R., and Karthikeyan, P. (2012), Environmental Impact Assessment of Cauvery River with Diatoms at Bhavani, Tamil Nadu, India, International Journal of Geology, Earth and Environmental Sciences, Vol. 2 (3): 36–42.

Venkatachalapathy, R., and Karthikeyan, P. (2013d), Benthic Diatoms in River Influenced By Urban Pollution, Bhavani Region, Cauvery River, South India, International Journal of Innovative Technology and Exploring Engineering, Vol. 2 (3): 206–210.

Venkatachalapathy, R., Nandhakumar, G., and Karthikeyan, P. (2013e), Diatoms Community Structure in Relation to Physico-Chemical Factors in Yercaud Lake, Salem District, Tamil Nadu, India, International Journal of Innovative Technology and Exploring Engineering Vol. 2 (4): 220–222.

Watanabe, T., Asai, K., and Houki, A. (1986), Numerical estimation of organic pollution of flowing waters by using the epilithic diatom assemblage-Diatom Assemblage Index (DIApo). Science of the Total Environment, Vol. 55: 209–218.

Zelinka, M., and Marvan, P. (1961), Zur Präzisierung der biologischen Klassifikation der Reinheit fliessender Gewässer. Arch. Hydrobiol. 57 389–407.

14 HEAVY METALS IN INDIAN MANGROVE ECOSYSTEM

Prabhat Ranjan and Ramanathan, A. L.
School of Environmental Science, Jawaharlal Nehru University, New Delhi
Email: alrjnu@gmail.com

ABSTRACT

Mangrove ecosystem, besides being among the world's most productive tropical ecosystem, is one of the most threatened tropical ecosystems. This study r reviews the current knowledge on heavy-metal pollution and its toxic effect in the Indian mangrove ecosystem. The literature confirms that the potential toxicity risk for Pichavaram, Coringa–Gaderu, Manakudy estuary mangrove and Vellar estuary mangrove is serious while for Sundarban, Muthupet, and Goa, it is of low level. This review highlights the major studies and data on heavy metals in the Indian mangrove ecosystem, their contamination, enrichment, risk, and toxic effect.

INTRODUCTION

Mangrove forests are one of the world's most productive tropical ecosystem confined to the tropics and subtropics, which dominate approximately 75% of the world's coastline between 25° N and 25° S and are estimated to cover an area of 1.7 to 2.0 × 10^5 km² (Borges et al. 2003). They act as a barricade against cyclones, protect coastal erosion, and provide habitat for a number of commercially important aquatic organisms (Yim and Tam 1999). In the last few decades, due to urbanization, industrialization, and developmental processes, mangroves are under serious threat of degradation. India lost 40% of mangrove cover within this century (Krishnamurthy et al. 1987).

Mangrove sediments are the final point of disembarkation of trace metals, as a result of adsorption, desorption, precipitation, diffusion processes, chemical reactions, biological activity, and a combination of these phenomena. Mangrove sediments, being anaerobic and reduced, are rich in sulphide and organic matter content, favouring the retention of heavy metals (Lacerda and Abrao 1984).

Description of Major Indian Mangrove

Pichavaram. Pichavaram mangrove forest is located between the Vellar and Coleroon estuaries at 11° 2' N, 79° 47' E. The forest occurs on 51 islets, separated by intricate waterways that connect the Vellar and Coleroon estuaries. The southern part near the Coleroon estuary is mainly mangrove vegetation while the northern part near the Vellar estuary is dominated by mudflats. The Vellar estuary opens into the Bay of Bengal at Parangipettai and connects with the Coleroon River, which is a distributary to the River Cauvery. The Pichavaram mangrove is influenced by the mixing of three types of waters: (1) neritic water from the adjacent Bay of Bengal through a mouth called Chinnavaikkal, (2) brackish water from the Vellar and Coleroon estuaries, and (3) fresh water from an irrigation channel (Khan Sahib canal), as well from the main channel of the Coleroon river. The mangrove covers an area of about 1,100 ha, of which 50% is covered by forest, 40% by waterways, and the remaining filled by sand flats and mudflats (Krishnamurthy and Prince Jayaseelan 1983).

Sundarbans. The Indian Sundarbans at the apex of the Bay of Bengal (between 21° 40' to 22° 40' N and 88° 03' E to 89° 07' E) is located on the southern edge of West Bengal, on the north-east coast of India. It is formed at the estuarine phase of the Hugli River of an area of 9,600 km^2 and is a mangrove wetland belonging to the low-lying coastal zone. It is a tide-dominated estuarine wetland at the lower deltaic plains of Ganges and Brahmaputra rivers. The wetland is featured by a complex network of tidal creeks which surround hundreds of tidal islands exposed to different elevations at high and low semidiurnal tides.

Coringa and Gaderu. The extensive estuarine areas to the north of Gautami–Godavari (82° 15' to 82° 22' E, 16° 43' to 17° 00' N) have an area of 132 km^2 and open into Kakinada Bay via the main branches, Gaderu (length: 11 km) and Coringa (length: 26 km). The area between Gautami–Godavari and Kakinada Bay has dense vegetation of mangrove forests and mudflats belong to Coringa Wildlife Sanctuary. The Gaderu and Coringa are the branches of Godavari River, the second largest river in India (Sreenivas 1998).

Goa. Along the entire course of Goan rivers, there exists an intricate network of creeks and backwaters. A luxuriant growth of mangroves and associated swamps can be observed along most of the water bodies within the estuarine reaches. The most prominent and extensive backwaters with mangroves are located along the east of the capital city Panaji. The total area covered by the estuaries in Goa, including the major Mandovi Zuari estuarine complex, is approximately 12,000 ha, of which the mangrove forest occupy 2000 ha. About 900 ha of mangroves are found along the Zuari estuary, 700 ha along the Mandovi estuary, and 200 ha along the Cumbarjua canal.

Bhitarkanika. Geographically, Bhitarkanika is located between 20° 4' to 20° 8' N and 86° 45' to 87° 50' E in the Kendrapara District of Orissa. It is the second largest mangrove ecosystem of India, consisting of mangrove forests, rivers, creeks, estuaries, backwater, accreted land and mudflats. Bhitarkanika mangrove was declared as a wildlife sanctuary with an area of 672 km^2 in 1975. It is a tide-dominated mangrove with areas of high tidal range of semidiurnal, with mean tide level of 1.5 to 3.4 m. The average annual rainfall is about 1,670 mm, of which ~70% is received during August and September. The relative humidity remains between 75 and 80% throughout the year.

Muthupet mangrove. The Muthupet wetland system is spread over an area of 68.03 km^2 and is fed by minor rivers Paminiyar, Koraiyar, Kandankurichanar, Kilaithangiyar, and Marakkakoraiyar, which form part of the tributaries of the Cauvery delta. Of this, some 10% is thick forest while 20% of the area is submerged underwater. These mangrove forests belong to one of India's most extended mangrove areas and are characterized by semidiurnal macrotides (average range of ~3 m).

MATERIAL AND METHOD

The sediments samples were of different depth, from 10 cm up to 5 m. The core samples of the study were taken with the help of PVC pipes. The samples were kept in analytical-grade polythene bags, and after sieving through 63 mm sieve, the sieved sediment samples were digested with a mixed acid such as HF, HCl, HNO$_3$, H$_2$O$_2$, aqua regia, H$_2$SO$_4$, or boric acid. Chemical-leaching methods using acetic acid (Loring 1978), weak HCl solutions (Luoma and Jenne 1976), and sequential extractions (Tessier et al. 1979) have been used to the partition of total metal concentrations into their loosely bound (acid-leachable) and residual phases, and the total metal concentrations were extracted using aqua regia and strong acid combination. Finally, the concentrations of metals were determined by ICP, ICP-MS, ICPAES, ICP-OES, CV-AAS, AAS, XFS, or XRF. These sample-processing methods and analytical tools are all acceptable.

ANALYTICAL METHODS

Contamination factor. The CF is the ratio obtained by dividing the mean concentration of each metal in the soil (Ci) by the baseline or background value (concentration in unpolluted soil) (Hokanson et al. 1980).

$CF = Cn / Bn$

Cn in the above formula is the concentration of the examined element n in the surface sediments, and Bn is the geochemical background concentration of metal n. Bn usually refers to the world's average shale or upper continental crust composition as a reference value.

CF is defined according to four categories. CF < 1 is low level, CF between 1 and 3 is moderate level, CF of 3 to 6 is considerable, and CF > 6 is very high in contamination level.

Pollution load index (PLI). The PLI of a place is calculated by obtaining the nth root from the CFs obtained from metals. PLI is developed by Tomlinson et al. (1980), which is as follows:

$$PLI = \sqrt[n]{(CF1 \times CF2 \times CF3 \times \dots \times CFn}$$

Where CF is the contamination factor of different metals in the samples. The PLI value of >1 is polluted, whereas <1 indicates no pollution.

Enrichment factor. EF is a geochemical index based on the assumption that under the natural sedimentation conditions, there is a linear relationship between a reference (RE) element and other elements. Elements which are most often used as reference ones are Al and Fe. (Mucha et al. 2003, Meza Figueroa et al. 2009, Bhuiyan et al. 2010, Esen et al. 2010, Seshan et al. 2010). The *EF* is defined as follows (Ergin et al. 1991):

$$EF = (M/Fe) \; samplet \; / \; (M/Fe) \; background$$

Where *(Me/Fe) sample* is the ratio of metal to Fe in the samples of interest and *(Me/Fe) background* is the geochemical background value of the ratio of metal to Fe.

Geoaccumulation index (I_{geo}). The index of geoaccumulation (I_{geo}) has been used as a measure of bottom sediment contamination since the 1970s. It determines contamination by comparing current metal contents with pre-industrial levels. The content accepted as background is multiplied each time by the constant 1.5 in order to take into account the natural fluctuations of a given substance in the environment as well as very small anthropogenic influences. The value of the geoaccumulation index is described by the following equation (Muller 1981):

$$I_{geo} = \log_2 (Cn \; / \; 1.5 \; Bn)$$

The interpretation of the obtained results is as follows: $I_{geo} \leq 0$ means practically uncontaminated, $0 < I_{geo} < 1$ means uncontaminated to moderately contaminated, $1 < I_{geo} < 2$ means moderately contaminated, $2 < I_{geo} < 3$ means moderately to heavily contaminated, $3 < I_{geo} < 4$ means heavily contaminated, $4 < I_{geo} < 5$ means heavily to very heavily contaminated, and $I_{geo} \geq 5$ means very heavily contaminated.

Potential ecological risk index (Eif). An ecological risk factor (Eif) to quantitatively express the potential ecological risk of a given contaminant suggested by Håkanson (1980) is as follows:

$$Eif = CF \times Tif$$

Tif is the toxic-response factor for a given substance. The toxic response index for different metals given by Håkanson (1980) are as follows: Hg (40); Cd (30); As (10); Cu, Pb, Ni (5), Cr (2); and Zn (1). And *CF* is the contamination factor.

The following terminologies are used to describe the risk factor: Eif < 40 means low potential ecological risk, $40 \leq$ Eif < 80 means moderate potential ecological risk, $80 \leq$ Eif < 160 means considerable potential ecological risk,

160 ≤ Eif < 320 means high-potential ecological risk, and Eif ≥ 320 means very high ecological risk.

Potential toxicity response index (RI). The potential toxicity response index (RI) was originally introduced by Håkanson 1980 to assess the degree of heavy metal pollution in soil, according to the toxicity of metals and the response of the environment. The calculating methods of RI are listed below:

$$RI = \Sigma Eif$$

There are four category of potential toxicity response index: RI < 150 means low grade, 150 ≤ RI < 300 means moderate, 300 ≤ RI < 600 means severe, and 600 ≤ RI means serious risk.

RESULT AND DISCUSSION

Metals distribution is very uneven within mangrove forest. It varies with depth, distance from coast, anthropogenic activities, types of vegetation, and hydrology (Chatterjee et al. 2009, Kehrig et al. 2003, Marchand et al. 2006). Its sources are usually difficult to identify as some have natural sources and others have anthropogenic both as point and non-point sources.

There were concentrations of Al, As, Cd, Cr, Cu, Co, Fe, Mn, Ni, Pb, and Zn in mangrove sediments at Sundarbans (Banerjee et al. 2012, Sarkar et al. 2004, Sarkar et al. 2008, Chatterjee et al. 2009, and Jonathan et al. 2010), Pichavaram (Ramanathan et al. 1999, Ranjan et al. 2008 and 2013), Coringa and Gaderu (Ray et al. 2006), Manakudy estuary mangrove (Kumar and Edward 2009), Vellar estuary mangrove (Palpandi and Keshavan 2012), Bhitarkanika (Sarangi et al. 2002), Muthupet (Raman et al. 2007), and Goa (Attri and Kerkar).

In all studies, it was found that Al shows the highest mean concentration in all areas, followed by Fe, Mn, and Cr. Al concentration in Sundarbans mangrove varied between 2.46% and 6.33% (Sarkar et al. 2004 and Chatterjee et al. 2009). Fe concentration in Sundarbans area was almost the same in all areas, ranging from 3.08% to 3.75%. Muthupet and Pichavaram also have the same value in tsunamigenic sediments of Pichavaram, where it is lower. Coringa–Gaderu, Manakudy estuary mangrove, and Vellar estuary mangrove show lower Fe concentration than other mangrove places, whereas Goa mangrove shows exceptionally high value of Fe concentration of 12.18%. The high values of Fe in the mangrove sediment could be attributed to the precipitation of the respective metal sulphide compounds in anaerobic sediments. These sulphides form a major sink for the heavy metals.

Mn values show a range of 0.06 to 0.16% with similar trend among all mangrove forests. Fe and Mn have fairly close distribution patterns in sediment, which indicate the strong association to the geochemical matrix between the two elements. This association has been previously recognized by several authors (Abu Hilal and Badran 1990, Nohara and Yokota 1978, El-Sayed 1982).

Cd concentration is lower in Sundarbans mangrove (ranging from 0.24 to 1.88 µg/g) and Muthupet (0.24 µg/g) than in Coringa–Gaderu (10.9 µg/g), Manakudy (2.67 µg/g), and Vellarmangroves (9.15 µg/g), but high variation was seen in Pichavaram area, from 6.6 µg/g (Ramanathan et al. 1999) to 34.74 µg/g (Ranjan et al. 2008). This may be due to synergistic effect of anthropogenic inputs (e.g. fertilizers driven by Vellar, Uppnar, and Coleroon river as well as from the tsunami-driven sediments derived from the deep ocean), and the concentration in tsunamigenic sediments is so high (Li et al. 2006, Seralathan et al. 2006).

Co concentration is higher in Pichavaram than in Sundarbans mangrove; its value is almost similar in all studies done in Sundarbans. Manakudy and Muthupet show similar concentration, whereas Pichavaram (35.3 µg/g) and Goa (34.36 µg/g) show comparatively higher values.

Cr concentration is low in Coringa-Gaderu mangrove in comparison to other mangrove, and it is highest in Tsunamigenic sediment of Pichavaram (Ranjan et al. 2008), which is 617 µg/g. This may be due to high amount of heavy metals which surfaced after tsunami waves in the south-east coast of India, and its higher presence can be attributed to the abundance of garnet mineral family. It is also high in Manakudy estuary mangrove (377.45 µg/g), which may be due to untreated waste discharge of industries.

Cu shows similar values in all the mangrove sites except in Tsunamigenic sediments of Pichavaram (132.2 µg/g) and Vellar estuary mangrove (16.28 µg/g), which show highest and lowest values respectively. High Cu concentration may be due to anthropogenic wastes (Vernet 1993) from nearby soils brought back by tsunami waves. Fungicides and algaecides used in fish-farming are other sources of pollutants, mainly consisting of copper compounds (Spencer and Green 1981).

The trend of Ni shows similar values in all mangrove sites except the tsunamigenic site with higher concentration and Vellar estuary mangrove with minimum concentration of 252.1 μg/g and 1.64 μg/g respectively. Higher Ni concentration may be mainly caused by the effluent discharge from nearby chemical industries.

Pb shows a range of 17.2 to 65.9 μg/g in Sundarbans area, with highest value of 65.9 μg/g in the study of Chatterjee et al. 2009. Pichavaram mangrove has lower value of Pb of 11.2 μg/g and 21 μg/g respectively in the study of Ramnathan et al. (1999) and Ranjan et al. (2013) respectively. Muthupet and Goa mangroves have Pb concentration in the same range, whereas Manakudy estuary mangrove has the highest concentration of 161.254 μg/g. Higher value of Pb is due to the local redox condition, which allowed Pb to coprecipitate with Mn during Mn oxide formation in superficial segment (Lee and Candy 2001).

Zn shows a range of 22.8 to 303.75 μg/g in Sundarbans area, with highest value found in the study of Sarkar et al. (2008). Pichavaram shows approximately the same in pre-tsunamic and tsunamic sediment (93 and 106 μg/g respectively), but it is very low in post-tsunamic study, which is 16 μg/g (Ranjan et al. 2013). Similar values are shown in Manakudy, Muthupet, and Goa, with lower value in Vellar. Higher concentration of Zn can be attributed to many sources, including sewage effluent and run-off.

Contamination factors of Al and As concentrations are low at all mangrove sites. Cd contamination is very high at Pichvaram, Coringa–Gaderu, Vellar estuary mangrove and Manakudy estuary mangrove. In most studies in Sundarbans, Cd contamination is low. Co, Cr, Mn, Ni, Pb, and Zn are in low to moderate range of contamination in most of the mangrove sites of India, whereas Fe is very high in all the sites except Coringa–Gaderu, Manakudy, and Vellar estuary mangrove, where it is in moderate range.

Al, As, Cu, Mn, Ni, Zn, and Co show minimal enrichment in all the sites. Cd in Manakudy, Vellar, and Pichavaram shows very high enrichment, and coring shows extremely high enrichment. Extremely high enrichment factor of Cd is of geogenic origin, and the tsunamic sediment can be attributed to the fact that marine sediments from the deep oceans, which are rich in Cd, might have been trapped in mangrove sediments after the tsunami.

In all the sites, Al and As accumulations are practically uncontaminated. Co, Cu, Zn geoaccumulation at Sundarbans mangroves mainly comes under practically uncontaminated level. At most sites, Co and Ni accumulations are in the range of uncontaminated to moderate. Fe, in almost all sites except Pichavaram (Ranjan et al. 2013) and Coringa–Gaderu, is in the range of moderate to strong, whereas Cd in Manakudy estuary mangrove and Fe in Goa are in strong to very strong accumulation class. Cd in all the studies in Pichavaram shows very strong accumulation. The same range of very strong accumulation is also seen in Cd of Coringa–Gaderu and Vellar estuary mangrove. High accumulation can be attributed to industrial waste and run-off, and tsunamigenic sediments can be attributed to wave-driven deep-sea sediments.

All metals except Cd and Pb show low potential of ecological risk at all sites, whereas Pb is in moderate potential of ecological risk in Pichavaram (Ranjan et al. 2008) and Manakudy estuary mangrove (Kumar and Edward 2009). Cd is also in moderate potential ecological risk in Sundarbans and Muthupet and of very high potential ecological risk in Pichavaram, Coringa–Gaderu, Manakudy, and Vellar mangrove.

Pollution load index shows the overall pollution level of the area. All sites except Vellar estuary mangrove indicate a polluted level in all the studies done so far in the mangrove area.

CONCLUSION

Increase of heavy metals in the mangrove sediment may be attributed to the abundance of fine particle with greater surface area and precipitation of metals as hydroxide coating (mainly Fe and Mn) over finely dispersed particles. Factors like high organic-matter content, flocculation due to varying salinity regions, and transportation of deep-shore sediments to the coastal zone also contribute significantly towards the enrichment of heavy metals in the sediments. The high values of metals like Fe in the mangrove sediment could be attributed to the precipitation of the respective metal sulphide compounds in anaerobic sediments. All sites show high correlation in the distribution pattern of Fe and Ni, showing strong association between them. Many heavy metals like Cd, Cu, Pb, and Zn have a wide range of sources, which mainly constitute anthropogenic sources like untreated waste discharge from industries, agricultural waste run-off, sewage effluent and run-off. Tsunamigenic sediments show higher contamination factor, enrichment factor, geoaccumulation index, potential ecological risk index, pollution load index, and potential toxicity risk index than other mangrove sediments. This may be due to the higher waste discharge at that time and tsunami-driven sediments derived from the deep ocean.

REFERENCES

Abu-Hilal, A. H., Badran, M. M. (1990), Effect of pollution sources on metal concentration in sediment cores from the Gulf of Aqaba (Red Sea). Mar Pollut Bull. 21 (4):190–7.

Ashokkumar, S., Mayavu. P., Sampathkumar. P., Manivasagam. P., Rajaram. G. (2009), Seasonal Distribution of Heavy Metals in the Mullipallam Creek of Muthupettai Mangroves (south-east coast of India). American-Eurasian Journal of Scientific Research 4 (4): 308–312.

Attri, K., and Kerkar, S. (2011), Seasonal Assessment of Heavy Metal Pollution in Tropical Mangrove Sediments (Goa, India) Journal of Ecobiotechnology, 3 (8): 09–15.

Banerjee, K., Senthilkumar, B., Purvaja, R., Ramesh, R. (2012), Sedimentation and trace metal distribution in selected locations of Sundarbans mangroves and Hooghly estuary, North-east coast of India. Environ Geochem Health 34:27–42.

Borges, A. V., Djenidi, S., Lacroix, G., Theate, J., Delille, B., and Frankignoule, M. (2003), Atmospheric CO2 fluxes from mangrove surrounding waters. Geophysical Research Letters, 30 (11), 12–14.

Chakraborty, R., Zaman, S., Mukhopadhyay, N., Banerjee, K., and Mitra, A. (2009), 'Seasonal variation of Zn, Cu and Pb in the estuarine stretch of west Bengal' Indian Journal of Marine Science 38 (1), 104–109.

Chatterjee, M., Filho, E. V. S., Sarkar, S. K., Sella, S. M., Bhattacharya, A., Satpathy, K. K., Prasad, M. V. R., Chakraborty, S., Bhattacharya, B. D. (2007), Distribution and possible source of trace elements in the sediment cores of a tropical macrotidal estuary and their ecotoxicological significance. Environment International 33:346–356.

Chatterjee, M., Massolo, S., Sarkar, S. K., Bhattacharya, A. K., Bhattacharya, B. D., Satpathy, K. K., Saha, S. (2009) An assessment of trace element contamination in intertidal sediment cores of Sunderban mangrove wetland, India for evaluating sediment quality guidelines. Environ Monitoring Assessment 150:307–322.

El-Sayed, M. K. (1982), Effect of sewage effluent on the sediment of Nordasvatnet (a land-locked fjord), Norway. Mar Pollut Bull. 13:85–8.

Håkanson, L. (1980), Ecological Risk Index for Aquatic Pollution Control, a Sedimentological Approach. Water Res., 14: 975–1001.

Jayaprakash, M., Jonathan, M. P., Srinivasalu, S., Muthuraj, S., Mohan, V. R., Rao, N. R. (2008), Acid-leachable trace metals in sediments from an industrialized region (Ennore Creek) of Chennai City, SE coast of India: An approach towards regular monitoring. Estuarine, Coastal and Shelf Science 76: 692–703.

Jonathan, M. P., Sarkar. S. K., Roy. P. D., Alam. Md. A., Chatterjee. M., Bhattacharya. B. D., Bhattacharya. A., Satpathy. K. K. (2010), Acid leachable trace metals in sediment cores from Sunderban Mangrove Wetland, India: an approach towards regular monitoring. Ecotoxicology 19:405–418.

Krishnamurthy, K., and Jeyaseelan, M. J. P. (1983), The Pichavaram (India) mangrove ecosystem. Int. J. Ecol. Envir. Sci. 9: 79–85.

Krishnamurthy, K., Choudhury, A., and Untawale, A. G. (1987), Status report. Mangroves in India, Ministry of Environment and Forests, Govt. of India, New Delhi: 150 pp.

Kumar, P. S., and Edward J. K. P. (2009), Assessment of metal concentration in the sediment cores of Manakudy estuary, south west coast of India. Indian Journal of Marine Sciences, vol. 38 (2) pp. 235–248.

Lacerda, L. D., and Abrao, J. J. (1984), Heavy metals accumulation by mangrove and salt marsh intertidal sediments. Revista Brasileira de Botanica, 7, 49–52.

Lee, S. V., and Candy, A. B. (2001), Heavy metal concentration and mixing processes in sediments from Humber estuary. Eastern England. Estuarine coast shelf science, 53: 619–636.

Li, X. D., Wai, O. W. H., Li, Y. S., Seralathan, P., Srinivasalu, S., Ramanathan, A. L., et al. (2006), Post tsunami sediments characteristics of Tamilnadu Coast. In G. V. Rajamanickam (Ed.) 26th December 2004 tsunami causes, effects remedial measures, pre and post tsunami disaster management, a geoscientific perspective (pp. 190–215). New Delhi: New Academic Publisher.

Liu, W. H., Zhao, J. Z., Ouyang, Z. Y., Solderland, L., and Liu, G. H. (2005), Impacts of Sewage Irrigation on Heavy Metal Distribution and Contamination in Beijing, China. Environ. Intl., 32: 805–812.

Loring, D. H. (1978), Geochemistry of zinc, copper, and lead in the sediments of the estuary and Gulf of St. Lawerence. Canadian Journal of Earth Sciences 15, 757–772.

Luoma, S. N., and Jenne, E. A. (1976), Estimating bioavailability of sediment bound trace metals with chemical extractants. In: Hemphill, D. D. (Ed.), Trace Substances in Environmental Health. Univ. Missouri Press, Columbia, MO, pp. 343–35.

Müller, G. (1981), Die Schwermetallbelastung derSedimentendes Neckars und Seiner Nebenflüsse. Chemiker-Zeitung 6, 157, 1981.

Nohara, M., Yokota. S. (1978), The geochemistry of trace elements in pelagic sediments from the central Pacific Basin. J. Geol Soc Japan. 84 (4):165–75.

Palpandi, C., and Kesavan, K. (2012), Heavy metal monitoring using Neritacrepidularia-mangrove molluscfrom the Vellar estuary, South-east coast of India. Asian Pacific Journal of Tropical Biomedicine S358-S367.

Raman, D. J., Jonathan, M. P., Srinivasalu, S., Armstrong-Altrin, J. S., Mohan, S. P., Ram-Mohan, V. (2007), Trace metal enrichments in core sediments in Muthupet mangroves, SE coast of India: Application of acid leachable technique. Environmental Pollution 145:245–257.

Ramanathan, A. L., Subramanian, V., Ramesh, R., Chidambaram, S., James, A. (1999), Environmental geochemistry of the Pichavaram mangrove ecosystem (tropical), south-east coast of India. Environmental Geology 37 (3).

Ranjan, R. K., Ramanathan, A. L., Singh, G., Chidambaram, S. (2008), Assessment of metal enrichments in tsunamigenic sediments of Pichavaram mangroves, south-east coast of India. Environmental Monitoring Assessment. 147:389–411.

Ray, A. K., Tripathy, S. C., Patra, S., Sarma, V. V. (2006), Assessment of Godavari estuarine mangrove ecosystem through trace metal studies. Environment International 32:219–22.

Rubio, B., Nombela, M. A., and Vilas, F. (2000), Geochemistry of major and trace elements in sediments of the Ria de Vigo (NW Spain): An assessment of metal pollution. Marine Pollution Bulletin, 40, 968–980.

Sarkar, S. K., Bilinski, S. F., Bhattacharya, A. K., Saha, M., Bilinski, H. (2004), Levels of elements in the surficial estuarine sediments of the Hugli River, north-east India and their environmental implications. Environment International 30: 1089–1098.

Sarkar, S. K., Cabral, H., Chatterje, E. M., Cardoso, I., Bhattacharya, A. K., Satpathy, K. K., AftabAlam, M. A. (2008), Biomonitoring of Heavy Metals Using the Bivalve Molluscs in Sunderban Mangrove Wetland,

North-east Coast of Bay of Bengal (India): Possible Risks to Human Health. Clean, 36 (2), 187–194.

Sreenivas, N. (1988), Zooplankton production and distribution in mangrove habitat of Godavari Estuary-Kakinada. PhD thesis, Andhra University, India.

Tam, N. F. Y., and Wong, Y. S. (1993), Retention of nutrients and heavy metals in mangrove sediments receiving wastewater of different strengths. Environmental Technology, 14, 719–729.

Tam, N. F. Y., and Wong, Y. S. (1995), Retention and distribution of heavy metals in mangrove soils receiving wastewater. Environmental Pollution, 94, 283–291.

Tam, N. F. Y., and Wong, Y. S. (2000), Spatial variation of heavy metals in surface sediments of Hong Kong mangrove swamps. Environmental Pollution, 110, 195–205.

Tessier, A., Campell, P. G. C., Bisson, M. (1979), Sequential extraction procedure for the speciation of particulate traces metals. Analytical Chemistry 51 (7), 844–851.

Tomlinson, D. L., Wilson, J. G., Harris, C. R., and Jeffney, D. W. (1980), Problems in the assessment of heavy metal levels in estuaries and the formation of a pollution index. Hel gol. Wiss. Meeresunters, Vol. 33, pp. 566–572.

15 POLLUTION THREATS TO COASTAL WETLANDS

P. Sampathkumar
CAS in Marine Biology, Annamalai University Parangipettai 608 502
Email: sampathcas@gmail.com

ABSTRACT

Coastal wetlands encompass diversified habitats with varied ecological processes that support a variety of marine and coastal species and open-sea habitats and ecosystems, and the wealth of ecological processes that support all of these. Since 1600s, extensive losses have occurred, with many of the original wetlands drained and converted to farmlands. Today, less than half of the nation's original wetlands remain. Conversion to agricultural usage of land was responsible for 54% of the losses of both fresh water and coastal wetlands, drainage for urban development was responsible for 5%, and 'unspecified usage' (planned development) was responsible for 41% of the losses. This is in contrast to the mid 1950 to mid 1970, when agricultural drainage of wetlands was responsible for 87% of the losses and urban development for 8%.

Activities resulting in wetland loss and degradation include agriculture; commercial and residential development; road construction; impoundment; resource extraction; industrial siting, processes, and waste; dredge disposal; silviculture; and mosquito control. The primary pollutants causing degradation are sediment, nutrients, pesticides, salinity, heavy metals, toxic chemicals from paints, cleaners, solvents, low dissolved oxygen, pH, and selenium. Dumping of wastes from fish-cleaning and discharge of human waste from marine operations and boats can increase the amount of nutrients and organic matter in wetlands and can lead to eutrophication.

The above pressures on natural habitats associated with increasing population and economic growth will continue to lead to the loss of biological diversity. Recognizing the problems, the nature of the underlying causes, and the limited resources available to counteract powerful destructive trends will definitely lead to a best way of conserving the biological diversity of the coastal wetlands.

INTRODUCTION

For the human society, coastal areas are an important interface between terrestrial and sea-based activities. Not by coincidence, a vast majority of the global population is concentrated along its interface; it is estimated that about 55% of the world's population lives in coastal areas. Our society is heavily dependent on coastal resources, often leading to intense competition for this resource between various activities like food production, urban development, transportation, recreation, and waste disposal. At the same time, it is ironic that about half of the world's coastal ecosystems face threats to the existence as a result of human activities.

Coastal wetlands encompass diversified habitats with varied ecological processes that support a variety of marine and coastal species and open-sea habitats and ecosystems, and the wealth of ecological processes. Among coastal wetlands, estuaries, mangroves and coastal lagoons are biodiversity-rich areas, whereas the other brackish habitats have only a few specialized species. Extensive losses have occurred, with many of the original wetlands drained and converted to farmlands. Today, less than half of the nation's original wetlands remain. The coastal wetlands plays a significant role in controlling floods, water storage or supply, water purification, retention of pollutants/nutrients/sediments, groundwater recharge or discharge, maintenance of underground water tables, freshwater cycle, staging ground for waterfowl, nurseries for fisheries and wildlife, stabilization of local climate, protecting biodiversity, recreation, tourism and cultural heritage, and providing livelihoods to local people.

Conservation and sustainable use of biological resources of these systems are of critical importance for meeting the food, health, and other needs of the human population. Nearly half of the world's coastal ecosystems face a significant risk of degradation due to human activities. In the absence of proper management, environmental degradation will continue to cause damage to the coastal biodiversity.

PRESENT STATUS

The coastal environment occupies 18% of the surface of the globe, the area where around a quarter of global primary productivity occurs and around 60% of the human population lives, where two-thirds of the world cities with population of over 1.6 million people are located, and where approximately 90% of the world's fish catch is supplied.

The coastal ocean accounts for 8% of the ocean surface, <0.5% of the ocean volume, around 14% of global ocean production, up to 50% of the global oceanic denitrification, 80% of the global organic matter burial, 90% of the global sedimentary mineralization, 75–90% of the global sink of suspended river load and its associated elements/pollutants, in excess of 50% of the present-day global carbonate deposition.

RESULT AND DISCUSSION

Although wetlands can improve water quality in watershed, their capacity to process pollutants without becoming degraded can be exceeded. Many wetlands have suffered functional degradation, although it is difficult to calculate the magnitude of the degradation. Wetlands are threatened by air and water pollutants and by hydrologic alteration (USEPA 1994b). Some researchers believe that a significant percentage of the nation's remaining wetlands has been substantially compromised in terms of hydrology.

Hydrological Alteration

Wetlands form as a result of certain hydrologic conditions which cause the water table to saturate or inundate the soil for a certain amount of time each year. The alteration of wetland hydrology can change the soil chemistry and the plant and animal community. Alteration which reduces or increases the natural amount of water entering a wetland or the period of saturation and inundation can, in time, cause the ecosystem to change to an upland system or, conversely, to a riverine or lacustrine system. This alteration can be natural, such as through the successional process of stream impoundment by beavers or climate change.

Wetland loss and degradation through hydrologic alteration by man has occurred historically through such actions as: drainage, dredging, stream channelization, ditching, levees, deposition of fill material, stream diversion, groundwater withdrawal, and impoundment. Habitat loss and fragmentation, water diversion structures, and impoundments are the implications of hydrologic alterations of wetlands.

Urbanization

Urbanization is a major cause of impairment of wetlands (USEPA 1994b). Urbanization has resulted in direct loss of wetland acreage as well as degradation of wetlands. Degradation is due to changes in water quality, quantity, and flow rates; increases in pollutant inputs; and changes in species composition as a result of introduction of non-native species and disturbance. The major pollutants associated with urbanization are sediment, nutrients, oxygen-demanding substances, road salts, heavy metals, hydrocarbons, bacteria, and viruses (USEPA 1994b). These pollutants may enter wetlands from point sources or from non-point sources. Construction activities are a major source of suspended sediments that enter wetlands through urban run-off.

Wastewater treatment plant effluent is a source of pollutants that continue to degrade wetlands (USEPA 1994b). Wastewater can alter the ecology of a wetland ecosystem if high-nutrient levels cause extended eutrophication and metals cause plant and aquatic-organism toxicity (Ewel 1990). Iron and magnesium, in particular, may reach toxic concentrations, immobilize available phosphorous, and coat roots with iron oxide, preventing nutrient uptake.

Heavy metals may bioaccumulate in estuarine wetlands, causing deformities, cancers, and death in aquatic animals and their terrestrial predators. Heavy-metal ingestion by benthic organisms (including many shellfish) in estuarine wetlands occurs because the metals bind to the sediments or the suspended solids that such organisms feed on or settle on the substrate where such organisms live.

Urban and industrial stormwater, sludge, and wastewater treatment plant effluent, which are rich in nitrogen and phosphorus, can lead to algal blooms in estuaries. Algal blooms deplete dissolved oxygen, leading to mortality of benthic organisms. Some algae are toxic to aquatic life (Kennish 1992). Excess algae can shade underwater sea grasses (part of the coastal wetland ecosystem), preventing photosynthesis and resulting in seagrass death (Batiuk et al. 1992, USEPA 1994b).

Landfills can pose an ecological risk to wetlands, and landfill construction may alter the hydrology of nearby wetlands. Mosquito-control efforts in urbanized and resort communities have resulted in wetlands loss and degradation through drainage, channelization, and use of toxic pesticides.

Marine Operations/Boats

Wetlands can be adversely affected by pollutants released from boats and marine operations. Pollutants include hydrocarbons, heavy metals, and toxic chemicals from paints, cleaners, and solvents (USEPA, 1993a). Dumping of wastes from fish-cleaning and discharge of human waste from marinas and boats can increase the amount of nutrients and organic matter in a wetland. The increased organic matter and nutrients can lead to eutrophication.

Industry

Adverse effects of industry on wetlands can include reduction of wetland acreage, alteration of wetland hydrology due to industrial water intake and discharge, water temperature increases, point and non-point source pollutant inputs, pH changes as a result of discharges, and atmospheric deposition.

Saline water discharges, hydrocarbon contamination, and radionuclide accumulation from oil and gas production can significantly degrade coastal wetlands (Rayle and Mulino 1992). Most petroleum hydrocarbon inputs into coastal wetlands are either from coastal oil industry activities, from oil spills at sea, from run-off, or from upstream releases (Kennish 1992). Oil can alter reproduction, growth, and behaviour of wetland organisms and can result in mortality. Plants suffocate when oil blocks their stomata (Dibner 1978).

Agriculture

Agriculture has been the major factor in freshwater and estuarine wetland loss and degradation. Certain exempted activities performed in wetlands can degrade wetlands: harvesting food, fibre, or forest products; minor drainage; maintenance of drainage ditches; construction and maintenance of irrigation ditches; construction and maintenance of farm or forest roads; maintenance of dams, dikes, and levees; direct and aerial application of damaging pesticides (herbicides, fungicides, insecticides, fumigants); and groundwater withdrawals.

These activities can alter a wetland's hydrology, water quality, and species composition. Excessive amounts of fertilizers and animal waste reaching wetlands in run-off from agricultural operations, including confined animal facilities, can cause eutrophication. Grazing livestock can degrade wetlands that they use as a food and water source. Urea and manure can result in high-nutrient inputs. Pesticides and fertilizers used during silvicultural operations can enter wetlands through run-off as well as through deposition from aerial application, and the fertilizers may contribute to eutrophication of wetlands.

Mining

Phosphate-mining has resulted in the loss of thousands of acres of wetlands, and other types of mining operations can also degrade wetlands through hydrologic alterations, high-metal concentrations, and/or decreased pH.

Acid drainage from active and abandoned mines causes extensive ecological damage and introduces high levels of acidity and heavy metals into the wetland environment through run-off and through direct drainage from mines into wetlands.

Atmospheric Deposition

Nitrous oxides, sulphurous oxides, heavy metals, volatilized pesticides, hydrocarbons, radionuclides, and other organics and inorganics are released into the atmosphere by industrial and agricultural activities and from locomotives. These compounds can enter wetlands through wet and dry atmospheric deposition and can adversely affect aquatic organisms and the terrestrial organisms that feed on them.

CONCLUSION

Many policies and legal instruments aim to improve the management of coastal areas, but they must be better streamlined in order to safeguard the coastal biodiversity. Coordinated action at global, regional, and local levels will be a key to sustainability. The above pressures on natural habitats, associated with increasing population and economic growth, will continue to lead to the loss of biological diversity. Recognizing the problems, the nature of the underlying causes, and the limited resources available to counteract powerful destructive trends will definitely lead to a best way of conserving the biological diversity of the coastal wetlands.

REFERENCES

Batiu, R. A., R. J. Moore, K. A. Dennison, W. C. Stevenson, J. C. Staver, L. W. Carter, V. Rybich, N. B. Hickman, R. E. Kollar, S. Bieber, S. Heasly (1992), Chesapeake Bay submergedaquatic vegetation habitat requirements and restorationtargets: a technical synthesis. US Environmental ProtectionAgency, Chesapeake Bay Program, Report CBP/TRS 83.

Dibner, P. C. (1978), Response of a Salt Marsh to Oil Spill and Cleanup. EPA: Cincinnati, OH.

Ewel, K. (1990), 'Multiple demands on wetlands; Florida cyprus swamps can serve as a case study', Bioscience 40: 660–666.

Kennish, M. J. (1992), Ecology of Estuaries: Anthropogenic Effects. CRC Press, Inc., Boca Raton, FL.

Rayle, M. F., M. M. Mulino (1992), Produced Water Impacts in Louisiana Coastal Waters. Environ Sci Research: Produced Water: Tech/Environ Issues and Solutions (Plenum). pp. 343–354.

USEPA. U. S. Environmental Protection Agency (1993a), Guidance Specifying Management Measures for Sources of Non-point Pollution in Coastal Waters. EPA: Washington DC. Available through EPA Wetlands Hotline. 1-800-832-7828.

USEPA. U. S. Environmental Protection Agency (1994b), National Water Quality Inventory. 1992 Report to Congress. EPA 841-R-94-001. EPA: Washington DC.

16 DISTRIBUTION OF OSTRACODS FROM PAZHAVERKADU (PULICAT LAGOON) TAMIL NADU, INDIA

P. Mahalakshmi and S. M. Hussain
Department of Geology, School of Earth and Atmospheric Sciences, University of Madras, Guindy Campus, Chennai 600 025
Email: smhussain7@hotmail.com

ABSTRACT

In order to study the systematic distribution of the recent brackish Ostracoda, a total of 17 surface sediment samples were collected from Pazhaverkadu (Pulicat lagoon). The Ostracod taxonomy was dealt using the classification proposed by Hartmann and Puri (1974). Accordingly, a total of 20 ostracod taxa belonging to 16 genera, 12 families, 2 superfamilies, and 2 suborders of the order Podocopida have been identified. Among these, *Cytherelloidea leroyi* belong to suborder Platycopa and the remaining 19 species to suborder Podocopa are recorded from Pazhaverkadu (Pulicat lagoon).

Sedimentological parameters such as $CaCO_3$, organic matter, and sand-silt-clay ratio were estimated. An attempt has been made to bring out the relation between the substrate and Ostracoda and to evaluate the congenial sediment type for the population abundance in the study area. From the distribution of microfauna, it is inferred that the most favourable sediment type for the population abundance is silty sand.

In the present work, the ratio between the carapaces and open valves of Ostracoda has been taken into consideration for determining the relative rate of sedimentation. Among a total of 8,384 Ostracod shells recovered in the surface samples, a total of 7,997 specimens are carapaces while the remaining 387 specimens are open valves. The distribution of carapaces and open valves, for all the stations put together, reveals that the carapaces outnumbered open valves which may be concluded that a relatively very rapid rate of sedimentation prevails in the Pulicat lagoon.

Keywords: Ostracoda, Sediment characteristics, Sedimentation rate, Pazhavekadu Pulicat, Tamil Nadu.

INTRODUCTION

Ostracods are an abundant and diverse group of tiny crustaceans with a long fossil record from Ordovician to Recent. About 50,000 species have been identified, grouped into several orders. Ostracods are small crustaceans, typically around 1 mm in size, laterally compressed and protected by a bivalve-like chitinous or calcareous shell known as carapace. The hinge of the two 'valves' is in the upper dorsal region of the body. The Ostracoda are one of the most successful crustacean groups with approximately 8,000 living species. Ostracods are generally small, ranging from 0.1 to 32 mm in length. Most ostracods live burrowed in the substrate or epibenthic crawlers; others are nektonic.

STUDY AREA

The proposed work envisages a detailed probe into microfaunal (Ostracoda) analysis of the sediments collected from Pazhaverkadu (Pulicat lagoon), near Chennai, Tamil Nadu (Figure 16.1).

The Pulicat is the largest south Indian coastal lake and a marshy mangrove wetland located in Chinglepet District of Tamil Nadu and Nellore District of Andhra Pradesh. The Pulicat lake estuary is a shallow tropical lagoon and lies between 13° 24' 42" to 13° 28' 40" N and 80° 18' 50" to 18° 20' 00" E (Survey of India toposheet No. 66 C/7), lying almost parallel to the Bay of Bengal. It extends over the Ponneri and Gummidipundi taluks of Thiruvallur District in Tamil Nadu and Sulurpet and Tada taluks of Nellore District in Andhra Pradesh and covers an area of about 461 km². The lake is separated from the Bay of Bengal by the barrier island of Sriharikota. It has a length of about 4.48 km, a width ranging from 0.3 to 102 km, and an area of about 5.38 km². This area is drained by the Buckingham Canal and the Araniar River. In most part of the wetland, *Avicennia marina* is the dominant mangrove species.

METHODOLOGY

A total of 17 surface sediment samples were collected from the Pazhaverkadu (Pulicat lagoon), to study the taxonomy and distribution of Recent Ostracoda, and its corresponding geocoordinates are given in Table 16.1. The Ostracod taxa were separated from the sediments, applying standard micropalaeontological techniques. Apart from the taxonomy of the individual species, their detail morphological, micro-structural characters were critically studied using stereobionocoular microscope and SEM (scanning electron microscope).

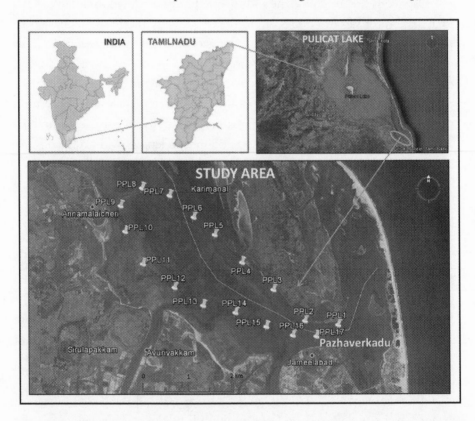

Figure 16.1. Geological map of study area Pazhaverkadu (Pulicat lagoon).

The taxonomy and systematics were dealt using Ostracod treatise by Hartmann and Puri (1974) and other recent literature. Distribution pattern of individual taxon was examined, and their sediment relationship was determined for ecologic/environmental interpretation.

Sand-silt-clay ratio estimation was carried out using the procedure of Krumbein and Pettijohn (1938). Organic matter was determined by titration method of Gaudette et al. (1974). Estimation of $CaCO_3$ was made by adopting the procedure proposed by Loring and Nota (1973).

Table 16.1 Geographical coordinates of grab samples collected from the Pazhaverkadu (Pulicat lagoon), Tamil Nadu.

L. No.	Latitude	Longitude	Depth (ft)	Temperature (°C)	DO (%)	Salinity (‰)
1	13° 25' 51" N	80° 18' 48" E	4	32	6.2	36
2	13° 25' 54" N	80° 18' 49" E	4	33	6.2	60
3	13° 25' 60" N	80° 17' 55" E	6	32	6.4	59
4	13° 26' 58" N	80° 17' 29" E	7	31	6.2	48
5	13° 26' 34" N	80° 17' 29" E	6	31	6.8	48.5
6	13° 26' 59" N	80° 16' 53" E	4	32	6.2	47.5
7	13° 27' 20" N	80° 16' 58" E	2.5	31	6.7	47.5
8	13° 27' 55" N	80° 16' 19" E	4	34	6.8	57
9	13° 28' 24" N	80° 15' 52" E	12	31	6.7	59
10	13° 28' 54" N	80° 15' 36" E	6	33	7.2	60
11	13° 29' 26" N	80° 15' 14" E	6	33	6.6	6.2
12	13° 29' 44" N	80° 15' 46" E	8	32	6.2	62
13	13° 29' 50" N	80° 15' 59" E	7	31	6.7	65
14	13° 29' 50" N	80° 15' 41" E	9	30	6.8	63
15	13° 28' 27" N	80° 15' 46" E	4	31	6.7	58
16	13° 28' 36" N	80° 16' 48" E	3	33	7.2	62
17	13° 27' 50" N	80° 16' 28" E	4	33	7.2	62

RESULT AND DISCUSSION

Micropalaeontology Study

All the sediment samples were subjected to standard micropalaeontological techniques, and calcareous microfauna (Ostracoda) were retrieved. The Ostracod taxonomy was dealt using the classification proposed by Hartmann and Puri (1974). Accordingly, a total of 20 ostracod taxa belonging to 16 genera, 12 families, 2 superfamilies, and 2 suborders of the order Podocopida have been identified. Among these, *Cytherelloidea leroyi* belong to suborder Platycopa, and the remaining 19 species to suborder Podocopa are recorded from Pazhaverkadu (Pulicat lagoon) (Table 16.2). The checklist of the same is presented below, and SEM photographs of a few selected species are presented in Plate I.

1. *Cytherelloidea leroyi*
2. *Hemicytheridea bhatiai*
3. *H. paiki*
4. *H. khoslai*
5. *Neomonoceratina iniqua*
6. *N. jaini*
7. *Jankeijcythere mckenziei*
8. *Neosinocythere dekrooni*
9. *Tanella gracilis*
10. *Cyprideis* sp.
11. *Keijella reticulata*
12. *K. karwarensis*
13. *Lankacythere coralloides*
14. *Hemikrithi peterseni*
15. *Caudites javana*
16. *Loxoconcha megapora indica*
17. *Semicytherura contraria*
18. *Paijenborchellina* sp.
19. *Kalingella mckenziei*
20. *Phlyctenophora orientalis.*

PLATE-I

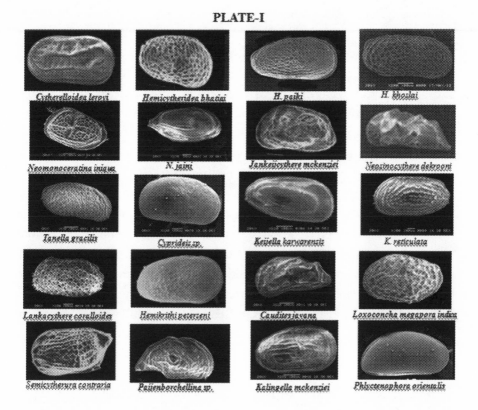

Cytherelloides leroyi	*Hemicytheridea bhatiai*	*H. paiki*	*H. khoslai*
Neomonoceratina inigua	*N. jaini*	*Jankeiicythere mckenziei*	*Neosinocythere dekrooni*
Tanella gracilis	*Cyprideis sp.*	*Keijella karsarensis*	*K. reticulata*
Lankacythere coralloides	*Hemikrithi peterseni*	*Caudites javana*	*Loxoconcha megapora indica*
Semicytherura contraria	*Paijenborchellina sp.*	*Kalingella mckenziei*	*Phlyctenophora orientalis*

Sediment Characteristics

Organic Matter

The ultimate source of organic matter incorporated in the sediments is some form of plant life thriving on the surface waters of the sea or on land or both. In shallow water sediments, the organic matter is, to a great extent, related to the plant material of terrigenous origin while for the ocean as a whole, it is the planktonic photosynthetic organisms, which are the chief source of organic matter. In either case, the amount of organic matter content of the sediments depends upon the following: (a) rate of deposition of organic matter, (b) rate of deposition of inorganic matter, and (c) rate of decomposition of organic matter, followed by deposition.

The rate of deposition of organic matter depends upon the production within the upper layers and the rate of destruction during descent through the water column. Abundant supply of oxygen will cause decomposition of the organic matter that has reached the bottom. The sediment texture also plays a role—i.e., comparatively coarse-grained sediments are more permeable than fine-grained ones, and hence, the latter are more suitable for preservation of organic matter. According to Sverdrup et al. (1942), the undermentioned conditions will favour the formation of sediments rich in organic matter: (a) good supply of organic matter, (b) relatively, a rapid rate of accumulation of organic material, especially of fine-grained sediments, and (c) less supply of oxygen to the water in contact with the sediments.

Subba Rao (1960) recorded 1.05% to 1.34% organic matter content for the sandy sediments collected from a depth of 10–15 fathoms off the east coast of India. However, he observed that the silt–clay materials of the Pennar, Krishna, and Godavari rivers, even though fine in nature, are poor in organic matter. In the sediments of Suddagedda river estuary, sandy sediments have been found to be poor in organic matter content while fine-grained materials are rich (Venkata Rao and Subba Rao 1974). They (1976), after analysing the Chipurupalle stream sediments, established that the sandy types are poor in organic matter while materials containing higher amount of clay are rich in the same.

According to Joy and Clark (1977), organic carbon being directly related to food supply is one of the major environmental parameters which influence the distribution of benthic ostracods. After analysing the organic matter content in 144 samples collected off Porto Novo (Bay of Bengal), Rasheed and Ragothaman (1978) stated that it shows a range from 0.10% to 2.72% by weight. They also observed that all the samples collected near the shore are poor in organic matter, and as depth increases, a gradual rise in the same is noticed.

Table 16.2 Taxonomic chart of the Ostracoda in the Pulicat lagoon

Order	Suborder	Superfamily	Family	Genus	Species
Podocopida	Platycopa		Cytherellidae	*Cytherelloidea*	*Cytherelloidea leroyi*
	Podocopa	Cytheracea	Cytheridae	*Hemicytheridea*	*Hemicytheridea bhatiai*
					H. paiki
					H. khosalai
				Neomonoceratina	*Neomonoceratina iniqua*
					N. jaini
				Jankeijcythere	*Jankeijcythere mckenziei*
			Sinocytheridae	*Neosinocythere*	*Neosinocythere dekrooni*
			Leptocytheridae	*Tanella*	*Tanella gracilis*
			Cytherideidae	*Cyprideis*	*Cyprideis* sp.
			Trachyleberididae	*Keijella*	*Keijella reticulata*
					Keijella karwarensis
				Lankacythere	*Lankacythere coralloides*
			Krithidae	*Hemikrithe*	*Hemikrithi peterseni*
			Hemicytheridae	*Caudites*	*Caudites javana*
			Loxoconchidae	*Loxoconcha*	*Loxoconcha megapora indica*
			Cytheruridae	*Semicytherura*	*Semicytherura contraria*
				Paijenborchellina	*Paijenborchellina* sp.
			Uncertain	*Kalingella*	*Kalingella mckenziei*
		Cypridacea	Candonidae	*Phlyctenophora*	*Phlyctenophora orientalis*

In the present study, organic matter content was determined for all the 17 surface sediment samples. The organic matter content in the surface sediments samples ranges from 0.12% to 2.73% (Table 3 and Figure 16.2). In general, the higher organic matter appears favouring the maximum ostracod population (standing crop) in the lagoon.

Calcium Carbonate

There have been previous studies pertaining to the calcium carbonate content of the sediments off the east coast of India from different localities. Subba Rao and Mahadevan (1957) analysed the distribution of calcium carbonate in the shelf sediments off Visakhapatnam in relation to the distance from the coast, configuration of the shelf, and the silty and clayey material of the sediments. They found that the calcium carbonate content increases from

5.0% (nearshore) to about 80.0% (at a depth of 60 fathoms), and beyond the continental shelf, it decreases to about 10%. In 1958 Subba Rao made a study of calcium carbonate content of the sediments collected off the east coast of India, north of Chennai. He stated that the sediments from the depths of less than 20 fathoms are, in general, poor in calcium carbonate content. Likewise, Madhusudana Rao and Murthy (1968) studied many sediment samples collected from off Chennai and Karaikal. They observed that samples collected from the depths of 36 ft and 54 ft (Madras) contain 1.75% and 3.0% calcium carbonate respectively, and sediments collected off Karaikal from the depths of 48 ft and 96 ft contain 6.0% and 8.0% calcium carbonate respectively.

Rasheed and Ragothaman (1978) observed that the calcium carbonate percentage varies from 0.5% to 5.5% in the inner shelf sediments off Porto Novo, Tamil Nadu. They found the same to show an increase seaward from the shore. They have also stated that, in general, the sediments off Porto Novo are poor in calcium carbonate content than those recorded from other localities off Tamil Nadu state. The sediment samples analysed for $CaCO_3$ content off the nearshore environments off Goa indicate high carbonate content (60–90%), attributable to the rich benthic fauna and shell fragments in the area.

Shankaranaraya Guptha (1979) used the degree of shell fragmentation, colour of skeletal fragments, and colouration of benthic foraminifera of carbonate sediments for inference of submerged terraces at the depths of –65, –75, –85, and –92 m in the region off Ratnagiri, which indicated different phases of eustatic sea levels. However, in the eastern continental shelf south of Andhra Pradesh, such studies are totally partial in the shelf environment.

In the present study, the calcium carbonate content determined for all the 17 surface samples in the Pazhverkadu Pulicat lagoon ranges from 6% to 16.5% (Table 16.3 and Figure 16.3). In the study area, the presence of $CaCO_3$ in the sediments has no impact on the distribution of Ostracoda as it is not showing any relationship with the standing crop of the Ostracoda.

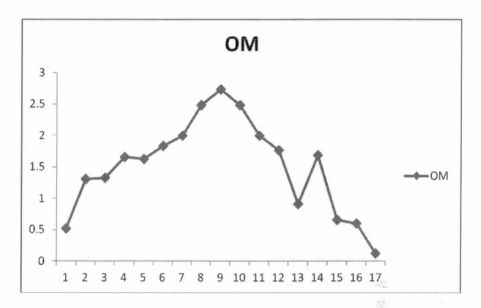

Figure 16.2. Distribution of organic matter in the surface
samples in Pazhaverkadu (Pulicat lagoon).

Substrate

The nature of bottom sediments—such as grain size, sorting coefficient, and the presence or absence of bottom vegetation—has an impact on the distribution of foraminifera. Rasheed and Ragothaman (1978), on the basis of foraminifer's studies, stated that silty sand and sandy, silty clay are more favourable for the abundance of living populations in the inner shelf sediments off Porto Novo.

Venkatesh Prabu et al. (1997) analysed the textural characteristics of nearshore sediments off Hannovar, south-west coast of India, and opined that the transportation agencies were incapable of separating the sediments into different size grades. Rajamanickam and Gujar (1997) collected 256 sediment samples, and based on detailed studies on textural parameters, they described the possible changes in the depositional environments on the nearshore sediments of Jaigad, Maharashtra. Puri (1966) stated that the nature of bottom sediments—such as grain size, sorting coefficient, and the presence or absence of bottom vegetation—affects the distribution of ostracods. Consequently, diverse sedimentary facies support distinct ostracod assemblages. According to

Annapurna and Rama Sarma (1982), ostracods prefer areas high in sand and clay rather than areas rich in silt, as in the Bimili backwaters and Balacheruvu tidal stream. Similar relationship has also been observed in marine marginal water bodies of other localities (Elofson, 1941, Benson 1959).

Buzas (1965) stated that since clay-size particles tend to bind the organic matter, the clay content of the sediment is considered to be an important factor for the distribution and quantity of benthonic organisms, and in Long Island Sound, where the silt and clay content of the sediment is less than 2%, there are usually no foraminifera. However, Murray (1968) found no obvious correlation between the nature of substrate and the composition of living fauna, in Christchurch Harbour area.

Rasheed and Ragothaman (1978), while dealing with foraminiferal studies in the inner shelf sediments off Porto Novo, stated that silty sand and sandy, silty clay are more favourable for the abundance of living population. The substrate sediment texture has a control on the kind of ostracod fauna that can colonize a particular sediment type (Brasier 1980). The texture stability of sediment composing the substrate exerts a strong influence on marine ostracods.

In the present work, an attempt has also been made to bring out the relationship between the substrate and Ostracoda population and to evaluate the congenial sediment type for the standing crop of Ostracoda for the present area of study. The relative abundance of sand, silt, and clay in the sediments for each of the 17 surface sediment samples has been estimated. The sand, silt, and clay ratios for the surface sediments samples range from 9.1% to 98.2%, 90.5% to 1.5%, and 0.1% to 0.3% respectively (Table 16.3). Trefethen's (1950) textural nomenclature has been used to describe the sediment types of the present area. Considering the possible sediment types of Trefethen (1950), the substrate of the Pazhaverkadu (Pulicat) samples consists of sand, silt, sandy silt, and silty sand (Figure 16.4).

Carapace–Valve Ratio

In recent years, the utility of statistical data on Ostracoda, such as juveniles and adults, closed and isolated valves, males and females, right and left valves, smooth and ornamented forms, besides colour variation, pyritization, and predation, to interpret the environment of deposition and rate of deposition and to assess the potentiality of sediments as source rocks for hydrocarbons has attained importance. The carapaces in ostracods open up, and intense bacterial activity separates the valves. In an environment where deposition of the sediment is low, the carapaces are likely to open up by bacterial action. But in an environment where deposition is very rapid, the carapaces will sink into the soft bottom and will be quickly covered by sediments. Thus, the carapaces will have less chances of opening up after the destruction of muscles and ligaments.

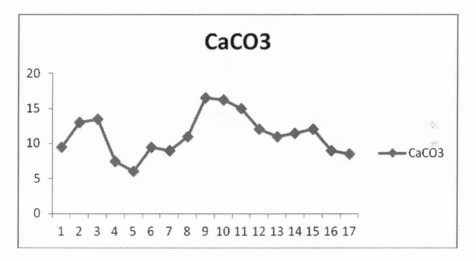

Figure 16.3. Distribution of CaCO$_3$ in the surface samples in Pazhaverkadu (Pulicat lagoon).

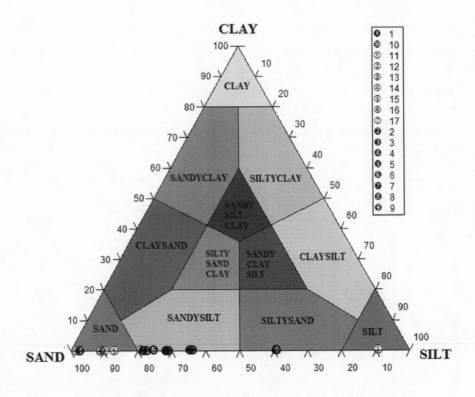

Figure 16.4. Trilinear plots of sand, silt, and clay ratios of surface samples of Pazhaverkadu (Pulicat lagoon) (after Trefethen 1950).

Table 16.3 Estimated percentage values of CaCO$_3$, OM, sand, silt, and clay of surface sediment samples of Pazhaverkadu (Pulicat lagoon), Tamil Nadu

S. No.	CaCO$_3$ (%)	OM (%)	Sand (%)	Silt (%)	Clay (%)	Ostracod population
1	9.5	0.52	71.8	28.0	0.1	26
2	13.0	1.31	78.4	21.4	0.1	232
3	13.5	1.33	97.0	2.8	0.1	79
4	7.5	1.66	70.9	28.9	0.1	28
5	6.0	1.63	77.2	22.6	0.1	117
6	9.5	1.83	75.1	24.5	0.2	106
7	9.0	2.0	64.6	35.0	0.3	1,168
8	11.0	2.48	63.8	35.8	0.3	1,889
9	16.5	2.73	38.9	60.7	0.2	2,323
10	16.2	2.48	39.4	60.2	0.2	1,748
11	15.0	2.0	9.1	90.5	0.3	207
12	12.0	1.76	78.9	20.7	0.2	225
13	11.0	0.91	90.8	8.9	0.1	78
14	11.5	1.69	91.1	8.6	0.1	26
15	12.0	0.66	87.0	12.7	0.1	30
16	9.0	0.6	98.2	1.5	0.1	18
17	8.5	0.12	89.8	9.9	0.1	84
Average	11.22	1.52	71.9	27.8	0.1	
Max.	16.5	2.73	98.2	90.5	0.3	
Min.	6.0	0.12	9.1	1.5	0.1	

Pokorny (1965) pioneered the usage of carapace–valve ratio to yield palaeoecological information. Oertli (1971) reviewed Pokorny's work and related the carapace–valve ratio to potential for the information of hydrocarbons. He summarized that when the ratio is high, the sedimentation is rapid, which minimizes disarticulation of carapaces into separate valves. With sufficiently rapid burial, organic matter is not absorbed by mineral particles and so retains potential for conversion into hydrocarbons. Honnappa and Venkatachalapathy (1978) studied the carapace–valve ratio to interpret the rate of deposition of sediments in the Mangalore Harbor area. They found that the occurrence of separate shells is much more in number than the closed shells (ratio being 24:1). According to them, this is indicative of a slow rate of sedimentation in more agitating waters.

From a study of the ostracod assemblages in the Pulicat lagoon sediments, Sreenivas et al. (1991) found the percentage of complete shells to be more in number when compared to the separate ones. According to them, it is an indication of comparatively rapid rate of sedimentation. While studying various aspects of ostracod assemblages in the Gulf of Mannar, off Tuticorin, Hussain et al. (2002) observed the ratio between the carapaces and open valves for evaluating the rate of sedimentation and found that the same is faster (or rapid). The ratio of carapaces to valves in the inner shelf of Gulf of Mannar has been estimated by him (Hussain et al. 2002) to be 4:1. An almost similar estimate was determined by Sridhar (1996) from the Palk Bay, where he observed the carapace to valve ratio to be 5:1, indicative of a fairly faster rate of sedimentation. Hussain and Rajeshwara Rao (1996) observed generally more number of closed carapaces than the open valves along the east coast inner shelf sediments while the number is so less from the sediments off the west coast. The above observation inferred that the rate of sedimentation is rapid in the east coast and slow in the west coast of India, which they attributed to more number of streams/rivers flowing and debouching the sediments into the Bay of Bengal. From off Karikkattukuppam, Bay of Bengal, Hussain et al. (2004) observed a slow rate of sedimentation in the study area.

In the present work, the ratio between the carapaces and open valves of Ostracoda has been taken into consideration for determining the rate of sedimentation. Among a total of 8,384 Ostracod shells recovered in the surface sample, 7,997 specimens are carapaces while the remaining 387 specimens are open valves (Table 16.4). The distribution of carapaces and open valves, for all the stations put together, reveals that the carapaces outnumbered open valves. From this observation, it may be concluded that a relatively rapid rate of sedimentation prevails in the Pazhaverkadu (Pulicat lagoon).

Table 16.4 Distribution of carapaces and open valves Ostracoda in the surface sediment samples of Pazhaverkadu (Pulicat lagoon), Tamil Nadu

S. No.	Carapace	Open valve	Total
1	22	4	26
2	222	10	232
3	77	2	79
4	28	0	28
5	106	11	117
6	92	14	106
7	1,127	41	1,168
8	1,842	47	1,889
9	2,290	33	2,323
10	1,588	160	1,748
11	172	35	207
12	213	12	225
13	77	1	78
14	23	3	26
15	27	3	30
16	15	3	18
17	76	8	84
Total	7,997	387	8,384

CONCLUSION

The taxonomy and systematics of Ostracod were dealt using treatise of Hartmann and Puri (1974). A total of 20 ostracod taxa belonging to 16 genera, 12 families, 2 superfamilies, and 2 suborders of the order Podocopida have been identified. Among these, *Cytherelloidea leroyi* belong to suborder Platycopa, and the remaining 19 species to suborder Podocopa are recorded from Pazhaverkadu (Pulicat lagoon).

Organic matter content for all the 17 surface samples ranges from 0.12% to 2.4%. The higher organic matter appears favouring the maximum population. Similarly, the calcium carbonate content in the surface sediments of Pazhaverkadu (Pulicat lagoon) ranges from 6% to 16.5%. The $CaCO_3$

in the sediments has no impact on the distribution of Ostracoda as it is not showing any relationship with the standing crop of the Ostracoda. The relative abundance of sand, silt, and clay in the sediments from each of the 17 surface sediment samples ranges from 9.1% to 98.2%, 90.5% to 1.5%, and 0.1% to 0.3% respectively, and the substrate of the Pazhaverkadu (Pulicat) samples consists of sand, silt, sandy silt, and silty sand. Among these, silty sand appears a favourable substrate for the ostracod fauna in the mangrove area. From the ratio of carapaces and open valves of Ostracoda in the present area of study, it is concluded that a comparatively rapid rate of sedimentation prevails in the Pazhaverkadu lagoon area, contributing the sediment flux mainly from the rivers Arani and Kalangi to the Pulicat lagoon.

ACKNOWLEDGEMENTS

The authors are highly thankful to UGC-CPEPA mangrove project for the financial support and to Prof. S. P. Mohan, head of the Department of Geology, University of Madras, for the facilities and SEM photomicrography.

REFERENCES

Annapurna, C., and Rama Sarma, D. V. (1982), Sediment-ostracod relationship in the Bimili backwaters and Balacheruvu tidal stream. *Proc. Ind. Acad. Sci. (Anim. Sci.)*, v. 91 (3), pp. 297–303.

Brasier, M. D. (1980), *Microfossils*, George Allen and Unwin Ltd., London, 193p.

Buzas, M. A. (1965), The distribution and abundance of foraminifera in Long Island Sound, *Smith. Misc. Coll.*, v. 149 (1), Publ. No. 4604, pp. 1–89.

Elofson, O. (1941), Zur kenntnis der marionen Ostracoden schwedens mitbesonderer Berucksichtingung des Skageraks, *Zool. Bidr. Uppsala Univ.*, v. 19, pp. 215–534.

Gaudette, H. E., Flight, W. R., Toner, L., and Folger, D. W. (1974), An inexpensive titration method for the determination of organic carbon in recent sediments, *J. Sed. Petrol.*, v. 44, pp. 249–253.

Hartmann, G., and Puri, H. S. (1974), Summary of Neontological and Palaeontological classification of Ostracoda. Mitt. Hamburg. Zool. Mus. Inst. 70: 7–73.

Honnappa and Venkatachalapathy, V. (1978), Paleoecological and ecological interpretations of sediments of Mangalore Harbour area, west coast of India, on the basis of colour variation of ostracod shells, *Curr. Sci.*, v. 47 (20), pp. 772–773.

Hussain, S. M., and Rajeshwara Rao, N. (1996), Faunal affinity, zoogeographic distribution and review on Recent Ostracoda from the east and west coasts of India, *Bull. Pure Appl. Sci.*, v. 15 (1), pp. 37–50.

S. M. Hussain, G. Ravi, S. P. Mohan, and N. Rajeshwara Rao, Recent benthic Ostracoda from the Bay of Bengal, off Karikkattukuppam (near Chennai), south-east coast of India, Implication on microenvironments. Journal of Environmental micropaleontology, Microbiology and Meiobenthology (JEMMM) (2004), vol. 1, pp. 105–121.

S. M. Hussain, S. P. Mohan, and V. Manivannan, Microenvironmental inferences of Recent benthic ostracoda from the Gulf of Mannar, off Tuticorin, south-east coast of India. *Proc. National Seminar on Management of Natural Resources* (2002), pp. 23–43.

Joy, J. A., and Clark, D. L. (1977), The distribution, ecology and systematics of the benthic ostracods of central Arctic Ocean, *Micropal.*, v. 23 (2), pp. 129–154.

Krumbein, W. C., and Pettijohn, F. J. (1938), *Manual of Sedimentary Petrography*, D. Appleton Century Co. Inc., New York, 549p.

Loring, D. H., and Nota, D. J. G. (1973), Morphology and sediments of the Gulf of St. Lawrence, *J. Fish. Res. Board Canada, Bull.*, v. 182, pp. 147.

Madhusudana Rao, Ch. and Murthy, P. S. N. (1968), Studies on the shelf sediments of the Madras coast, *Bull. Nat. Inst. Sci. India*, 38, pp. 442–448.

Murray, J. W. (1968a), The living Foraminiferida of Christchurch Harbour, England. *Micropal.*, v. 14, pp. 83–96.

Oertli, H. J. (1971), The aspects of ostracod faunas: a possible new tool in petroleum sedimentology, *Bull. Centre. Rech. Pau-SNPA*, 5, Suppl., pp. 137–151.

Pokorny, V. (1965), *Principles of Zoological Micropaleontology*, 2, Pergamon Press, London, 465 p. (Translation of German edition).

Puri, H. S. (1966), Ecologic and distribution of Recent Ostracoda, *Proc. Symp. Crustacea*, Pt. I., *Mar. Biol. Assoc. India*, Mandapam, pp. 457–495.

Rajamanickam, G. V., and Gujar, A. R. (1984), Sediment depositional environments in some bays in Central West coast of India. *Ind. Jour. of Mar. Sci.* v. 14, pp. 13–19.

Rasheed, D. A., and Ragothaman, V. (1978), Ecology and distribution of Recent foraminifera from the Bay of Bengal, off Porto Novo, Tamil Nadu State, India. *Proc. VII Indian Colloq. Micropal. Strat.*, pp. 263–298.

Shankaranaraya Guptha, M. V. (1979), Sediments of the Western continental shelf of India Environmental Significance. *Jour. Geol. Soc. India*, v. 20, pp. 107–113.

Sreenivas, K., Raju, B. N., Honappa and Reddi, K. R. (1991), Ostracoda in the estiuraine sediments, Pulicat Lake estuary, east coast of India. Jourl. Geol. Soc. India, 37 (5): 492–499.

Sridhar, S. G. D. (1996), *Ecology, distribution and systematics of Recent Ostracoda from the Palk Bay, off Rameswaram, Tamil Nadu*, Published PhD thesis, University of Madras, Chennai.

Subba Rao, M. (1960), Organic matter in marine sediments off east coast of India, *Bull. AAPG.* v. 44 (10), pp. 1705–1713.

Subba Rao, M., and Mahadevan, C. (1957), Distribution of calcium carbonate in the marine sediments off Visakhapatnam, *Geol. Dept., Andhra Univ.,* Waltair, pp. 149–152.

Sverdrup, H. V., Johnson, M. W., and Fleming, R. H. (1942), The *Oceans,* Prentice Hall, New York, 1087 p.

Trefethen, J. M. (1950), Classification of sediments. *Amer. Jour. Sci.,* v. 248, pp. 55–62.

Venkata Rao, T., and Subba Rao, M. (1974), Recent foraminifera of Suddagedda Estuary, east coast of India, *Micropal.,* v. 20 (4), pp. 398–419.

Venkatesh Prabhu, H., Hariharan, V., Katti, R. J., and Narayana, A. C. (1997), Textural characteristics of nearshore sediments of Honnavar, south-west coast of India, *Indian Jour. Mar. Sci.,* v. 26, pp. 392–394.

17 LAGENID FORAMINIFERA FROM THE INNER SHELF OFF CHENNAI, BAY OF BENGAL

N. Rajeshwara Rao
Department of Applied Geology, University of Madras, Guindy Campus, Chennai 600 025
Email: raonandamuri@gmail.com

ABSTRACT

L agenids constitute an extensive group of vitreous benthic foraminifera and are characterized primarily by the calcareous and finely perforated tests and terminal apertures. Fossil lagenid foraminiferal species are sometimes very useful and are a key biomarker for age determination and stratigraphic correlation. This is because many lagenid species have short stratigraphic ranges. It was, therefore, decided to prepare an inventory of the lagenid species (suborder Lagenina Delage and Hérouard 1896) and investigate their ecological preferences on the inner shelf off Chennai in the Bay of Bengal. In all, 56 surface sediment samples collected during October, January, April, and July were studied, lagenid species inventoried, and the 'living' and total populations counted. Accordingly, 58 species belonging to 17 genera and 7 families were identified; all of them belong to the superfamily Nodosariacea (Ehrenberg 1838). These population counts were correlated with such ecological parameters as water depth, pH, bottom water temperature (BWT), dissolved oxygen (DO), salinity, sand, silt, clay, $CaCO_3$ and organic matter (OM) contents. The results indicate that lagenids prefer muddy substrate, relatively calm conditions, and deeper parts of the inner shelf, thereby emphasizing the significance of this group of benthic foraminifers in interpreting palaeoenvironmental conditions of deposition.

INTRODUCTION

Foraminifera are single-celled organisms (protists) with exoskeletons called tests. They are abundant as fossils for the last 540 million years since they evolved during the Cambrian period. The tests are commonly divided into chambers that are added during growth, though the earliest species were simple forms that are open tubes or hollow spheres. Fully grown individuals range in size from about 100 µm to almost 20 cm long. Some species have symbiotic relationship with blue-green, green, brown, and red algae. Foraminifers are among the most abundant shelled organisms in many marine environments. There are an estimated 4,000 species living in the world's oceans and seas today. Of these, 40 species are planktic—that is, they float in the water column at different depths. The remainder lives on or in the sand, mud, rocks, and plants at the bottom of the ocean. Foraminifera are found in all marine environments, from the intertidal to the deepest ocean trenches and from the tropics to the poles, but species of foraminifera can be very particular about the environment in which they live. Some are abundant only in the deep ocean, others are found only on coral reefs, and still other species live only in brackish estuaries or intertidal salt marshes and mangroves.

As different species of foraminifera are found in different environments, they are very useful to determine palaeoenvironmental conditions. These microorganisms have thus been used to map past distributions of the tropics, locate ancient shorelines, and track global ocean temperature changes during the ice ages. Therefore, they assume considerable significance in biostratigraphy, palaeoecology, palaeobiogeography, palaeoceanography, and most importantly, oil exploration. There are many major groups of foraminifers (called suborders), and different environments are characterized by different groups of species (assemblages). The assemblage found in the littoral zone, for example, will be different from the one from the inner shelf. In this study, a particular group of benthic foraminifers belonging to the suborder Lagenina have been studied from surface sediment samples collected from the inner shelf for their systematic palaeontology, distribution, and ecology to assess their utility in palaeoenvironmental investigations.

STUDY AREA

The Bay of Bengal forms the north-eastern part of the Indian Ocean and has several interesting features. The offshore regions that lie between 8° and 22° N resemble clear blue tropical water, whereas the nearshore waters undergo seasonal cycles of colour varying from deep-blue to the greenish hue of plankton and the brown of coastal drainage (La Fond 1958). The physical and chemical properties and circulation of the surface waters of the Bay of Bengal are greatly influenced by the meteorological conditions associated with the monsoon system (Rao and Jayaraman 1968). A number of river systems that drain into the bay contribute considerably to the dilution of the waters. All these aspects make the Bay of Bengal a very complex hydrographic setting.

Based on the climatic classification on the amounts of precipitation proposed by Landsberg et al. (1966), particularly on the lengths of dry and wet seasons, the rivers that flow across the south-east Indian coast and drain into the bay are associated with land masses of climatic group V3 and V4 (tropical semi-deserts of dry climates with humid winters). In general, surface salinity distributions in the Bay of Bengal follow the seasonally changing current patterns. The low salinity tongue extending down to Visakhapatnam from the north is caused by the southward flowing coastal part of the gyre in the north-western bay. The high salinities in the southern region are caused by the northward extension of the Indian monsoon current (Varkey et al. 1996).

The subsurface waters of the bay are very uniform in all parts of the Bay of Bengal north of 5° N and can be identified as the Indian equatorial intermediate water (Gallagher 1966), which penetrates into the bay at depths greater than 100 to 150 m. In the central and southern Bay of Bengal, this water mass is present up to 1,000 m, with its temperature decreasing from 15° to 5 °C, and salinity remaining nearly constant (35.0 to 35.1‰).

METHODOLOGY

Bottom sediment and water samples were collected from 15 stations, between depths ranging from 7 to 55 m, with an interval of 1 km every three months for a period of one year, representing the four seasons— October (north-east monsoon), January (winter), April (summer), and July (south-west monsoon)—in a single transect approximately perpendicular to the coastline, off Karikkattukuppam, a few kilometres south of Chennai (Figure 17.1). Petersen grab and Nansen reversible water samplers were used for collecting sediment and water samples respectively. Sediment samples could not be collected at the fourth station due to underlying rock exposures that rendered the grab ineffective. Thus, 56 bottom sediment samples and 60 water samples (from the sediment–water interface) were obtained for the entire period. Sediment samples were preserved in a mixture of one part of buffered formalin in nine parts of water (4% solution) with a pinch of calcium chloride to achieve neutrality (Walker et al. 1974). Water samples were preserved by adding a few millilitres of chloroform (Newcombe et al. 1939).

Bottom water temperature and pH were measured on board, the former from the built-in thermometer in the water sampler and the latter using an ELICO portable water quality analyser. Salinity was estimated using the standard titration method and equation proposed by Knudsen (1901). Dissolved oxygen was determined UV-spectrophotometrically (Duval et al. 1974). Calcium carbonate and organic matter in the sediment samples were estimated, adopting methodology after Loring and Rantala (1992) and Gaudette et al. (1974) respectively. Sand, silt, and clay percentages were computed from a combination of sieving and pipette procedures, the latter in accordance with Krumbein and Pettijohn (1938) (tables 17.1a to 1d).

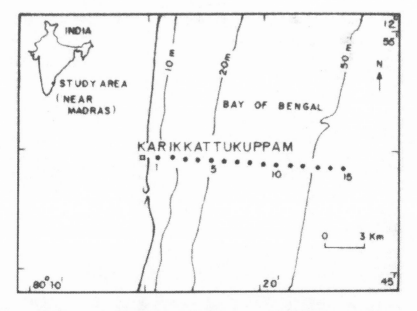

Figure 17.1. Map of the study area showing the sample locations.

The preserved sediment samples were subjected to the rose bengal staining technique, first described by Walton (1952), in order to differentiate the 'living' from the dead foraminifera. In spite of its limitations, the rose bengal technique is still widely employed as it is not as cumbersome as other staining techniques (Murray 1991); moreover, staining in tests of agglutinated species is easily recognized if rose bengal is used (Bernhard 1988). Foraminiferal tests were separated from the residue using carbon tetrachloride as the floatation reagent (Cushman 1959). The residue after floatation was checked for tests that might have escaped floatation using a Nikon stereomicroscope. The separated tests were subsequently hand-picked using a .00 Winsor–Newton sable hairbrush.

The hand-picked faunal specimens from each sample (25 ml of wet sediment) were transferred to 24-chambered micropalaeontological slides and mounted over a thin layer of gum tragacanth according to the family, genus, and species wherever possible. The different genera and species were identified; type specimens of each species were selected and transferred to round punch microfaunal slides with cover slips. Later they were mounted on brass stubs (1 cm in diameter) using a double-sided adhesive carbon tape and coated with gold for about three to four minutes (JEOL JFC-1100E ion-sputtering device) to render the surface of the foraminiferal tests conductive for scanning. To obtain lucid illustrations, microphotographs of different views of all the foraminiferal species present were taken using a scanning electron microscope (JEOL JSM-5300) with camera attachment (JEOL MP-35051, Asahi Pentax SF-7, Nova FP-4-125 black-and-white film).

Table 1a Ecological parameters of the samples (water and sediment) from off Chennai – NE Monsoon

	STATION NUMBERS														
Water	1	2	3	4	5	6	7	8	9	10	11	12	13	14	15
Depth (m)	7	10	14	18	21	24	28	34	38	41	45	48	51	53	55
pH	8.4	8.3	8.3	8.4	8.3	8.3	8.4	8.3	8.3	8.3	8.4	8.4	8.4	8.4	8.4
BWT (°C)	24.9	24.9	24.8	24.6	24.6	24.6	24.6	24.5	24.5	24.4	24.4	24.4	24.3	24.2	24.2
Salinity ‰	32.6	32.2	32.9	33.1	32.8	32.9	32.9	32.8	32.9	32.8	32.9	32.5	32.8	32.9	32.6
DO (ml/L)	4.8	4.7	5.1	5.3	5.2	5.3	5.3	5.4	5.1	5.2	5.2	5.0	5.1	5.3	5.3
Sediment				*** Sample could not be collected due to rocky bottom											
OM (%)	0.9	1.0	0.8	***	0.9	1.0	0.9	1.2	1.1	1.3	1.2	1.3	1.4	1.5	1.7
CaCO₃ (%)	3.1	3.4	3.0	***	3.3	3.4	3.5	3.9	4.1	4.2	4.1	4.4	4.3	4.4	4.6
Sand (%)	47.0	17.0	96.0	***	97.5	96.5	95.0	95.0	89.0	81.0	76.0	64.0	21.5	11.5	24.5
Silt (%)	51.5	79.0	3.5	***	2.0	3.0	4.0	3.5	6.5	14.0	18.5	28.5	73.5	83.0	68.0
Clay (%)	1.5	4.0	0.5	***	0.5	0.5	1.0	1.5	4.5	5.0	5.5	7.5	5.0	5.5	7.5

Table 1b Ecological parameters of the samples (water and sediment) from off Chennai – Winter

	STATION NUMBERS														
Water	1	2	3	4	5	6	7	8	9	10	11	12	13	14	15
Depth (m)	7	10	14	18	21	24	28	34	38	41	45	48	51	53	55
pH	8.2	8.1	8.2	8.2	8.3	8.3	8.2	8.3	8.2	8.3	8.3	8.3	8.2	8.3	8.2
BWT (°C)	24.1	24.1	24.0	24.0	23.9	23.9	23.8	23.7	23.7	23.6	23.6	23.6	23.5	23.5	23.4
Salinity ‰	31.5	31.2	31.9	31.6	31.7	31.6	31.7	31.5	31.7	31.6	31.1	31.9	31.4	32.2	32.0
DO (ml/L)	2.7	3.3	3.1	3.1	3.2	3.0	3.1	3.2	3.1	3.2	3.2	3.3	3.2	3.2	3.2
Sediment				*** Sample could not be collected due to rocky bottom											
OM (%)	1.3	1.9	1.3	***	1.8	2.0	2.1	2.3	2.4	2.9	3.2	3.1	3.0	3.3	3.5
CaCO₃ (%)	2.5	3.2	2.6	***	2.8	2.9	3.1	2.8	3.2	3.4	3.3	3.5	3.4	3.3	3.4
Sand (%)	55.5	20.0	97.5	***	96.0	95.5	94.0	93.5	91.0	78.0	73.0	66.0	24.5	14.0	23.0
Silt (%)	42.0	75.5	2.0	***	2.5	3.0	4.0	4.0	6.0	16.0	21.5	28.5	71.0	79.5	71.5
Clay (%)	2.5	4.5	0.5	***	1.5	1.5	2.0	2.5	3.0	6.0	5.5	5.5	4.5	6.5	5.5

Table 1c Ecological parameters of the samples (water and sediment) from off Chennai – Summer

Water	1	2	3	4	5	6	7	8	9	10	11	12	13	14	15
STATION NUMBERS															
Depth (m)	7	10	14	18	21	24	28	34	38	41	45	48	51	53	55
pH	8.6	8.5	8.5	8.6	8.6	8.6	8.5	8.6	8.6	8.6	8.5	8.6	8.6	8.6	8.6
BWT (°C)	28.6	28.5	28.6	28.5	28.3	28.3	28.2	28.0	27.9	27.9	27.7	27.7	27.6	27.6	27.5
Salinity ‰	34.9	35.2	35.8	35.2	35.1	35.1	35.2	34.8	35.1	34.9	35.1	35.2	35.2	35.1	35.2
DO (ml/L)	8.4	8.5	8.5	8.6	8.6	8.6	8.7	8.6	8.7	8.6	8.7	8.7	8.6	8.7	8.7
Sediment															
OM (%)	0.4	0.5	0.4	***	0.5	0.5	0.4	0.5	0.5	0.5	0.6	0.7	0.8	0.8	1.0
CaCO₃ (%)	5.5	5.3	5.5	***	5.6	5.5	5.6	5.9	6.1	6.2	6.5	6.6	7.0	6.8	7.2
Sand (%)	50.5	19.0	97.5	***	98.0	96.0	96.0	95.0	80.5	76.5	66.0	52.5	13.5	5.0	20.5
Silt (%)	47.5	77.5	1.5	***	1.5	2.5	3.0	3.5	14.0	17.5	25.5	41.0	78.5	85.5	66.5
Clay (%)	2.0	3.5	1.0	***	0.5	1.5	1.0	1.5	5.5	6.0	8.5	6.5	8.0	9.5	13.0

*** Sample could not be collected due to rocky bottom

Table 1d Ecological parameters of the samples (water and sediment) from off Chennai – SW Monsoon

Water	1	2	3	4	5	6	7	8	9	10	11	12	13	14	15
STATION NUMBERS															
Depth (m)	7	10	14	18	21	24	28	34	38	41	45	48	51	53	55
pH	8.4	8.3	8.5	8.4	8.5	8.4	8.5	8.5	8.4	8.5	8.4	8.5	8.5	8.5	8.5
BWT (°C)	26.1	25.8	26.0	26.0	25.9	25.9	26.0	25.9	25.8	25.7	25.7	25.5	25.5	25.2	25.2
Salinity ‰	33.1	32.9	33.5	33.6	33.9	33.6	33.8	33.5	33.6	33.9	33.9	33.5	33.8	34.1	33.6
DO (ml/L)	6.3	6.4	6.4	6.5	6.4	6.5	6.5	6.5	6.6	6.7	6.7	6.8	6.7	6.7	6.8
Sediment															
OM (%)	0.5	0.5	0.4	***	0.6	0.7	0.6	0.7	0.8	0.8	1.0	0.8	1.0	1.0	1.2
CaCO₃ (%)	4.6	4.4	4.7	***	5.0	5.3	5.0	5.2	5.3	5.9	6.1	6.2	6.1	5.8	5.9
Sand (%)	58.0	22.5	96.0	***	96.5	95.0	94.5	92.0	84.0	80.5	72.0	61.5	15.0	10.0	26.0
Silt (%)	39.0	72.5	2.5	***	2.0	3.5	3.0	5.5	12.5	13.5	21.0	32.0	77.5	83.0	64.5
Clay (%)	3.0	5.0	1.5	***	1.5	1.5	2.5	2.5	3.5	6.0	7.0	6.5	7.5	7.0	9.5

*** Sample could not be collected due to rocky bottom

BRIEF SYSTEMATIC PALAEONTOLOGY

The widely utilized classification proposed by Loeblich and Tappan (1987) was followed in the present study. A species has been regarded as the sum total of specimens sharing all test characters, with such measurable, countable, or otherwise observable variation in size and shape of some elements or of proportions between the latter in different ontogenic stages, which fits a pattern of normal distribution and whereby these specimens are separable from other similar groupings regarded as distinct species (Hottinger et al. 1993). In a relatively few cases, subspecies have been recognized that is assemblages of specimens differing from the typical species in a minor but recognizable modification of a test character, like ornamentation and chamber inflation, especially if there is an overlap between the subspecies and if they occur both together and separately in different samples. The identification of the species recorded in this study is based on comparison with the Catalogue of Foraminifera by Ellis and Messina (1940 onwards), and innumerable publications/atlases from several parts of the world.

There are 58 species belonging to the suborder Lagenina (Delage and Hérouard 1896) and the superfamily Nodosariacea (Ehrenberg 1838) identified; these belong to 17 genera and 7 families. The list of synonymies has been restricted to original citations, and descriptions have been given only for those species that are considered new. Their brief systematic palaeontology is given below:

Order: Foraminiferida (Eichwald 1830)
Suborder: Lagenina (Delage and Hérouard 1896)
Superfamily: Nodosaricea (Ehrenberg 1838)
Family: Nodosariidae (Ehrenberg 1838)
Subfamily: Nodosariinae (Ehrenberg 1838)
Genus: *Laevidentalina* (Loeblich and Tappan 1986)
Laevidentalina communis (d'Orbigny 1826)
Original citation: *Nodosaria (Dentalina) communis* (D'Orbigny 1826, vol. 7, p. 254, no. 35).

Laevidentalina filiformis (d'Orbigny 1826)
Original citation: *Nodosaria filiformis* (D'Orbigny 1826, vol. 7, p. 235, no. 14).

Laevidentalina ittai (Loeblich and Tappan 1953)
Original citation: *Dentalina ittai* (Loeblich and Tappan 1953, vol. 121, no. 7, p. 56, pl. 10, figs 10–12).

Genus: *Nodosaria* (Lamarck 1812)
Nodosaria catenulata (Brady 1884)
Original citation: *Nodosaria catenulata* (Brady 1884, vol. 9, p. 134, pl. 63, figs 32, 33).

Nodosaria catesbyi (d'Orbigny 1839)
Original citation: *Nodosaria* (*Nodosaria*) *catesbyi* (D'Orbigny 1839, v. 7, p. 16, pl. 11, figs 8–10).

Nodosaria radicula var. *glanduliniformis* (Dervieux 1893)
Original citation: *Nodosaria radicula* (Linne) var. *glanduliniformis* (Dervieux 1893, v. 12; 1894, p. 599).

Nodosaria cf. *vertebralis* (Batsch 1791)
Original citation: *Nautilus* (*Orthoceras*) *vertebralis* (Batsch 1791, pp. 1–2, figs 6a, b).

Genus: *Pyramidulina* (Fornasini 1894)
Pyramidulina catesbyi (d'Orbigny 1839)
Original citation: *Nodosaria catesbyi* (D'Orbigny 1839, p. 16, pl. 1, figs 8–10).

Family: Vaginulinidae (Reuss 1860)
Subfamily: Lenticulininae (Chapman, Parr and Collins 1934)
Genus: *Lenticulina* (Lamarck 1804)
Lenticulina calcar (Linnaeus 1758)
Original citation: *Nautilus calcar* (Linnaeus 1758, v. 1, p. 709).

Lenticulina gibba (d'Orbigny 1826)
Original citation: *Cristellaria gibba* (D'Orbigny 1826, p. 292, no. 17; 1839a, p. 40, pl. 7, figs 20, 21).

Lenticulina limbosa (Reuss 1863)
Original citation: *Cristellaria* (*Robulina*) *limbosa* (Reuss 1863, v. 48, p. 55, pl. 6, figs 69a, b).

Lenticulina macrodiscus (Cushman 1948)
Original citation: *Lenticulina macrodiscus* (Cushman 1948, pl. 20, fig. 1).

Family: Lagenidae (Reuss 1862)
Genus: *Lagena* (Walker and Jacob 1798)
Lagena acuticosta (Reuss 1861)
Original citation: *Lagena acuticosta* (Reuss 1861, v. 44, pt. 1, p. 305, pl. 1, fig 4).

Lagena annulopeculiaris sp. nov.

Description: The unilocular test is globular and flask-shaped with a slender, slightly tapering neck and a truncated aboral end. The calcareous wall is hyaline, and the test surface is ornamented by about 18 to 20 costae that do not continue over the entire length of the test but are terminated at the point where the chamber attains its maximum diameter. The aperture is terminal, and the neck is furnished by about 12 to 14 well-developed annuli.

Remarks: The most remarkable feature of this species is the presence of an exquisitely decorated neck that possesses at least a dozen well-developed annuli. This species is similar to *Lagena peculiariformis* in having longitudinal costae (almost the same number) and annuli on the neck. However, it differs from the latter in having costae that are terminated at the point where the test attains its greatest diameter, in having a truncated aboral end, in possessing more number of annuli on the neck that are more closely spaced, and in the absence of a polygonal collar.

Etymology: after the nature and number of annuli on the neck
Type level: Recent
Type locality: off Karikkattukuppam, at depths between 34 and 55 m
Holotype: 0.38 mm in length, 0.21 mm in diameter
Paratype: 0.36 mm in length, 0.19 mm in diameter
Repository: NRR–AG–182

Lagena blomae (Albani and Yassini 1989)
Original citation: *Lagena blomae* (Albani and Yassini 1989, v. 40, p. 377).

Lagena doveyensis (Haynes 1973)
Original citation: *Lagena doveyensis* HAYNES 1973, p. 82, pl. 12, figs 7, 8.

Lagena interrupta (Williamson 1848)
Original citation: *Lagena striata* (Montagu) var. *interrupta* (Williamson 1848, v. 1, p. 14, pl. 1, fig. 7).

Lagena laevis (Montagu 1803)
Original citation: *Vermiculum laeve* (Montagu 1803, p. 524).

Lagena cf. *oceanica* (Albani 1974)
Original citation: *Lagena oceanica* (Albani 1974, pp. 37–38, pl. 1, figs 7–11).

Lagena ovoidea sp. nov.

Description: The unilocular test is perfectly ovoid in shape and tapers to a long, slender neck which is almost cylindrical. The calcareous, hyaline test is smooth and unornamented except in the aboral region where a few faint costae are seen. The costae end at the point where the test attains its greatest diameter. The aboral region is rounded. The aperture is terminal, rounded, and without a lip.

Remarks: Sufficient number of specimens of this form has been obtained, and all of them consistently exhibit the characteristic ovoid shape, faint costae that terminate at the point where the test attains its greatest diameter, and the long, slender, cylindrical neck with a terminal aperture without a lip.

Etymology: after the typical shape of the test
Type level: Recent
Type locality: off Karikkattukuppam, at depths between 24 and 55 m
Holotype: 0.28 mm in length, 0.13 mm in diameter
Paratype: 0.27 mm in length, 0.13 mm in diameter
Repository: NRR–AG–188

Lagena pacifica (Sidebottom 1912)
Original citation: *Lagena pacifica* (Sidebottom 1912, p. 398, pl. 16, fig 29).

Lagena perlucida (Montagu 1803)
Original citation: *Vermiculum perlucidum* (Montagu 1803, p. 525, pl. 14, fig 3).

Lagena scalariata sp. nov.

Description: The unilocular test is globular and flask-shaped, tapering to a rather short neck. The aboral end is rounded. The calcareous, hyaline wall is smooth and unornamented, except in the oral region, where the neck is furnished by several scaly secretions of irregular size and shape, one below the other. The aperture is terminal and rounded, with a thick rim but without an everted lip.

Remarks: The perfect globular shape of the chamber, the lack of any ornamentation on the test, and the typical scaly neck are the characteristic features of this species. This species is quite rare in the inner shelf sediments off Karikkattukuppam.

Etymology: after the scaly nature of the neck.
Type level: Recent
Type locality: off Karikkattukuppam, at depths between 34 and 55 m.
Holotype: 0.25 mm in length, 0.18 mm in diameter
Paratype: 0.24 mm in length, 0.17 mm in diameter
Repository: NRR–AG–191

Lagena setigera (Millett 1901)
Original citation: *Lagena clavata* (d'Orbigny) var. *setigera* MILLETT 1901, p. 491, pl. 8, figs 9a, b.

Lagena cf. *spiratiformis* (McCulloch 1981)
Original citation: *Lagena spiratiformis* (McCulloch 1981, p. 96, pl. 32, figs 15–16).

Lagena striata (d'Orbigny 1839)
Original citation: *Oolina striata* (d'Orbigny 1839, p. 21, pl. 5, fig. 12).

Lagena striatapaucistriata (Yassini and Jones 1995)
Original citation: *Lagena striatapaucistriata* (Yassini and Jones 1995, p. 106, figs 323–325).

Lagena striata var. *strumosa* (Reuss 1858)
Original citation: *Lagena strumosa* (Reuss 1858, v. 10, p. 434).

Lagena substriata (Williamson 1848)
Original citation: *Lagena substriata* (Williamson 1848, v. 1, p. 15, pl. 2, fig. 12).

Lagena sulcata var. *interrupta* (Williamson 1848)
Original citation: *Lagena striata* (Montagu) var. *interrupta* (Williamson 1848, v. 1, p. 14, pl. 1, fig. 7).

Lagena sulcata var. *peculiaris* (Cushman and McCulloch 1950)
Original citation: *Lagena sulcata* (Walker and Jacob) var. *peculiaris* (Cushman and McCulloch 1950, v. 6, p. 361, pl. 48, figs 11–13).

Lagena sulcata var. *spicata* (Cushman and McCulloch 1950)
Original citation: *Lagena sulcata* (Walker and Jacob) var. *spicata* (Cushman and McCulloch 1950, v. 6, no. 6, p. 360).

Lagena torquata sp. nov.

Description: The unilocular test is globular and flask-shaped. The aboral region is rounded. The calcareous, hyaline wall is smooth and unornamented, except in the oral region where the short neck exhibits a twisted appearance. The aperture is terminal and consists of a rounded opening with a fairly thick everted lip.

Remarks: The characteristic feature of this species is the peculiar twisted appearance of the neck as if a torque action has been imparted to it. This species is rare in the bottom sediments of the inner shelf off Karikkattukuppam.

Etymology: after the twisted nature of the neck, as if due to torque action
Type level: Recent
Type locality: off Karikkattukuppam, at depths between 45 and 55 m
Holotype: 0.23 mm in length, 0.14 mm in diameter
Paratype: 0.24mm in length, 0.13 mm in diameter
Repository: NRR–AG–201

Genus: *Procerolagena* (Puri 1954)
Procerolagena distomapolita (Parker and Jones 1865)
Original citation: *Lagena sulcata* (Walker and Jacob) var. *distomapolita* (Parker and Jones 1865, v. 155, p. 357, pl. 13, fig. 21; pl. 18, fig. 8).

Procerolagena elongata (Ehrenberg 1844)
Original citation: *Miliomilidaelongata* (Ehrenberg 1844, p. 274, pl. 25, fig. 1).

Procerolagena gracillima (Seguenza 1862)
Original citation: *Amphorinagracillima* (Seguenza 1862, p. 51, pl. 1, fig. 37).

Genus: *Pygmaeoseistron* (Patterson and Richardson 1987)
Pygmaeoseistron hispidulum (Cushman 1913)
Original citation: *Lagena hispidula* (Cushman 1913, p. 14, pl. 5, figs 2, 3).

Family: Polymorphinidae (d'Orbigny 1839)
Subfamily: Polymorphininae (d'Orbigny 1839)
Genus: *Globulina* (d'Orbigny 1839)
Globulina gibba (d'Orbigny 1826)
Original citation: *Polymorphina* (*Globulina*) *gibba* (d'Orbigny 1826, v. 7, p. 266; figured by d'Orbigny 1846, pl. 13, figs 13, 14).

Globulina minuta (Roemer 1838)
Original citation: *Globulina minuta* (Roemer), in Cushman and Ozawa 1930, v. 77, art. 6, p. 83.

Genus: *Guttulina* (d'Orbigny 1839)
Guttulina pacifica (Cushman and Ozawa 1928)
Original citation: *Sigmoidella* (*Sigmoidina*) *pacifica* (Cushman and Ozawa 1928, v. 4, p. 19, pl. 2, fig. 13).

Genus: *Sigmoidella* (Cushman and Ozawa 1928)
Sigmoidella elegantissima (Parker and Jones 1865)
Original citation: *Polymorphina elegantissima* (Parker and Jones 1865, v. 155, p. 438).

Family: Ellipsolagenidae (A. Silvestri 1923)
Subfamily: Oolininae (Loeblich and Tappan 1961)
Genus: *Favulina* (Patterson and Richardson 1987)
Favulina hexagona (Williamson 1848)
Original citation: *Entosolenia squamosa* (Montagu) var. *hexagona* (Williamson 1848, v. 1, p. 20, pl. 2, fig. 23; 1858, p. 13, pl. 1, fig. 31).

Genus: *Oolina* (d'Orbigny 1839)
Oolina cf. *botelliformis* (Brady 1881)
Original citation: *Oolina botelliformis* (Brady), in Barker 1960, pl. 56, fig. 6.

Oolina globosa (Montagu 1803)
Original citation: *Vermiculum globosum* (Montagu 1803, p. 523).

Oolina laevigata (d'Orbigny 1839)
Original citation: *Oolina laevigata* (d'Orbigny 1839, v. 5, pt. 5, p. 18).

Oolina ovoidea (Yassini and Jones 1995)
Original citation: *Oolina ovoidea* (Yassini and Jones 1995, p. 113, fig 381).

Genus: *Vasicostella* (Patterson and Richardson 1987)
Vasicostella inflatiperforata (McCulloch 1977)
Original citation: *Lagenosolenia inflatiperforata* (McCulloch 1977, p. 62, pl. 64, fig. 28).

Subfamily: Ellipsolageninae (A. Silvestri 1923)
Genus: *Fissurina* (Reuss 1850)
Fissurina annectens (Burrows and Holland 1895)
Original citation: *Lagena annectens* (Burrows and Holland 1895, pt. 2, p. 203, pl. 7, figs 11a, b).

Fissurina cucullata (Silvestri 1902)
Original citation: *Fissurina cucullata* (Silvestri 1902, p. 146, figs 23–25).

Fissurina laevigata (Reuss 1850)
Original citation: *Fissurina laevigata* (Reuss 1850, p. 366, pl. 46, fig. 1).

Fissurina marginato-perforata (Seguenza 1880)
Original citation: *Lagena marginato-perforata* (Seguenza 1880, p. 332, pl. 17, fig. 34).

Fissurina quadrata (Williamson 1858)
Original citation: *Lagena quadrata* (Williamson 1858, p. 11, pl. 1, figs 27, 28).

Fissurina quiltyi (Albani and Yassini 1989)
Original citation: *Fissurina quiltyi* (Albani and Yassini 1989, v. 40, p. 398, figs 6i–j).

Genus: *Pseudoolina* (R. W. Jones 1984)
Pseudoolina fissurinea (Jones 1984)
Original citation: *Pseudoolina fissurinea* (Jones 1984, p. 119, pl. 4, figs 19, 20).

Family: Glandulinidae (Reuss 1860)
Subfamily: Glandulininae (Reuss 1860)
Genus: *Glandulina* (d'Orbigny 1839)

Glandulina glans (d'Orbigny 1826)
Original citation: *Nodosaria* (*Glandulina*) *glans* (d'Ordigny 1826, p. 252, model no. 51).

Glandulina laevigata (d'Orbigny 1839)
Original citation: *Nodosaria* (*Glandulina*) *laevigata* (d'Ordigny 1839, v. 7, p. 252, pl. 10, figs 1–3).

Glandulina spinata (Cushman 1935)
Original citation: *Glandulina spinata* (Cushman 1935, v. 91, no. 21, p. 8, pl. 3, figs 8, 9).

Genus: *Globulotuba* (Collins 1958)
Globulotuba entosoleniformis (Collins 1958)
Original citation: *Globulotuba entosoleniformis* (Collins 1958, p. 385, pl. 4, fig. 5).

RESULTS AND DISCUSSION

Lagenid Populations—NE Monsoon

Of the 58 lagenid species identified for all the four seasons, 46 were observed to occur during NE monsoon, out of which 26 were found to be 'living' in the 14 surface sediment samples; the tests of the remaining 20 taxa were unstained by rose bengal and, hence, were considered dead at the time of sampling. The most abundant species was *Fissurina cucullata*, followed by *Lagena* cf. *spiratiformis*, *Lagena striata* var. *strumosa*, *Lagena striata*, *Lagena ovoidea* sp. nov., *Glandulina spinata*, *Nodosaria catesbyi*, *Lagena annulopeculiaris* sp. nov., *Pseudoolina fissurinea*, and *Glandulina laevigata*. These 10 species accounted for 73.7% of the total lagenid population of 670 tests.

Lagenid Populations—Winter

During winter period, it was observed that tests of 40 species were present, indicating reduced lagenid species diversity when compared to NE monsoon. Among these, only 7 taxa were found in 'living' condition while the tests of as many as 33 species were not stained. The overall populations were also found to be much less compared with the earlier sampling period. The populations were so low that 10 or more tests (total populations) were counted only in the following species: *Fissurina cucullata*, *Nodosaria catesbyi*, *Glandulina spinata*, *Lagena perlucida*, and *Pseudoolina fissurinea*. These 5 taxa accounted for exactly 50% of the total lagenid population numbering 240 tests.

Lagenid Populations—Summer

Of the 58 lagenid species identified for all the four seasons, as many as 55 were observed to occur during summer, out of which 29 were found to be 'living' in the 14 surface sediment samples; the tests of the remaining 26 taxa were unstained by rose bengal and, hence, were considered dead at the time of sampling. The most abundant species was again *Fissurina cucullata*, followed by *Lagena setigera*, *Lagena ovoidea* sp. nov., *Lagena striata* var. *strumosa*, *Lagena striata*, *Pseudoolina fissurinea*, *Glandulina laevigata*, *Glandulina spinata*, *Nodosaria catesbyi*, and *Lagena annulopeculiaris* sp. nov. These 10 species accounted for ~70% of the total lagenid population of 1,639 tests.

Lagenid Populations—SW Monsoon

In the SW monsoon period, it was observed that tests of 49 species were present, indicating reduced lagenid species diversity when compared to NE monsoon. Among these, 23 taxa were found in 'living' condition while the tests of 26 species were not stained. The overall populations were found to be slightly less compared with the earlier sampling period but very much higher than the counts for NE monsoon and winter. The most abundant species was again *Fissurina cucullata*, followed by *Lagena setigera*, *Lagena striata* var. *strumosa*, *Lagena ovoidea* sp. nov., *Lagena striata*, *Nodosaria catesbyi*, *Pseudoolina fissurinea*, *Lagena perlucida*, *Glandulina laevigata*, and *Glandulina spinata*. These 10 species accounted for 73.9% of the total lagenid population numbering 1,319 tests. The order of abundance was observed to be more or less similar to that of the summer season.

Ecological Consideration

The pH values for all the four seasons were in a range of 8.1 to 8.6, the least being in winter and highest during summer. As per the general trend, below water temperature (BWT) was comparatively lower in NE monsoon and winter than during the summer and SW monsoon and generally decreased with the increase in depth. Similarly, the salinity values were also higher during these latter seasons as the rate of evaporation is enhanced during this part of the year; the highest range was in summer. Dissolved oxygen values were, however, slightly higher in SW monsoon than in summer; they were in a lower range during the NE monsoon and winter. On the other hand, organic matter content was higher during the NE monsoon and winter than in summer and SW monsoon. In general, however, the OM values were higher at greater depths, particularly in the samples that had increased mud content (silt + clay). This positive correlation between the mud content and organic matter has been reported by several earlier workers. For example, Burone et al. (2003) analysed the organic matter content in 101 surface sediment samples from the Ubatuba Bay, Brazil, and used Pearson correlation, regression, and principal component analysis (PCA) to analyse the data. They observed strong correlations between organic matter and fine sediment fractions. Calcium carbonate contents showed trends very much similar to salinity, being higher during the relatively hotter months, with the highest range in summer. The sand-silt-clay contents reveal that, irrespective of the season, the mud content increases generally with depth, particularly in the range between 38 and 55 m (figures 17.2a–d).

Both living and total lagenid populations are much higher in summer and SW monsoon than in NE monsoon and winter. Similar observations were made by Manivannan et al. (1996), who attributed higher benthic foraminiferal populations during the summer to increased DO and $CaCO_3$ contents and stated that the latter parameter was the major factor controlling the foraminiferal populations in the Gulf of Mannar, off Tuticorin. However, the spatial distributions of lagenid populations exhibit a considerable increase, particularly in the depth range of 38 to 55 m during all the four seasons, the same depth range of increased mud content (figures 17.3a–d). The nearshore area constitutes a dynamic environment and is more suited to species that are robust and to those that adopt an attached mode of life. In the study area, lagenids are very poorly represented or not present at all. Their considerably enhanced populations in the samples collected from a water depth range of 38 to 55 m reveal that these smaller and more-fragile taxa prefer calmer and comparatively deeper waters, with a definite preference for muddy substrates.

Figure 17.2 a – d Sand-Silt-Clay variation with depth

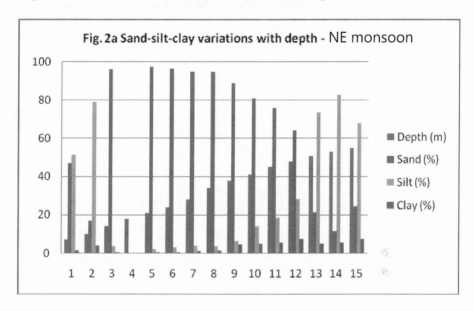

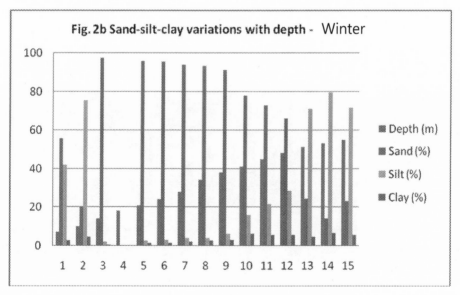

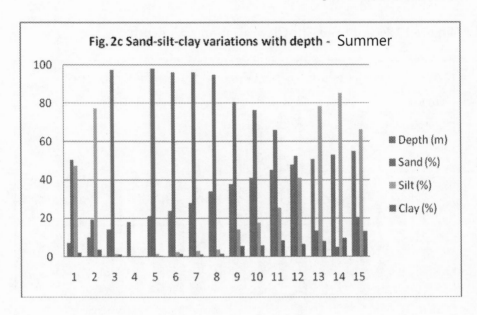

Fig. 2c Sand-silt-clay variations with depth - Summer

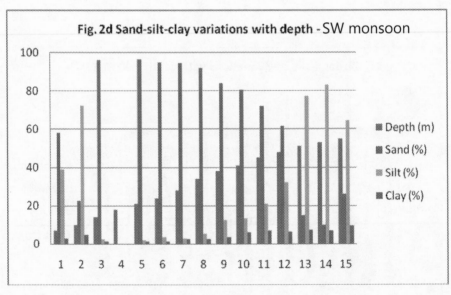

Fig. 2d Sand-silt-clay variations with depth - SW monsoon

Figure 17.3 a – d Lagenid population

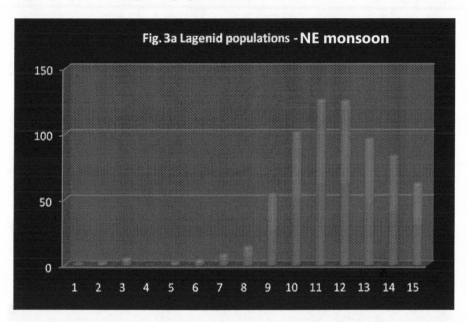

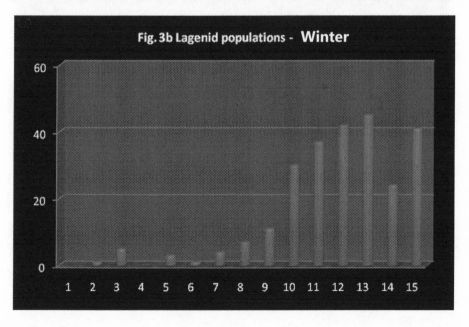

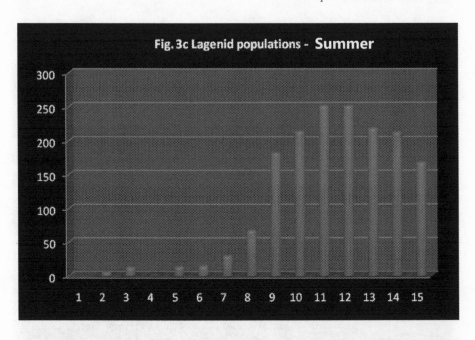

Fig. 3c Lagenid populations - **Summer**

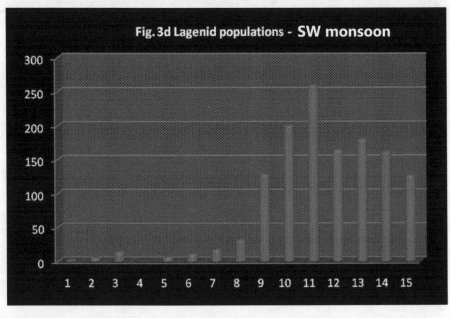

Fig. 3d Lagenid populations - **SW monsoon**

CONCLUSION

The examination of the seasonal and spatial distribution of lagenid populations on the inner shelf in the Bay of Bengal has revealed that, among the various ecological parameters determined, water depth and muddy substrate are the principal controlling factors for this particular group of hyaline, calcareous, benthic foraminifers. These results imply that the occurrence of fossil lagenids in ancient strata could be reliably utilized as depth and environment markers.

REFERENCES

Bernhard, J. M. (1988), Post-mortem vital staining in benthic foraminifera: duration and importance in population and distribution studies. *Jour. Foram. Res.*, v. 18, pp. 143–146.

Burone, L., Muniz, P., Pires-Vanin, A. M. S., and Rodrigues, M. (2003), Spatial distribution of organic matter in the surface sediments of Ubatuba Bay (south-eastern Brazil), *An. Acad. Bras. Ciênc.*, v. 75, no. 1, http://dx.doi.org/10.1590/S0001-37652003000100009.

Cushman, J. A. (1959), *Foraminifera. Their Classification and Economic Use.* 4[th]Edn., with *An Illustrated Key to the Genera*, Harvard Univ. Press, Massachusetts, 588 p.

Duval, W. S., Brockington, P. J., von Melville, M. S., and Geen, G. H. (1974), Spectrophotometric determination of dissolved oxygen concentration in water. *Jour. Fish. Res. Bd. Canada*, v. 31, pp. 1529–1530.

Ellis, B. F., and Messina, A. R. (1940), et seq., *A Catalogue of Foraminifera.* Amer. Mus. Natl. Hist., 30 vols. and supplements.

Gallagher, J. F. (1966), *The Variability of Water Masses in the Indian Ocean.* Natl. Oceanogr. Data Centre, Washington DC.

Gaudette, H. E., Flight, W. R., Toner, L., and Folger, D. W. (1974), An inexpensive titration method for determination of organic carbon in Recent sediments. *Jour. Sed. Petrol.*, v. 44, pp. 249–253.

Hottinger, L., Halicz, E., and Reiss, Z. (1993), *Recent Foraminiferida from the Gulf of Aqaba, Red Sea.* Ljubljana: Slovenska Akademija znanosti in umetnisti, 179 p.

Knudsen, M. (1901), *Hydrographical Tables.* G. M. Mfg. Co., New York, 63 p.

Krumbein, W. C., and Pettijohn, F. J. (1938), *Manual of Sedimentary Petrography.* D. Appleton Century Co. Inc., New York, 549 p.

La Fond, E. C. (1958), On the circulation of the surface layers on the east coast of India. *Andhra Univ. Mem. Oceanogr.*, 2, pp. 1–11.

Landsberg, H. E., Lippmann, H., Paffen, K. H., and Troll, C. (1966), *World Maps of Climatology.* Springer, Berlin.

Loeblich, A. R., and Tappan, H. (1987), *Foraminiferal Genera and their Classification.* Von Nostrand Reinhold, New York, 970 p.

Loring, L. H., and Rantala, R. T. T. (1992), Manual for the geochemical analyses of marine sediments and suspended particulate matter. *Earth Sci. Rev.*, v. 32, pp. 235–283.

Manivannan, V., Kumar, V., Ragothaman, V., and Hussain, S. M. (1996), Calcium carbonate, A major factor in controlling foraminiferal population in the Gulf of Mannar, off Tuticorin, Tamil Nadu. *Proc. XV Ind. Colloq. Micropal. Strat.*, Dehra Dun, pp. 381–385.

Murray, J. W. (1991) *Paleoecology of Benthic Foraminifera*. Longman Group, London, 397 p.

Newcombe, C. L., Horne, W. A., and Shepherd, B. B. (1939), Studies on the physics and chemistry of estuarine water in Chesapeake Bay. *Jour. Mar. Res.*, v. 11, pp. 87–116.

Rao, G. L. V., and Jayaraman, R. (1968), Hydrographical features of the southern and central Bay of Bengal during the transition period between winter and summer. *Bull. Natl. Instt. Sci. India*, 38, pp. 184–205.

Varkey, M. J., Murty, V. S. N., and Suryanarayana, A. (1996), Physical oceanography of the Bay of Bengal and Andaman Sea. In: Oceanography and Marine Biology: an Annual Review, A. D. Ansell, R. N. Gibson and Margaret Barnes (Eds.), UCL Press, 34, pp. 1–70.

Walker, D. A., Linton, A. E., and Schafer, C. T. (1974), Sudan Black B: a superior stain to rose Bengal for distinguishing living and non living foraminifera. *Jour. Foram. Res.*, v. 4, pp. 205–215.

Walton, W. R. (1952), Techniques for recognition of living foraminifera. *Contr. Cush. Found. Foram. Res.*, v. 3, pp. 56–60.

18 DISTRIBUTION AND ENVIRONMENTAL IMPLICATIONS OF FORAMINIFERA IN THE CORE SAMPLES OF KOLLIDAM AND MARAKKANAM MANGROVE LOCATIONS, TAMIL NADU, SOUTH-EAST COAST OF INDIA

S. M. Hussain, N. Mohammed Nishath and Jyothi Srivastava[1]
Department of Geology, University of Madras, Guindy Campus, Chennai 600 025
[1] Birbal Sahni Institute of Paleobotany, Lucknow 226 007
Email: hussain.sm7@gmail.com

ABSTRACT

To study the distribution of Foraminifera in the subsurface sediments of mangrove environment, two core samples have been retrieved near boating house of Pichavaram from Kollidam estuary (C1) and Marakanam (C2) with the help of a PVC core sampler. The length of the core varies from 60 to 65 cm. Both the core samples are subsampled at an interval of 5 cm. Thus, a total of 25 samples were obtained, and they were subjected to standard micropalaeontological and sedimentological analysis for the evaluation of different sediment characteristics. The core sample C1 (Pichavaram/Kollidam) yields only foraminifera, whereas the other core C2 (Marakkanam) has both foraminifera and Ostracoda. However, in the present study, only the distribution of foraminifera is discussed. The widely utilized classification proposed by Loeblich and Tappan (1987) has been followed in the present study for Foraminiferal taxonomy, and accordingly 23 foraminiferal species belonging to 18 genera, 10 families, 8 superfamilies, and 4 suborders have been reported and illustrated. Sedimentological parameters such as $CaCO_3$, organic matter and sand-silt-clay ratios were also estimated, and their down-core distribution is discussed. An attempt has been made to evaluate the favourable substrate for the abundance of Foraminifera population in the area of study. From the overall distribution of foraminifera in different samples of Kollidam estuary (Pichavaram area) and Marakanam estuary, it is observed that silty sand and sandy silt are more accommodative substrate for the population of foraminifera.

Keywords: distribution, foraminifera, mangrove areas, Tamil Nadu, environmental implications.

INTRODUCTION

The present study was conducted in two tropical dry evergreen forests in the Coromandel Coast of Tamil Nadu in southern India. These are reserved forests with disturbances like cattle-grazing, browsing and gathering of medicinal plants, and twig collection for burning as fuel wood by the local people. The Pichavaram mangrove wetland is located about 200 km south of Chennai in the northernmost part of the Cauvery delta. It is situated between the river Vellar in the north and river Kollidam (Coleroon) in the south and is connected to the estuaries of these two rivers by large brackish water canals called Khan Sahib backwaters. The backwater canal which joins the mangroves with river Kollidam is large and very deep. The Pichavaram mangrove wetland consists of three reserve forests (RF), namely Killai RF, Pichavaram RF, and Pichavaram extension area. Currently, 12 true mangrove plant species are present in the mangrove wetland. A mangrove tree species, namely *Excoecaria agallocha*, which is locally called Thillai, has been worshiped as a temple tree (sthala viruksham) at the Lord Nataraja temple at Chidambaram. The images of the Thillai are seen carved in rock sculptures and are being worshipped. Among the 12 species found in Pichavaram, *Avicennia marina* (*Venkandal*) alone constitutes 74% of the tree population. Marakkanam reserve forest (MRF) is located about 40 km north of Pondicherry in South Arcot District of Tamil Nadu. Out of the three sections of MRF, Agaram and Marakkanam regions have been converted to plantations of casuarina and eucalyptus.

Foraminifers are predominantly marine organisms living on the sea floor or floating in the water column. In spite of their small size and unicellular nature, foraminifera dwell in a variety of habitats. Some of them are, however, quite large, and species of the genus *Marginopora* from the Great Barrier

Reef, Australia, reach 25 mm in diameter. They are predominantly marine, although a few of them have been reported from brackish waters of lagoons, estuaries, low salinity lakes, and even some groundwater wells in Asia and Northern Africa. Foraminiferal tests are readily preserved and record evidence of environmental stores through time, thus providing historical baseline data even in the absence of background studies. Many species of foraminifera are geologically short-lived, and others are only found in specific environments, so a palaeontologist can examine the specimens in a sample and determine the geological age and environment when the rock formed. Sufficient literature is available on foraminifera and their distribution from the inner shelf region of the east coast of India (Kathal 2002). Much work is being carried out on Recent foraminifera from the surface samples of Tamil Nadu coast (Ragothaman and Kumar 1985, Manivannan et al. 1996, Rajeshwara Rao 1998). The data on their distribution in the subsurface samples of brackish water environment preferably mangrove areas are lacking, and hence, the present study has been taken up.

MATERIALS AND METHODS

The proposed work envisages a probe into foraminifera of the sediments collected from the subsurface (core sample) samples of Kollidam estuary of Pichavaram area, near Chidambaram, Cuddalore District (11° 29' N, 79° 46' E), and Marakanam estuary (11° 25' N, 79° 46' E), Villupuram District in Tamil Nadu, Chennai region (Figure 18.1). The fieldwork has been carried out in the month of March 2012, and two core samples have been retrieved near boating house in Pichavaram from Kollidam estuary (C1) and Marakanam (C2) with the help of a PVC core catcher. The geographical coordinates recorded using GPS for the core samples collection are given in Table 18.1. The length of the core varies from 60 to 65 cm. Both the core samples are subsampled at an interval of 5 cm. Thus, a total of 25 samples were obtained. The measured sediment characteristics for all sediment samples for two cores have been incorporated in this study.

RESULT AND DISCUSSION

All the samples are subjected to standard micropalaeontological techniques, and the calcareous microfauna (foraminifera) are recovered. According to Loeblich and Tappan (1987) classification, a total of 23 foraminiferal species belonging to 18 genera, 10 families, 8 superfamilies, and 4 suborders have been reported and illustrated. (Table 18.2) Scanning electron microphotographs (SEM) depicting different views of selected species are presented in Plate I.

Explanation to Plate I

1. *Spiroculina orbis* (Cushman 1921), apertural view
2. *Quinqueloculina polygona* (d'Orbigny 1839), side view
3. *Triloculina tricarinata* (d'Orbigny 1826), side view
4. *Triloculina Tricarinata* (d'Orbigny 1826), apertural view
5. *Nonionella stella* (Cushman and Moyer 1930), side view
6. *Nonionoides elangatum* (d'Orbigny 1826), side view
7. *Ammonia beccarii* (Linné 1758), dorsal view
8. *Asterorotalia inflata* (Millett 1904), ventral view
9. *Pararotalia nipponica* (Asano 1936), ventral view
10. *Pseudorotalia schroeteriana* (Carpenter, Parker, and Jones 1862), dorsal view
11. *Cribrononian simplex* (Cushman 1933), side view
12. *Elphidium crispum* (Linné 1758), side view
13. *Elphidium advenum* (Cushman 1922), side view
14. *Parrallina hispidula* (Cushman 1936), side view
15. *Rosalina globularis* (d'Orbigny 1826), ventral view
16. *Rosalina globularis* (d'Orbigny 1826), dorsal view
17. *Cibicides lobatulus* (Walker and Jacob 1798), side view

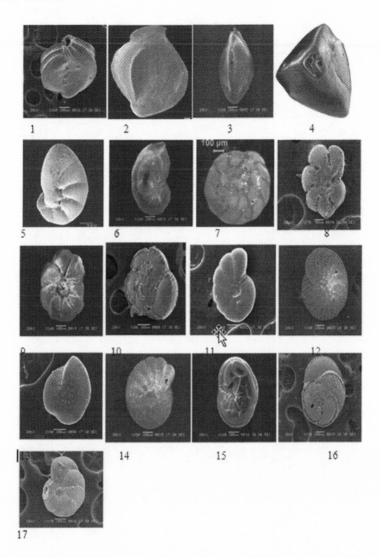

Plate I Scanning electron microphotographs (SEM) depicting different views of selected species

Table 18.1 Location of core samples collected in the Kollidam estuary in Pichavaram area (C1) and Marakanam estuary near Chennai (C2)

No. of core Samples	No. of Subsamples	Latitude	Longitude	Length of the core
C1	13	11° 25' 929" N	079° 46' 442" E	65 cm
C2	12	11° 29' 105" N	079° 46' 042" E	60 cm

Table 18.2 Taxonomic chart of foraminifera of the study area

Order	Suborder	Superfamily	Family	Genus	Species
Foraminifera	Textularina	Lituolacea	Textularidae	*Textularia*	*Textularia agglutinans*
	Miliolina	Miliolacea	Spiroloculidae	*Spiroculina*	*Spiroculina orbis*
			Hauerinidae	*Quinqueloculina*	*Quinqueloculina polygona*
					Quinqueloculina tropicalis
				Miliolinella	*Miliolinella elongata*
				Triloculina	*Triloculina tricarinata*
	Rotalina	Noionacea	Nonionidae	*Nonionellina*	*Nonionella stella*
				Nonionoides	*Nonionoides elongatum*
		Rotaliacea	Rotalidae	*Ammonia*	*Ammonia beccarii*
					Ammonia tepida
				Asterorotalia	*Asterorotalia inflata*
				Pararotalia	*Pararotalia nipponica*
				Pseudorotalia	*Pseudorotalia schroeteriana*
			Elphididae	*Cribrononion*	*Cribrononion simplex*
				Elphidium	*Elphidium crispum*
					Elphidium discoidale
					Elphidium norvangi
					Elphidium advenum
				Parrellina	*Parrallina hispidula*
		Buliminacea	Rosalinidae	*Rosalina*	*Rosalina globularis*
		Planorbulinacea	Cibicididae	*Cibicides*	*Cibicides lobatulus*
		Nonionacea	Gavelinellidae	*Hanzawa*	*Hanzawa concentrica*
	Globigerinina	Globorotaliacea	Globorotaliidae	*Neogloboquadrina*	*Neogloboquadrina dutertrei*

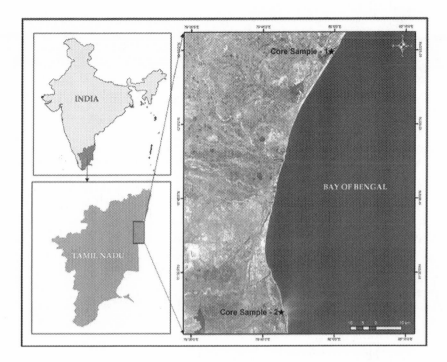

Figure 18.1. Location of the core sample collection in the study area.

Sedimentological Parameters

Sedimentological parameters such as $CaCO_3$, organic matter, and sand-silt-clay ratios were estimated and their down-core distribution is discussed. An attempt has been made to evaluate the favourable substrate for the population abundance of foraminifera in the present area of study. The study of organic matter and calcium carbonate in estuarine and coastal environments are important as organic carbon is used as a tool for predicting the impact of pollution (Shimp et al. 1971, Schoettle and Griedman 1973). Murray (1982) stated that foraminifera live in an environment in which the controlling factors are temperature, bottom topography, depth, salinity, pH, alkalinity, dissolved oxygen, food supply and substrate, and sediment organic matter content. In order to find out the role of organic matter and calcium carbonate contents in the sediments and the nature of substrate reflects on the abundance of foraminifera, and effort has been made to determine the same in all the subsurface sediment samples collected from the mangrove location of Kollidam estuary and Marakanam estuary.

321

Organic Matter

The readily oxidizable organic carbon content is determined by the Walkey–Black method, as outlined by Jackson (1958). This method differentiates humus matter from extraneous sources of organic carbon, such as graphite and coal. Gaudette et al. (1974) found that this method provided excellent agreement with the LECO combustion method of organic carbon analysis; this procedure has been followed in the present study. The organic matter in the sediments of Kollidam estuary (Pichavaram area) ranges from 0.98% to 4.34% while the organic matter in the sediments of Marakanam estuary ranges from 1.51% to 3.33% (tables 18.3 and 18.4, Figure 2). The organic matter in both cores is generally low, and it appears that the organic matter is not considered as a controlling factor on the distribution of foraminifera in the study area.

CaCO$_3$

The sediment CaCO$_3$ is measured by adopting the procedure proposed by Loring and Rantala (1992). The calcium carbonate in the subsurface sediments of Kollidam estuary (Pichavaram area) ranges from 7.3% (Sample No. 10) to 14.8%, whereas in the Marakanam estuary, the CaCO$_3$ values ranges from 12.5% to 22.5% (tables 18.3 and 18.4, Figure 18.3). The lowest values of CaCO$_3$ were recorded in C1, collected at Pichavaram estuary, and the highest values of CaCO$_3$ in C2, in the Marakanam estuary. From the foraminiferal faunal distribution, it appears that higher value of CaCO$_3$ favours maximum population.

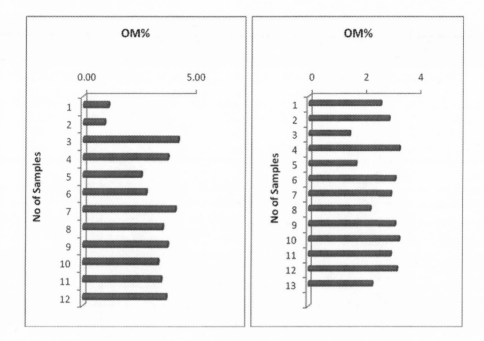

Figure 18.2. Histogram showing the distribution of OM in the core samples of Kollidam estuary (left) and Marakkanam estuary (right).

Table 18.3 Distribution of sand, silt, clay, OM, and $CaCO_3$ in the core samples of Kollidam area along with foraminiferal population

Sample No.	Depth (cm)	Sand (%)	Silt (%)	Clay (%)	Organic matter (%)	$CaCO_3$ (%)	Population of foraminifera
1	0–5	82.50	7.50	10.0	1.16	12.8	14
2	5–10	47.80	32.20	20.0	0.98	10.8	18
3	10–15	44.10	20.90	35.0	4.34	11.8	15
4	15–20	40.85	44.15	15.0	3.88	13.8	12
5	20–25	42.72	20.28	37.0	2.66	14.8	16
6	25–30	30.88	29.12	40.0	2.89	8.3	13
7	30–35	42.96	10.04	47.0	4.22	14.8	15
8	35–40	43.08	11.92	45.0	3.65	11.8	12
9	40–45	42.79	47.21	10.0	3.88	14.8	17
10	45–50	60.61	4.39	35.0	3.45	7.3	19
11	50–55	40.53	29.47	30.0	3.59	13.8	15
12	55–60	42.27	17.73	40.0	3.82	13.3	14
Maximum		82.50	47.21	47.0	4.34	14.80	
Minimum		30.88	4.32	10.0	0.98	7.30	

Table 18.4 Distribution of sand, silt, clay, OM, and CaCO$_3$ in the core samples of Marakanam area along with foraminiferal population

Sample No.	Depth (cm)	Sand (%)	Silt (%)	Clay (%)	Organic matter (%)	CaCO$_3$ (%)	Population of foraminifera
1	0–5	50.10	19.90	30.0	2.65	12.5	19
2	5–10	67.04	17.96	15.0	2.95	13.5	17
3	10–15	70.10	9.90	20.0	1.51	14.5	15
4	15–20	62.30	18.20	19.5	3.33	22.5	22
5	20–25	70.40	9.60	20.0	1.74	14.5	16
6	25–30	68.70	16.30	15.0	3.18	15.5	17
7	30–35	68.51	21.49	10.0	3.03	17.5	15
8	35–40	71.80	8.20	20.0	2.27	19.5	16
9	40–45	76.92	18.08	5.0	3.18	20.5	19
10	45–50	52.93	17.07	30.0	3.33	16.5	17
11	50–55	60.90	14.10	25.0	3.03	17.5	18
12	55–60	82.30	12.70	5.0	3.26	14.5	15
13	60–65	74.32	15.68	10.0	2.35	13.5	14
Maximum		82.30	21.49	30.0	3.33	22.50	
Minimum		50.10	8.20	5.0	1.51	12.50	

Sand-Silt-Clay Ratio

The sand-silt-clay analysis is done with the procedure of Krumbein and Pettijohn (1938). In the C1 samples of Pichavaram area in Kollidam estuary, sand ranges from 30.88% to 82.50%, silt content varies from 4.32% to 47.21% with a mean average of 21.48%, and clay contents varies from 10.0 to 82.50 with a mean average of 31.5% (Table 18.3). The down-core variation of sand, silt, and clay are shown, and their relative abundance is plotted on a trilinear diagram (Trefthen 1950) to know the sediment type (figures 18.4 and 18.5). In C2 samples of Marakanam estuary, sand ranges from 50.10% to 82.30% with a mean average of 67.61%, silt content varies from 8.20% to 21.49% with a mean average of 14.93%, and the clay content values ranges from 0.05% to 8.20% with a mean average of 17.5% (Table 18.4, figures 18.4 and 18.5). Maximum silt values are encountered at depth of 45 cm. Maximum sand values are encountered at depth of 15 cm. Maximum clay values are encountered at depth of 65 cm, and the clay content is less in all those samples. From the sand-silt-clay analysis, sand, sandy silt, sandy clay, silty sand, clays, silty clays, and substrates have been found in these core samples. From the overall distribution of foraminifera in different samples of Pichavaram area in Kollidam estuary and Marakanam estuary, it is observed that silty sand is more accommodative substrate for the population of foraminifera in Marakanam and silty clay sand in Kollidam samples.

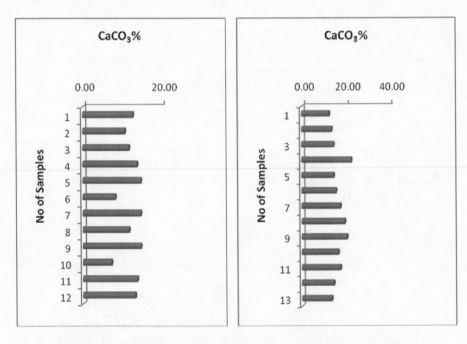

Figure 18.3. Histogram showing the down-core distribution of CaCO$_3$ in the core sample of Kollidam estuary (left) and Marakkanam estuary (right).

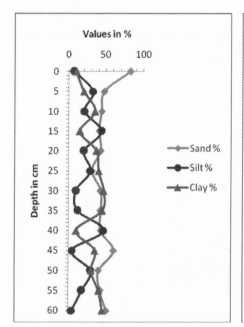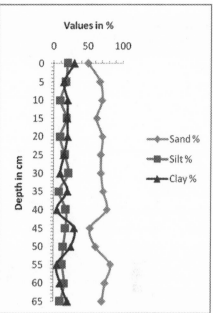

Figure 18.4. Down-core variation of sand, silt, clay in the Kollidam
mangrove area (left) and Marakanam mangrove area (right).

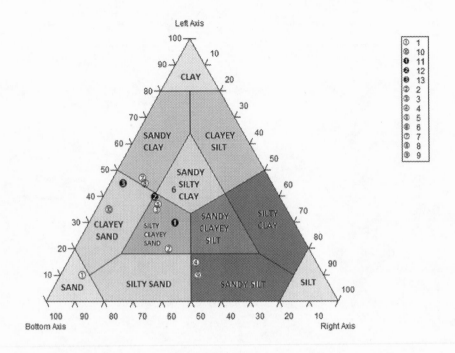

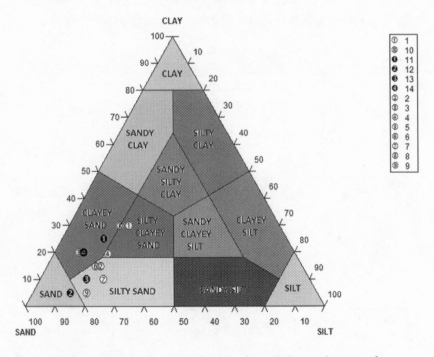

Figure 18.5. Trilinear plot of sand, silt, and clay in the core of
Kollidam (left) and Marakanam (right) (after Trefethen 1950).

CONCLUSION

The widely utilized classification proposed by Loeblich and Tappan (1987) has been followed in the present study for foraminiferal identification and taxonomy. In the present study, 23 foraminiferal species belonging to 18 genera, 10 families, 8 superfamilies, and 4 suborders have been reported and illustrated. The species of foraminifera recorded are characteristic of shallow inner shelf to marginal marine and tropical in nature. Sedimentological parameters like organic matter and $CaCO_3$ have been measured. The sand-silt-clay ratios were also estimated, and all the substrate has been found in the study area. In the present study, organic matter content determined in the sediments of Pichavaram area Kollidam estuary ranges from 0.98% to 4.34%, and in Marakanam estuary, it ranges from 1.51% to 3.33%. The organic matter in all the two cores is generally low, and it appears that the organic matter is not considered as a controlling factor on the distribution of foraminifera in the study area. Further, it has been found that the calcium carbonate in the subsurface sediments of Pichavaram area in Kollidam estuary ranges from 7.3% to 14.8%. In the Marakanam estuary, the $CaCO_3$ values range from 12.5% to 22.5%. The lowest values of $CaCO_3$ were recorded in C1, collected at Pichavaram estuary, and the highest values of $CaCO_3$ in C2, in the Marakanam estuary. From the foraminiferal faunal distribution, it appears that higher value of $CaCO_3$ favours maximum population.

From the sand-silt-clay analysis, silty sand, clay-sand, and silt-clay-sand substrates have been found in the core samples. The fine-grained nature of the sediments in the core reflects the low energy conditions prevailing in the mangrove locations. From the overall distribution of foraminifera in different samples of Pichavaram area in Kollidam estuary and Marakanam estuary, it is observed that silty sand is more accommodative substrate for the population of foraminifera in Marakanam, and silty clay sand in Kollidam samples. The distribution of foraminifera in the core samples indicates that the sediments are deposited under normal oxygenated environmental conditions. The colour of the foraminiferal tests is white and pale-yellow, which infers that there is no indication of pollution in the study area. The ratio of backwater (brackish) foraminiferal species to marine species is found lesser. Marine species are more dominant than the brackish water forms, particularly in the upper layers (top portion) of the core. This may be due to tidal influence.

ACKNOWLEDGEMENTS

Authors thank Prof. S. P. Mohan, head of the Department of Geology, University of Madras, for the permission, for the facilities provided to carry out the work, and for the SEM photography. The help rendered by Mr P. Loganathan in the field work is also acknowledged.

REFERENCES

Cushman, J. A., and Bronnimann, P. (1948), Some new genera and species of foraminifera from brackish water of Trinidad. *Contributions from the Cushman Laboratory for Foram. Res.*, v. 24, pp. 15–21.

D'Orbigny, A. (1826), Tableau methdique de la classes des Cephalopodes, Ann. Sci. Natur. V. 7, pp. 245–314.

Gaudette, H. E., Flight, W. R., Toner, L., and Folger, D. W. (1974), An inexpensive titration method for the determination of organic carbon in recent sediments, *J. Sed. Petrol.*, v. 44, pp. 249–253.

Jackson, M. L. (1958), Soil chemical analysis. Prentice Hall, New York, 485 p.

Kathal, P. K. (2002), Distribution and ecology of Recent foraminifera from littoral sediments of Eastern India. *Jour. Geol. Soc. India*, v. 6, pp. 429–454.

Kumar, V., and Manivannan, V. (2001), Benthic foraminifera responses to bottom water characteristics in the Palk Bay, off Rameshwaram, Southeast Coast of India. *Ind. Journ. Mar. Sci.*, v. 30, pp. 173–179.

Kumar, V., and Srinivasan, D. (2004), Factor analysis of Recent benthic foraminifera from the Coleroon river estuary, Tamilnadu, *Jour. of Geological Society of India*, v. 63 (3), pp. 299–312.

Kumar, V., and Priya, R. (2000), Epiphytic foraminifera and relation to algae, in the Palk Bay off Rameswaram, Tamil Nadu. *Journ. Nat. Con.*, v. 12 (2), pp. 245–253.

Kumar, V., and Sivakumar, K. (2001), Influence of estuarine environment on the benthic foraminifera. A case study from the Uppanar river estuary of Tamil Nadu. *Journ. Env. and Poll.*, v. 3, pp. 277–283.

Kumar, V., Manivannan, V., and Ragothaman, V. (1990), Distribution and species diversity of Recent foraminifera from the Thamirabarani river estuary, Punnaikkayal, Tamil Nadu. *Jour. Pal. Soc. India*, v. 35, pp. 53–60.

Kumar, V., Manivannan, V., and Ragothaman, V. (1996), Spatial and temporal variations in foram. abundance and their relation to substrate characteristics in the Palk Bay off Rameswaram, Tamil Nadu. Proceedings of the XV *Indian Colloquium on Micropal. and Stratigraphy*, Dehradun, pp. 367–379.

Krumbein, W. C., and Pettijohn, F. J. (1938), Manual of Sedimentary Petrography, D. Appleton Century Co. Inc., New York, 549p.

Loeblich, A. R., and Tappan, H. (1964), Sarcodina, chiefly Thecamoebians and Foraminiferida. *In*: R. C. Moore (ed.), *Treatise on Invertebrate Paleontology*, Part C. Geol. Soc. America, New York, 900p.

Loeblich, A. R., and Tappan, H. (1987), *Foram. genera and their classification*. Von Nostrand Reinhold, New York, 970pp.

Loring, D. H., and Rantala, R. T. T. (1992), Manual for the geochemical analyses of marine sediments and suspended particulate matter. Earth Sci. Rev., v .32, pp. 235–283.

Manivannan, V., Kumar, V., Ragothaman, V., and Hussain, S. M. (1996), Calcium carbonate: A major factor in controlling foraminifera population, in the Gulf of Mannar, off Tuticorin, Tamil Nadu. *Proc. XV Indian Colloq. Micropal. and Stratigraphy*, Dehra Dun, pp. 381–385.

Manivannan, V. (1989), *Ecology, distribution and systematics of Recent benthic foraminifera from the Gulf of Mannar, off Tuticorin, India*. PhD thesis, Univ. of Madras, Madras, India.

Murray, J. (1982), Benthic foraminifera: the validity of living/dead or total assemblages for the interpretation of Paleocology. Jour. Micropal., v. 1, pp. 137–140.

Murray, J. W., and Alve, E. (1999b), Taphonomic experiments on marginal Mar. foram. assemblages: how much ecological information is preserved? *Palaeogeography, Palaeoclimatology, Palaeoecology*, v. 149, pp. 183–197.

Raghothaman, V. (1974), The study of foraminifera from off Porto Novo, Tamil Nadu State. PhD thesis, Univ, Madras, Madras, 246p.

Ragothaman, V., and Kumar, V. (1985), Recent foraminifera from off the coast of Rameshwaram, Palk Bay, Tamil Nadu. Bull. Geol. Mi. Met. Soc. India, v. 52, pp. 122–146.

Rajeshwara Rao, N. (1998), Recent foraminifera in the inner shelf of the Bay of Bengal, off Karikattukuppam, unpublished PhD thesis submitted to the University of Madras, 273p.

Rasheed, D. A. (1967–68), Some foraminifera belonging to Miliolidae and Ophthalmidiidae from the Coral Sea, south of Papua (New Guinea). Part 2. *Jour. Univ. Madras*, v. 37–38, pp. 19–68.

Rasheed, D. A. (1969–70), Some Recent arenaceous foraminifera from the Coral Sea, south of Papua (New Guinea), Part 3, *J. Univ. Madras*, v. 39–40, pp. 41–58.

Rasheed, D. A., and Ragothaman, V. (1978), Ecology and distribution of Recent foraminifera from the Bay of Bengal, off Porto Novo, Tamil Nadu State, India. *Proc. VII Indian Colloq. Micropal. Strat.*, pp. 263–298.

Reiss, Z., and Hottinger, L., eds. (1984), The Gulf of aqaba. Ecological Micropal Springer-Verlag, Berlin, 355p.

Schoettle, M., and Griedman, G. M. (1973), Organic carbon in sediments of Lake George, New York: Relation to morphology of lake bottom, grain-size of sediments and man's activities. Bull. Geol. Soc. Amer., v. 84, pp. 191–198.

Scott, D. B., and Medioli, F. S. (1980), Quantitative studies of marsh foraminferal distribution in Nova scotia; implications for sea level studies. *Cushman Foundation for Foraminieral Res., Spl. Publ.* v. 17, p. 58.

Scott, D. B., Suter, J. R., and Kosters, E. C. (1991), Marsh foraminifera and arcellaceans of the lower Mississippi Delta: Controls on spatial distributions. *Micropal.*, v. 37 (4), pp. 373–392.

Shimp, N. F., Schweicher, J. A., Ruch, R., Heck, D. B., and Leland, H. V. (1971), Trace elements and organic carbon accumulation in most recent sediments of southern lake, Michigen: III Geological Survey. Env. Geol. Note, 41:25.

Todd, R., and Low, D. (1971), Foraminifera from the Bahama Bank, west of Andross Island. *USGS Prof. Paper* p. 683-C.

Trefethen, J. M. (1950), Classification of sediments. *Amer. Jour. Sci.*, v. 248, pp. 55–62.

19 SEASONAL CHANGES IN PHYSICO-CHEMICAL CHARACTERISTICS OF COASTAL ENVIRONMENT AT PICHAVARAM MANGROVE, SOUTH-EAST COAST OF INDIA

T. Ramkumar, S. Vasudevan, B. Chinnaraja, G. Gnanachandrasamy, and M. Bagyaraj
Department of Earth Sciences, Annamalai University 608002
Email: tratrj@gmail.com

ABSTRACT

The mangrove plants occur in the Pichavaram along the coastal area of Tamil Nadu in the south India, and this present study is aimed to analyse the physico-chemical parameters of estuarine water in two locations of Pichavaram mangroves. In the present study, the physico-chemical parameters, such as temperature, pH, salinity, dissolved oxygen, and total dissolved solids, were analysed during 2012. The locations selected for the present study area were the dense of mangrove region (Location 1) and mudflats in estuary (Location 2). During summer season, the temperature, pH, and salinity were high while dissolved oxygen and total dissolved solids were low.

Keywords: physico-chemical parameters, coastal environment, pichavaram mangroves.

INTRODUCTION

The mangrove environment has some special physico-chemical characteristics of salinity, tidal currents, winds, high temperatures, and muddy anaerobic soil. The salinity plays a vital role in the distribution of species, their productivity, and growth of mangrove forests (Twilly and Chen 1998). Changes in salinity are normally controlled by climate, hydrology, rainfall, and tidal flooding. The temperatures in the mangrove attain climate growth only under tropical conditions, where atmospheric temperature in the coldest months is greater than 20 °C and the seasonal fluctuation does not exceed 5 °C. Mangroves have been reported to grow in latitudes where the average sea surface temperature is 24 °C. Any further rise in temperature may lead to spreading of only some species into higher latitudes, provided that the direction of the ocean currents facilitates the dispersal of their seeds. However, very high temperatures are not favourable as leaves of mangroves are sensitive to temperature and their photosynthetic capacity gets reduced, falling to zero, at leaf temperatures of 38 °C to 40 °C, as against the optimum leaf temperature for photosynthesis, which is 28 °C to 32 °C (Clough et al. 1982 and Andrews et al. 1984).

Mangrove forests are one among the most productive ecosystems, lying between the land and sea in the tropical and subtropical latitudes (Kathiresan and Bingham 2001, Kathiresan 2002, and Harty 1997). Mangrove ecosystems are known for their activities such as primary producers, shoreline protectors, nursery grounds, and habitats for a variety of animals. They also maintain the coastline from erosion by reducing the influence of continuous wave action (Bunt 1992). One of the important functions of mangroves to the environment is to provide a mechanism for trapping sediment, and thus the mangrove forests are believed to be an important sink of suspended sediment (Woodroffe 1992, Wolanski Mazda and Ridd 1992, and Wolanski 1994). There are three different types of mangroves in India, viz. deltaic, backwater estuarine, and insular categories.

India is one among the 25 hotspots of the richest and highly endangered eco-regions of the world (Myers et al. 1994 and Agoramoorthy and Hsu 2002a). India's diverse plant species are mainly found in various types of forest such as tropical, subtropical, temperature, subalpine, alpine, dry open, open, evergreen, deciduous, littoral, and mangrove, which occupy 20% of the total geographical area (Negi 1993).

STUDY AREA

The Pichavaram mangroves (11° 25' N, 74° 47' E) are situated about 190 km south of Madras at the mouth of the Vellar, Coleroon, and Uppanar rivers on the south east coast of India, known as the Coramandal coast (Bay of Bengal) (Figure 19.1). Pichavaram is the second largest mangrove of India, covering an area of 1100 ha. It has islets ranging in size from 10 m², to 2 km² separated by intricate waterways that connect the Vellar estuary in the north and the Coleroon estuary in the south. The Coleroon estuary part is largely dominated by mangroves while the vellar estuary is dominated by mudflats. The sprawling mangrove is criss-crossed by numerous channels and creeks linking other water bodies in this region. The tides are semidiurnal, with a range of 0.5±1.0 m. Spreading over an area of 11 km², the site is covered by tide-dominated forests (50%), urban waterways (40%), and mud and sand flats (Kathiresan 2000). The annual temperature ranges from 18 to 36 °C. The lithology of the Pichavaram area includes gneiss, charnockite, granite, quartzite, limestone, and alluvium (Ramanathan 1993). Alluvium is dominated in the western part, whereas fluviomarine beach sands cover the eastern part. The geology of the area is dominated by quaternary sediments. This small ecosystem is playing an important role in sustaining coastal natural resources by providing detritus, nutrient salts, trace elements, etc. The structure and integrity of this dynamic but fragile ecosystem is influenced by various meteorological factors such as rainfall and wind, and it is also subjected to anthropogenic pressure of diverse variety.

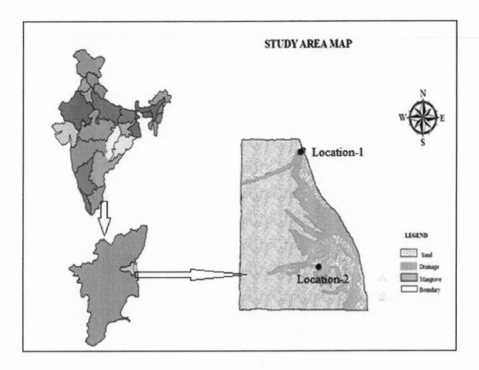

Figure 19.1. Location map of the study area.

MATERIALS AND METHODS

One litre of surface water samples was collected from two locations monthly from January to December 2012, using pre-washed polyethylene bottles from the mangrove environments. Each water sample was analysed to identify the physico-chemical parameters such as temperature, pH, salinity, dissolved oxygen, and total dissolved solid. The parameters were analysed using thermometer, ecotester, hand-held refractometer, and Thermo Orion DO Probe (080510), adopting the method of APHA (1995). Results of the physico-chemical analyses were interpreted using excel software.

RESULT AND DISCUSSION

Temperature

The physico-chemical parameters were shown in Figure 19.2 for locations 1 and 2. The physico-chemical analysis of water revealed that the temperature ranges from 21 °C to 36 °C in Pichavaram mangroves. In Location 1, the temperature ranged from 21 °C to 36 °C. The maximum water temperature (36 °C) was observed during June, and the minimum temperature (21 °C) was observed during October. In Location 2, the temperature ranged from 22.3 °C to 29.3 °C. Maximum temperature was observed during July (29.3 °C), and minimum temperature was observed during January (22.3 °C).

Location 1

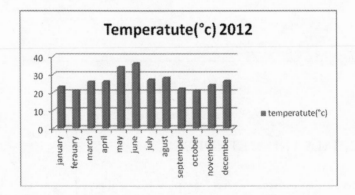

Location 2

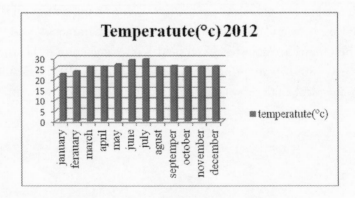

Figure 19.2. Column chart for temperature in locations 1 and 2.

pH

The pH ranges from 7.6 to 8.6 in the two locations of Pichavaram mangroves. In Location 1, the pH value ranges from 7.6 to 8.5. The maximum value 8.5 during on May and minimum value 7.6 during on January. In Location 2, the pH value ranges from 7.9 to 8.6. Maximum value of 8.6 was observed during July, and minimum value of 7.9 was observed during November.

Location 1

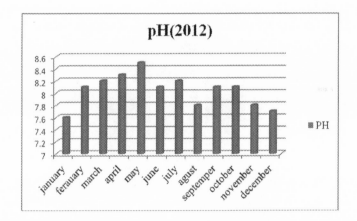

Location 2

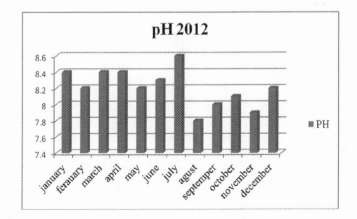

Figure 19.3. Column chart for pH in locations 1 and 2.

Salinity

The salinity ranges from 1.4% to 1.9% in both locations of Pichavaram mangroves. In Location 1, the salinity value ranges from 1.4% to 1.9%. Maximum value of salinity of 1.9% was identified during April, and minimum value of 1.4% was identified during November and December. In Location 2, the salinity value ranges from 1.56% to 1.86%. Maximum value of 1.86% was identified during February, and minimum value of 1.56% was observed during July and November.

Location 1

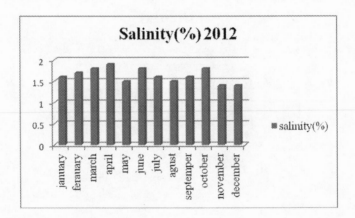

Location 2

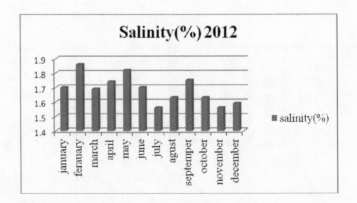

Figure 19.4. Column chart for salinity in locations 1 and 2.

Dissolved Oxygen

The dissolved oxygen ranges from 7.48 to 8.26 mg/l in two locations of Pichavaram mangroves. In Location 1, the dissolved oxygen ranges from 7.7 mg/l to 8.4 mg/l, with the maximum value of 8.4 mg/l during April and December. In Location 2, the dissolved oxygen ranges from 7.48 mg/l to 8.26 mg/l, with maximum value of 8.26 mg/l during March and May and minimum value of 7.48 mg/l during June.

Location 1

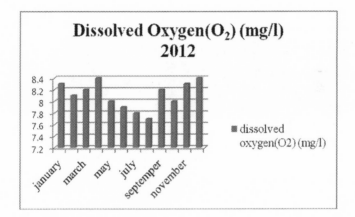

Location 2

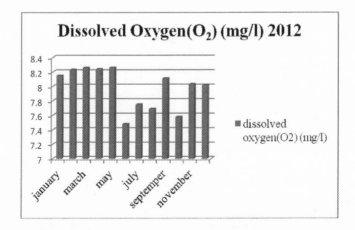

Figure 19.5. Column chart for dissolved oxygen in locations 1 and 2.

Total Dissolved Solid

The total dissolved solid ranges from 2.2 mg/l to 3.8 mg/l in two locations of Pichavaram mangroves. In locations 1 and 2, the maximum value of the total dissolved solid value was observed during March (3.8 mg/l), and the minimum value (2.2 mg/l) was observed during May.

Location 1

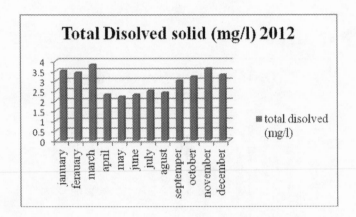

Location 2

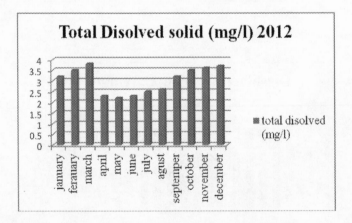

Figure 19.6. Column chart for total dissolve solid in locations 1 and 2.

CONCLUSION

The present study reveals that the temperature ranges from 21 °C to 36 °C in June and July, and the pH value ranges from 7.6 to 8.6 in the two locations of Pichavaram mangrove regions. The pH level of water was relatively high in the summer season from May to July and low in the monsoon and post-monsoon seasons. Salinity ranges from 1.4 to 1.9% during the study period in both locations of Pichavaram coastal mangrove environments. This may be the nature of the salt accumulated in the soil. Low amount of dissolved oxygen was observed in Pichavaram area in June and August 2012. The low dissolved oxygen is common in aquatic system, especially in estuarine and marine system that have high nutrient loading and are seasonally stratified into water with different densities. On the both locations, the maximum amount of total dissolved solid was observed in March because of the high amount of supply of suspended sediments and organic materials mixing with aeolian deposits from post-monsoon season, and minimum amount of total dissolved solid was during summer period.

REFERENCES

Agoramoorthy, G., Hsu, M. J., Biodiversity surveys are crucial for India. Current Science 82: 244–245, 2002a.

Andrews, T. J., Clough, B. F., and Muller, G. J., Photosynthetic gas exchange properties and carbon isotope ratios of some mangroves in North Queensland. In Physiology and management of mangroves (Teas, H. J. ed.) 15–23, 1984.

Bunt, J. S., How can fragile ecosystems best be conserved? In: Hsu, K. J., Thiede, J. (eds), Use and misuse of the seafloor (Dahlem workshop reports: environmental science research report 11), Wiley, Chichester 229–242, 1992.

Clough, B. F., Andrews, T. J., and Cowan, I. R., Physiological processes in mangroves: Mangrove ecosystem in Australia: structure, function and management Australian National University Press, Canberra 193–210, 1982.

Harty, C., Mangrove in New South Wales and Victoria. Vista Publication, Melbourne. 47, 1997.

Kathiresan, K., and Bingham, B. L., Biology of mangroves and mangrove ecosystems. Advances in marine biology 40: 81–251, 2001.

Kathiresan, K. A., Review of Studies on Pichavaram Mangrove, south-east India. Hydrobiologoa 30:185–205, 2000.

Kathiresan, K., Why are mangroves degrading? Current Science 83: 1246–1249, 2002.

Myers, N., Mittermeier, R. A., Mittermeier, C. G., Fonseca, G. A. B., Kent, J., Biodiversity hotspots for conservation priorities. Nature 403:853–856, 1994.

Negi, S. S., Biodiversity and its Conservation in India. Indus Publishing Company, New Delhi 1993.

Ramanathan, A. L., Vaidyanathan, P., Subramanian, V., and Das, B. K., Geochemistry of the Cauvery estuary, East coast of India. Estuaries 16, 459–474, 1993.

Twilly, R. R., and Chen, R. A., water budget and hydrology model of a basin mangrove forest in Rookery Bay, Florida. Marine and Freshwater Research 49: 309–323, 1998.

Wolanski, E., Y. Mazda, and P. Ridd, Mangrove hydrodynamics. In A. I. Robertson and D. M. Alongi (eds.), Tropical mangrove ecosystem, American Geophysical Union, Washington 436–46, 1992.

Wolanski, E., In Physical oceanography processes of the Great Barrier Reef. CRC, Boca Raton, Florida 1994.

Woodroffe, C., Mangrove sediments and geomorphology. In A. I. Robertson and D. M. Alongi (eds.), Tropical mangrove ecosystem, American Geophysical Union, Washington DC, 7–41, 1992.